For Walter,
who spurred this on,
with warm affection,

Bob

Gray Agonistes

Gray Agonistes

Thomas Gray and Masculine Friendship

Robert F. Gleckner

The Johns Hopkins University Press

Baltimore and London

The Johns Hopkins University Press
2715 North Charles Street
Baltimore, Maryland 21218-4319
The Johns Hopkins Press Ltd., London

Library of Congress Cataloging-in-Publication Data
will be found at the end of this book.

A catalog record for this book is available from the
British Library.

ISBN 0-8018-5433-4

For Glenda Jean Karr Gleckner

Contents

Acknowledgments

Although my life-long interest in William Blake and John Milton has always provided me the opportunity to reacquaint myself with the literature and art of the latter half of the eighteenth century, this book's venture into the decades before Blake's birth in 1757 was precipitated less by that involvement than by an eye-opening graduate seminar some years ago on the elegiac mode from Milton to Wordsworth that I co-taught with my colleague Wallace Jackson. I am greatly indebted to him for restimulating my interest particularly in the poetry of Thomas Gray, on whom he was working and publishing at the time. While that interest has moved me in critical directions quite different from Jackson's, this book's inception I owe largely to him. My debts to other Gray scholars and, more broadly, eighteen-century scholars-critics are registered in my text and notes, but more personal thanks are due to my former colleagues Lee Patterson and Stanley Stewart, both of whom provided me vigorous, challenging, and encouraging critical reading of an early, inchoate draft of what was essentially a prospectus, and the latter especially extended continuing moral support throughout the work's completion. At a crucial stage of final revisions Willis B. Regier, newly appointed director of the Johns Hopkins University Press, read the entire manuscript with a shrewdly critical eye and sharp blue pencil enabling me thereby to attend to an embarrassing host of stylistic gaucheries that escaped my eye. Those that remain, of course, are mine alone.

The research and much of the writing of the book were facilitated by generous annual research grants from the Duke University Faculty Enhancement Fund, a Mellon Research Fellowship at the Henry E. Huntington Library, and two summer appointments as an Honorary Fellow at the Center for Ideas and Society at the University of California, Riverside, courtesy of the center's director, Bernd Magnus. The Huntington staff and its resident research associates were helpful as always, as were the staffs of the University of California Riverside library and the Duke University library. Roz Wolbarsht, Deborah Carver, and Catherine Allen performed extraordinary feats in word-processing my dauntingly scribbled manuscript into its multiple hard-copy drafts and emergent final copy.

Finally, my wife, to whom this book is dedicated, ever quietly abided my irritations with myself, my mood swings and absences, and my neglect. There would be no book without her understanding.

Gray Agonistes

Introduction

Along with two very recent books, Wallace Jackson's series of es-
says[1] has called welcome attention to the fact that the "case"
of Thomas Gray needs to be reopened. As Jackson properly
notes, the fifty-year critical debate over, broadly speaking, the conflict be-
tween Gray's private and public voices has not got us very far toward
grasping the indefinable elusiveness of Gray's total poetic achievement,
not to say the depths of his intensely personal struggles. Nor have we
made signal advances during this same half-century toward understanding
or defining the poetic age in which Gray was the most prominent figure
among an array of others rarely, if ever, acclaimed as pace setters, innova-
tors, originals, even really interesting poets—the Wartons, Akenside, Beat-
tie, Shenstone, and others less memorable. There is, of course, the excep-
tion of Collins, who at twenty-nine concluded his career, and his life to all
intents and purposes, in madness. The varied terms in which the larger
definitional debate has been conducted need not detain us here beyond
my noting the unilluminating disparateness between, say, Northrop Frye's
1956 positioning of the "age" as a discrete, internally coherent, and self-
sustaining literary period (neither pre- nor post-)[2] and John Sitter's opting
twenty-six years later for "post-Augustan" as peculiarly appropriate (albeit
with qualifications) to the midcentury poets' "flight from history." Some-
where in between is Marshall Brown's courageous, if finally self-defeating,
attempt to resuscitate "preromanticism" (now in new terminological ves-
sel) as still appropriate to the age. Sitter's terminology, it should be
noted, derives from Cassirer's defense of Burkhardt's use of the term "Re-
naissance."[3] What we try to give expression to by such naming, writes
Cassirer, "is a unity of *direction*, not *actualization*. The particular individu-
belong together, not because they are alike or resemble each other, but
because they are *cooperating in a common task*, which . . . we perceive to be
new and to be the era's distinctive 'meaning' " (Cassirer's italics).

1

My own sense is that Frye leans rather precariously toward the pole o
actualization. And even Howard Weinbrot, in his recent attack on Frye'
mode of actualization, reasserts the validity of actualization itself by ar
guing the internal coherence of eighteenth-century poetry on the basis o
its *all* being "the poetry of process," which Frye had claimed was precisel\
what differentiates late-eighteenth-century poetry from its Augustan fore
bears' "poetry of product."[4] My own aim is narrower, yet one that may
contribute in modest ways to this continuing debate, the furtherance o
which was, I believe, Frye's deep-seated hope in claiming his "age of sen-
sibility's" distinctiveness in the first place. This narrower aim is anothe
look at what Jackson calls Gray's "failed enterprise that of its kind is unri
valed within the century"[5]—a look different from though not entirel\
unrelated to his, since mine also focuses on the voice (rather than th\
voices) of Gray and his almost debilitating sense of belatedness.

The still persistent view of Gray's two voices—one "private," one "pub
lic"—originated in Lord David Cecil's suggestive 1945 formulation c
three "categories" of poetry in Gray's work, though the idea languishe\
for almost twenty years before it was picked up, and variously modulatec
by F. Doherty (1963), Patricia Spacks (1965), Roger Lonsdale (1973), Leo
Guilhamet (1974), and Paul Fry (1980).[6] Indeed, even Suvir Kaul's 199\
Thomas Gray and Literary Authority[7] does not completely escape this crit
cal paradigm, although his terms are substantially more sophisticated. Th
two-voice theory, despite its seductive neatness, is far too constricted
overfocused to account for Gray's distinctive poetic achievement or i
ultimate truncation, or for its moments of moving puissance in virtual\
all the individual poems. Jackson's counterargument consists of examini\
the poetry in terms of the progress myth and of Gray's inveterate defle
tion of desire, which "creates the elegiac poet who will be neither t\
poet of romance . . . nor the bard of the sublime." That is to say, su
deflection is his "desired mode of encounter, and evasion or incapacity
the satisfactory figure of fulfillment"—the haunting and often crippli
sense that the only presence is absence.[8] While this general propositi\
seems to me unexceptionable as far as it goes, I should prefer to pu\
another way, in terms suggested by the subtitle of Jackson's 1986 ess\
"Drowning in Human Voices": Gray hears Eliot's "mermaids singing"
merely "each to each" but even more insistently to him (*pace* Prufroc
thinking otherwise); they are generative yet paradoxically oppressive su\
ings of the poetic voices of the illustrious dead. But rather than th\

voices constituting, as Kaul suggests (*Literary Authority*, 91), a "vocational anxiety" that for Gray was a product of "the increasing professionalism of poetry" threatening his cherished independence as a "gentleman-poet"— a matter, then, of "class"—the siren "mermaid" who sings most seductively to Gray is the magnificently yet forbiddingly laureled Milton. While that is a critical commonplace, it has been pursued far less adequately than, for example, Paul Sherwin does in his fine book on Collins, *Precious Bane*.[9]

For Gray, even more powerfully than for Collins, Milton is that Lycidean "Genius of the shore" who ought to "be good / To all that wander in [the] perilous flood," whose response to Moschus's question in "Epitaph for Bion" ("Ah, who will make music on thy pipe, O thrice desired Bion. . . . Who is so bold?") is ringingly self-affirming, and whose "goodness" opens out to both the "fresh woods, and pastures new" of poetic futurity (*Lycidas*, 183–85, 193) as well as to "something like prophetic strain" (*Il Penseroso*, 174). But how to tap the divine sources of that Genius "That from beneath the seat of Jove doth spring" (*Lycidas*, 16) is a question that all but paralyzingly haunts Gray, whose poetic self-characterizations more tellingly reflect the beseechment of Milton's earlier lines in *Lycidas* rather than the triumph of his conclusion:

> So may some gentle Muse
> With lucky words favor my destined urn,
> And as he passes turn,
> And bid fair peace be to my sable shroud.
> (*Lycidas*, 19–22)

If there is no doubt that Gray in the *Elegy Written in a Country Churchyard* was variously indebted to Blair, Akenside, Collins, the Wartons, and Hervey (among a host of others cited, or silently appropriated, by Gray himself), there is no doubt either, as countless critics have pointed out, that the final thirty lines or so of the *Elegy* extrapolate on these very lines from *Lycidas*—"*some* fond breast," "*Some* kindred spirit," and "*some* hoary-headed swain" serving in lieu of "*some* gentle Muse" or of *the* (not some) glorious, divinely voiced Milton.[10]

If, indeed, Norton Nicholls recollected correctly that Gray once told him "he never sat down to compose poetry without reading Spencer *[sic]* for a considerable time previously" (a "fact" for which I see little evidence), I shall attempt to demonstrate that Gray never sat down to write without Milton's *voice* echoing in his consciousness—as well as in an ear fully as "exquisite" as Milton's own.[11] So far as we know, Gray himself never said *that* to anyone, his very silence with respect to Milton's ubiquitous role in his poetry in itself constituting an eloquent absence or omission—matching the absence of Gray's saying to anyone that he always *read* Milton "for a considerable time" prior to composing. But Nicholls is also responsible for the myth that Gray not only had a poor verbal memory but that he "congratulated himself on not having" a better one. Such an alleged statement, I would argue, is evasion by commission, for there is absolutely no doubt (witness Lonsdale's editorial superabundance of allusions, echoes, analogs) that Gray had both an acute aural, as well as an extraordinarily rich and discriminating verbal, memory which precluded the necessity of rereading the poetry of others to fire his inspiration.[12]

It is less easily demonstrable that some of those ancestral voices habitually drowned out others, and that the recollection of some poetic texts often elbowed aside the intrusion of others. Without some textual self-selection or deliberate authorial choice, Gray's ear would have been dinned to deafness and his hand frozen to near immobility by the cacophony of voices and tunes battling for attention. Or, were composition even possible amid what Keats in "How Many Bards" called "disturbance rude" and "wild uproar," the niagara of vividly remembered words and phrasings would inundate authorial verbalizations to the point of indistinguishability. Something like this phenomenon is what Lonsdale characterizes as "a kind of literary kleptomania" (xvii), a compositional helplessness so acute, so powerful, as to erase all vestiges of an independently creative self.[13] But to suggest that Gray was unaware of most of his thefts is as absurd as implying (as Lonsdale does) that he was so unsure of himself that he had to "[depend] on the phrasing and thoughts of other poets" (xvii).

My intention is to argue precisely the opposite case—that Gray was acutely aware of the vast bulk of his borrowings and that he rarely had to submissively "depend" on other poets to speak ventriloquistically for him. My procedure in the pages that follow, then, runs sharply counter to the habitual tendency in Gray studies to offer, explicitly or implicitly, apologies for Gray's alleged derivativeness.[14] His allusive practice, however, *is* considerably complex, and at times seems to acknowledge that complexity by taking pains to acknowledge a borrowing. To choose one at random, lines 14–15 of the *Ode on the Spring* read:

Where'er the rude and moss-grown beech
O'er canopies the glade.

Pressured to acknowledge his debts in the 1768 *Poems of Mr. Gray*, he cited *Midsummer Night's Dream* 2. 1. 249–51, an acknowledgment that, under no pressure, he had made to Walpole over twenty years earlier.[15] What is interesting about this one, and indeed most of Gray's acknowledgments, is their common pedantry, for it is clearly his purpose here to present Shakespeare as *the* authority for the unusual (and, in reality, redundant) phrase "o'er canopies." Gray's other confessed debts in the Spring Ode have the same tenor: his translation of a phrase from Virgil's *Georgics*, an echo of *Paradise Lost* 7. 405–6, and a "thought" (as Gray puts it) from Matthew Green's *The Grotto* (Lonsdale, 51–52n). Missing in Gray's 1768 notes, however, are far more telling allusions: an exact quotation from *Comus*, an antecedent text whose core concerns have a strong impact on Gray's entire conception; a clear evocation of *L'Allegro* (again of obvious pertinence to Gray's ideas in the Spring Ode); a substantial allusion to *Paradise Lost*, Book 4, in lines 5–7; and, of crucial importance, demonstrable references to Richard West's poem *Ad Amicos* (sent to Gray five years earlier) and to West's own spring ode entitled *Ode on May* (sent to Gray scarcely a month before Gray wrote his "response").[16]

One could argue from this, of course, that Gray's acknowledging in 1768 his allusions to West's poems would have been gratuitous since they were unpublished. But the substantial (if not obvious) contextualizing of the *Ode on the Spring* in *Comus* and *Paradise Lost* (Adam and Eve in the garden, Satan's first sight of them and it, Satan's first temptation into Eve's sleeping ear), not to mention elements of *L'Allegro* and *Il Penseroso*, bespeaks the presence of a complex subtextuality in the poem. On its surface, however, the Spring Ode does evince what Lonsdale (and a host of others) accurately describe as "richness of effect . . . achieved by the deliberate echoing and evocation of earlier classical and native descriptions of the spring, both in details of phrasing and in the basic situation of the retired poet contemplating the frivolity of the world as represented by the 'insect youth' " (48). In fact, it is precisely this masquerading that has led so many to rather wistfully lament, as George Whalley does, that Gray "seems never quite to have fashioned for himself the words and rhythms he needed to declare the force and subtlety of his inner life or of his poetic intelligence." Or to say, even more helplessly—and erroneously—that Gray's borrowings, like those of Collins, the Wartons, Akenside, Mason, and Macpherson, "remain more a matter of style and genre than of specific reference. They add to the feel of the poem, not its content, and they are consequently less interesting uses of the past than are classical borrowings" (that is, borrowings by classical authors from classical authors).[17]

One other example of this sort of thing will suffice. To the Eton College Ode Gray in 1768 added a note to explain that the Henry of line 4 is "King Henry the Sixth, Founder of the College." At the same time he avoids *any* acknowledgment of his numerous borrowings from Milton— not to mention those from Pope and Dryden, and still others that pointedly evoke once again Richard West's *Ad Amicos*. While one might argue that Gray expected his readers to readily recognize echoes of and allusions to Pope and Dryden (and possibly other contemporary poets as well), there is a consistent pattern of evasion or effacement inherent in Gray's most telling allusions. They (especially those to Milton and West) are, more often than not, deliberately obscured (or violently misshaped) by other elements of Gray's context, a tactic precisely parallel to the constructed self-protectiveness of all his references to West. To put the matter oversimply, if Milton's poetry represents the "voice as of the cherub-choir" that Gray almost desperately aspires to, his relationship with West and (especially) the impact on him of West's early death, constitute the tragic subject that voice sings. And unlike the recognition of those allusions that either need no acknowledgment because of their commonplaceness in Augustan poetic idiom or simply pay homage to felicitousness, acknowledging the abundant Miltonisms Gray feared would surely lead "some Magazine or Review" to call him "Plagiary" and citing those from West would destroy the very fiber of his moral being. That is to say, to attempt to be Milton and to fail is not Andrea del Sarto-like heroism at all but rather utter failure to be *a* poet; and to love another man in an age when ostracism and possibly severe legal punishment could result from public discovery and exposure, and to *write* of that relationship would be to court personal infamy, not merely poetic or personal failure.[18] Only in the "blooming Eden" that Milton dared to imagine and explore could Gray's transgressive love for West be both possible and guiltless.

Paul Sherwin concluded in his book on Collins and Milton that this poetic contemporary of Gray "never comprehend[ed], as do Milton and the Romantics, that his own personal history, in its totality, might serve as the starting point for a coherent body of poetry at once mythical and true."[19] And, several years later, Richard Wendorf similarly argued that "the few facts we possess about Collins's life in the 1740s [can] not support the conclusion that the poetry written during these years was produced by the writer's sense of 'personal torment' [Sherwin's phrase] (at least not by those conventional torments—disappointed love, the loss of family or friends, severe illness, even madness—that we consider most basic)."[20] Where Sherwin finds a certain "coherence" in Collins' frustration and despair in attempting to rival Milton, Wendorf finds it in Collins' self-consciousness of being "entirely an Author." In Gray I find a powerful and moving coherence in the body of his poetry, forged out of many of those "personal torments" Collins had but didn't write about, as well as out of Gray's sense of being, or aspiring to be, entirely an author. That is to say, Gray's poetry enacts a double narrative of interlocking "personal histories":[21] (1) his heroic engagement with the reigning power of Milton's achievement and with his precedential model for a literary career, both fueling Gray's drive toward the status of Poet in his own right, not of mere Miltonic imitator; and (2) his equally heroic struggle to come to terms with his own sexuality, with his love for West, with his all-absorbing grief at West's early death, and finally with his late-life love of, and abandonment by, Bonstetten.

Both of these narratives are underwritten by fear more than mere anxiety. If Milton's riding sublime "Upon the seraph-wings of Ecstasy" enabled him to pass "the flaming bounds of place and time" and to see "The living throne, the sapphire-blaze, / Where angels tremble while they gaze," for Gray it also led to his being "blasted with excess of light," his eyes "Closed . . . in endless night." The analogy of his own aspiration to Milton's was patently clear to Gray: riding sublime on Milton's seraph-wings may well enable him to pass beyond the "limits of [the] little reign" of his poetic contemporaries, but the cost of such a trespass loomed as the "endless night" into which the Bard plunges—that very phrase no coincidental repetition of Milton's recompense in *The Progress of Poesy*. Concomitantly, for Gray to transgress both God's law and man's law against homosexual relationships meant to risk personal self-destruction—at best being branded criminal, sinner, pervert, fraud, failed human being.

Both of these anxieties (somehow a pale word to use here), of course, have been recognized by Gray scholars, but no one has studied the Gray-Milton relationship with anything like the intensity and meticulousness of Sherwin's charting of the Collins-Milton relationship. Moreover, as George Haggerty has written more recently, "the homosexuality of a group of important mid- to late-eighteenth-century writers [including Gray] has been the best secret of literary studies" until a few years ago—

and even then by far the major attention has been accorded to such figures as Beckford, Walpole, and M. G. Lewis.[22] What I propose here, then, is in its simplest sense twofold: (1) to chart what I called above, neutrally, "the Gray-Milton relationship" (more accurately, perhaps, Gray's struggle with Milton's ghost) and to particularize its impact on, and in, Gray's poetry from his earliest efforts to his last; and (2) to chart in the poetry and the letters Gray's relationship with West (with some reference to Gray's friendship with Walpole and Thomas Ashton, the other two members of the self-styled Etonian "Quadruple Alliance") and its impact on his life and poetic career as well as on individual poems.

Of even greater concern to me, however, is the particular nature of the impingement of the Gray-Milton "narrative" upon the Gray-West narrative and vice versa—that is to say, the extent to which these two interlock, intersect, interanimate with, even at times serve as surrogates (or metonymies) for, each other. Needless to say, neither relationship is fully knowable: we can not read Gray's mind even with the help of the splendidly edited letters. Complicating, and often frustrating, any concerted effort to elucidate with absolute certainty these dual relationships is the fact that what I have called the narratives of both are so buried in the texts available to us, poetry and letters, that excavation demands studied attention to precisely those textual details that have long been allowed to remain quiescent beneath Gray's familiar exquisite control, decorousness, and overall sensibility. Whereas what has been referred to in the past almost ad nauseam as Gray's "artifice" has been increasingly fissured in recent years,[23] the persistent subversiveness of its subtextuality has remained largely unplumbed—in large measure because Gray himself (with major assists from his friend and editor Mason) deliberately obscured or disguised it sufficiently to deflect our attention from it through a variety of brilliant poetic and allusional strategies. While I shall try to articulate later in greater detail what those are and how they work, let me briefly describe a few of those strategies here.

The Gray-Milton relationship/narrative has been muddied by the source-hunting industry that has uncovered in Gray's poetry hundreds of allusions, echoes, parallels, imitations, emulations, coincidental correspondences, accidental similarities, outright thefts, and verbal bows of homage—all to an astonishing array of writers in several languages, by a man who seemingly did little else but read from the day he learned how until he died at almost fifty-five. What is conjured up here is precisely the Thomas Gray, Scholar, of the title of William Powell Jones' 1937 book. By contrast, relatively little has been done to help us understand *why* Gray "alluded" so much, why he would want to clutter his work with the language and ideas of others, or (of greater importance to any clear estimate of his poetic achievement) how all these allusion, echoes, and so on function in the poetry, how Gray may be seen to "use" them rather than merely adorning his verse with a borrowed luster.[24] Gray himself, as I have already noted, did his best to cloud this entire issue even more by publicly acknowledging his habitual "borrowing." His oft-quoted letter to Bedingfield in August 1756 is the best case in point. There, with respect to his "Pindarics," Gray admits to borrowing from *Paradise Lost*, Cowley's *The Mistress*, Dante's *Purgatorio*, Shakespeare's *King John* and *Julius Caesar*, not to mention a painting by Raphael and another by Parmigiano (from the first of which he says he "took" an "image" while the second, he explained, "comes still nearer to my meaning" in *The Bard*). Then he adds that he could show his readers and reviewers "a hundred more instances, which they never will discover themselves" (*CTG*, 476–77).

Why this boastfulness—or self-deprecation? What are we now to think of this oddly mixed bag of sources acknowledged, not to mention the "hundred" others that no one will ever "discover"? Are they *that* obscure? Are they even there? Or is all this but a ruse to deflect attention from those borrowings/allusions that, once discovered and contextualized, can have demonstrably determinate effects on our reading and our full understanding of the poem in ways that the "sources" Gray cites rarely, if ever, do—if indeed they don't confound "full understanding"? What does it mean for Gray to "say," for example, via his allusion to *Paradise Lost*, that the Bard's "beard and hoary hair" were somehow "like" Satan's "standard," raised by Azazel and, unfurled and "full high advanced / Shone like a meteor streaming to the wind, / With gems and golden luster rich emblazed"? While some sense is extractable from the comparison (beard = banner streaming like a meteor), the full Miltonic picture applied to Gray's scene is even more ludicrous than what Lonsdale delicately calls the "distracting parallel" from the patently ludicrous *Hudibras*: "This hairy meteor [i.e., Hudibras's beard] did denounce / The fall of sceptres and of crowns" (Lonsdale, 186). At the very least Gray seems to be at some pains (like a magician) to flourish one hand in such a way as to deflect our attention from what the other (subtextual) hand is doing.[25] And clearly a constituent part of that flourishing is the mishmash of allusions, echoes, parallels, and the like to which we are directed by Gray himself (as well as by his commentators) in the face of which any subtext,

Miltonic or otherwise, becomes, in effect, both invisible and mute.

The subtextual Gray-West narrative, on the other hand, is literally un-spoken except via a remarkable repertoire of encodings: private languages, idioms, phrases, words; epistolary communication in languages other than English—especially Latin and occasionally Greek, the former sometimes so colloquial (or grammatically unusual or strange) as to suggest something beyond ostensible meaning; English translations of Latin poems with tell-ing omissions, substitutions, and even apparently intentional mistransla-tions; brief references or allusions to Latin poems the complete version and substance of which the knowledgeable recipient is called upon to supply as part of the letter; and so on. For all my suspicion that some sort of private language (as it were), other than the above encodings, may well have been developed in the correspondence of Gray and West, I confess my inability to discover any translatable "passwords" or "passphrases" into anything like the crypto-language Louis Crompton discovered in By-ron's correspondence with certain of his friends.[26] It is clear, however, that homosexuality in the eighteenth century was always couched in what Crompton calls "vague and mysterious" language: "genders were changed in poems, codes used in letters, references made purposely ambiguous in autobiographical notes," and so on. So with Gray and West, as I shall try to show—with some lesser attention as well to the other two members of the Quadruple Alliance and to certain aspects of the cultural context of early-eighteenth-century society and of Eton.

On this last, since I cannot essay here a detailed history of eighteenth-century life and society in England, I shall be relatively brief. In Maccub-bin's eye-opening collection of essays, *"'Tis Nature's Fault": Unauthorized Sexuality during the Enlightenment,*[27] for example, George S. Rousseau's sweeping survey, "The Pursuit of Homosexuality in the Eighteenth Cen-tury," does part of the job for me. Although what little he has to say of Gray is drawn from Hagstrum, his portrait of "the school experience" is particularly apropros. If, as numerous studies have shown, many of the public-school boys "were primarily homoerotic," Rousseau argues that most "remained anything but libertine: men who were at best homosexual in the Platonic sense—that is, homoplatonic—and who romantically ideal-ized same-gender friendships." At the same time, he points out that it is impossible to deny that English schools in Gray's day were "a breeding ground for all . . . varieties" of male-male relationships.[28] T. A. J. Burnett, in his fine biography of Scrope Davies, spells this out in some detail. While Gray's Eton was not "quite so appalling" as it became at the "nadir" to which it had sunk by the end of the century, living conditions prior to that descent were not fundamentally different: "Well might a boy abandon hope who entered there," Burnett writes; "the surroundings, the routine and the diet ... must have struck terror" into any boy who entered Eton and confronted there, likely for the first time, "the other face of the eighteenth century." The students were locked in their quarters, virtually all in the "infamous Long Chamber" some 172 by 27 feet in size, between eight o'clock in the evening and seven in the morning. "The total lack of privacy [added to the absence of any form of supervision] ... not only meant that study was virtually impossible, but also resulted in cruel bullying and sexual malpractices." [29]

Unfortunately there is extant but one letter from Gray during his years at Eton, which he left in September 1734. It is inconceivable that he wrote no more. This eight-year-or-so gap in the complete three-volume *Correspondence* must, I believe, be chalked up to Mason's admitted "selection" of only those letters he "thought would be most likely to please the generality of readers; omitting, though with regret, many of the more sprightly and humorous sort, because either from their personality, or some other local circumstance, they did not seem so well adapted to hit the public taste." [30] Mason's professed aim of hitting the public taste aside, one must wonder what "personality" means here, and, even more tantalizingly, what "other local circumstance" refers to if not, at least in part, Gray's "circumstances" at Eton. Some of those may well be of the sort chronicled in Royston Lambert's *The Hothouse Society: An Exploration of Boarding-school Life through the Boys' and Girls' Own Writings*, writings that graphically, and often chillingly, illuminate life in such public schools. Typical, and among the most moving in the book, is a confession by a particularly withdrawn, isolated, and self-suppressive boy who wrote that his "feelings [for another boy] let themselves out in a sort of minor neurosis. ... No poetry produced, but sometimes a musical composition with [the] affair in the *back* of the mind, which is soon burnt." [31] Such boy-boy "affairs," however, are not the entire story. In Raymond Flower's *Oundle and the English Public School*, he reminds us that a master's flagellation of a boy (not an uncommon occurrence, of course) was all too often a kind of "Paphian pleasure ... over which for centuries had been drawn a decorous veil"—a pleasure at least on occasion intensified into active pederasty, as in the famous case of Headmaster Nicholas Udall at Eton. [32]

In any case, from all accounts of Eton and other public schools in Gray's time (including prominently, in light of Crompton's study, Byron's Har-

row), "excepting a code of laws of their own, there was no help or redress"
for the boys. The "system" was "protected . . . by a taboo of silence which
boys feared to break" (Flower, 50, 52). In such circumstances it is not
difficult to understand the formation of the Quadruple Alliance (Gray,
West, Walpole, and Ashton), its very militaristic title implicitly their com-
munal defense against invasion of their group by other boys—and, no
doubt, more broadly against that "other face of the eighteenth century"
characterized hyperbolically, but possibly no less accurately" by Flower as
"birch, boorishness, buggery and the bottle" (48).

If one may not concur completely with G. S. Rousseau's judgment
(based on little evidence) that "Walpole . . . was patently homocentric and
did little to conceal his propensity among his intimates," we may still ac-
cede to Eve Sedgwick's notion of Walpole's "close protective coloration
given by his aristocratic milieu . . . [which] came to be seen [by whom?]
as ethereal, decorative, and otiose." [33] The fact remains, however, that
Walpole was (like Gray) devotedly attached to his mother, who died sud-
denly when he was only twenty, and, according to Arthur C. Benson, even
at Eton "some of his friends were as effeminate in appearance and in
manner as himself." [34] Walpole never married, but for a number of years
he did carry on an extended platonic affair, in person and by letter, with a
Parisian marquise considerably his senior, Madame du Deffand, whom he
met in 1765. From her reading of the Walpole-Deffand letters, Anna de
Koven argues that they reveal Walpole's progressive seeking of a mother-
figure. Du Deffand herself says that Walpole "suppressed his feelings and
checked his conduct for fear of being ridiculed . . . and . . . he had a horror
of affectionate friendships caused by some great grief which he was un-
willing to impart." As a result, according to Martin Kallich, her romantic
exuberance exasperated and embarrassed Walpole to the point of his for-
bidding her to use the word *love* in her letters, and, later, even the word
friendship. In a letter of 16 October 1767, for example, Walpole circum-
spectly addresses her as "dear grandmaman" and closes with his being her
"devoted . . . affectionate grandson." [35]

It is hardly coincidental, then, that Walpole's famous *Castle of Otranto*
(1764) is in many ways a typical oedipal romance, as is his less famous
novel of incest, *The Mysterious Mother*, written three years later. [36] On the
other hand, Rousseau fudgingly claims that Gray "probably *was* exclu-
sively homosexual, especially in his attachment to his Cambridge pupil
Charles Victor de Bonstetten"—a moderation, in fact, of Hagstrum's
firmer case for Gray's homosexuality throughout his life. Hagstrum sums

up the "pattern" of Gray's life as follows: "the late-life passion for a young man; an excessive love of his mother; fear of the father; a witty, passionless heterosexual friendship [with Henrietta Jane Speed]; and cold-hearted impoliteness in contemplating the marriage of [Mason]." In fact, as early as Gray's Cambridge days, Hagstrum argues, his homoerotic emotions "were . . . overwhelming and obsessive." [37] George Haggerty goes even further, claiming (without pursuing the matter) that except in the sonnet on West's death and the *Elegy,* "Gray's internal conflict is played out *in each of his poems* in vivid and at times painful ways. . . . His feelings about his own dark and troubling sexuality are *everywhere apparent in his poetry.*" [38]

No such judgments, conjectures, or suspicions seem to have been leveled at West or Ashton—though I shall argue strongly for the former's inclusion in these terms in the Quadruple Alliance, and I will assume some degree of "propensity" on Ashton's part as well, if only on the grounds of the suspiciously few letters that have survived (and the mysteriousness of several of these), of his late marriage (at age forty-four) about which we know nothing, and of the fact that "English boys who awakened to their sexual difference by intimate bonding were often drawn to the clergy [as Ashton was, with Walpole's help] precisely because it offered them, in adulthood, shelter and refuge from the disappointments of the outside heterosexual world. This may be why so many homosexual students, at least in Britain [in the eighteenth century], were attracted to the posts of school-master, private tutor, and chaplain." [39]

The fourth and by far the most influential figure in the Alliance for understanding Gray's life, poetry, and career was Richard West. A "delicate" youth (as he is virtually always described), West was raised from age ten on by his mother, his father having died in 1726. His close friend at Eton, William Cole, described him as "slim, of a pale and meagre look and complexion," and from the mid-1730s to his death he was frequently ill, often debilitatingly. Unfortunately we know little else about him personally except what is derivable from his letters, his poetry, and assorted comments by the other members of the Quadruple Alliance. That "little," however, will suffice to enable a reasonably accurate history of his relationships with the other Alliance members, the most intense and complex, of course, being with Gray. While all these relationships emerge out of their Eton days together, in the case of Gray, particularly but not exclusively, they grow well beyond the fundamental defensiveness of the Quadruple Alliance. That bonding was conceived to solve what Alan Bray, in his landmark study *Homosexuality in Renaissance England,* calls "the most pressing problem" for homosexuals in early- to mid-eighteenth-century England: "not physical persecution; in the end only a minority had to face that. It was rather in the confusion and guilt that had to be faced in the conflict between homosexual desire and the manifest disapproval of the world about the frightened individual." [40]

"Manifest disapproval," however, was clearly not limited to overt, public (or semipublic) displays of homosexual attachments. As William Epstein has recently reminded us, the age was notorious for "the ubiquitous interception and opening of mail in England and throughout the Continent." [41] For example, West closes one of his letters to the touring Gray and Walpole with (the letter is entirely in French except for this), "I hope this silly, unmeaning thing won't be open'd & stop't at the post" (*CTG*, 120). In writing Walpole from Cambridge in 1764 Gray concludes with: "All letters to & from this place, that seem to promise any thing, are open'd (I hear) at the Gen: Post-Office" (*CTG*, 831); and a few months later he acknowledges receipt of a letter and parcel from Walpole "unrifled" (*CTG*, 834). Even as early as 1736 Gray had cautioned Walpole to fold his letters "with a little more wit, for your last had been open'd without breaking the Seal" (*CTG*, 48).

Such fears and anxieties, however, seem hardly to justify Epstein's main point about the Quadruple Alliance, namely that their "shared intellectual, emotional, and (in a few instances, probably) physical intimacies" were the root cause of their forming a secret "intelligence community" that Epstein aligns with cold-war conspiracies and intelligence communities. This is why their correspondence was "metaphorically interconnected by assumed identities, disguises, secrecy, surveillance, intrigue, and 'intelligence.'" Epstein goes on to argue, then, that "although there is as yet no convincing biographical evidence" to prove "Gray's obvious homoeroticism led to same-sex intimacy," scholars need now to assume rather than extenuate "the possibility." [42]

While I am unconvinced that such an assumption will especially illuminate the interconnectedness of Gray's life and poetic career, it will be clear that I place plus or minus zero value in assuming the opposite, the certain absence of same-sex intimacy between the several pairs of the Alliance. If "surveillance" and "intrigue" in their correspondence tends to overstate the case, there is no doubt of their efforts to maintain secrecy despite the fact that the Alliance's pet names and efforts to achieve an "intelligence community" were generally known at Eton—and possibly even at Cambridge. [43] In the *Monthly Review* of August 1775, for example, Mason's quotation of an anonymous judgment of Gray's personal deportment in public is said to have left "his friend and poet under the idea of a *fastidious fribble*. . . . It is true, the world knew it. When he entered Peter House, his effeminacy and fair complexion drew upon him the name Miss Gray." And when he returned from his European tour with Walpole, Gray is reported to have worn a "muff . . . , an object of no small derision with the university lads!" (101–2). That there were only about a dozen undergraduates in residence at Peterhouse when Gray first entered seems, at least, to render the nicknaming more legendary than factual, though the charge of effeminacy is one that punctuates gossip about him throughout his life. And we do know that, until Walpole's arrival at King's College nine months after Gray's, Gray hobnobbed almost exclusively with Ashton (who had gone up earlier)—no doubt, as Ketton-Cremer says, "to talk of Eton days, and revive the jokes and slang of the Quadruple Alliance."[44]

Gray's seemingly congenital "despondence and morose self-image" that are ubiquitous throughout his correspondence were clearly fueled, though probably did not originate, here.[45] In fact, Roger Martin, in his 1935 *Essai sur Thomas Gray* contends that "Gray's neurosis stemmed from an unfortunate childhood and a congenital nervous disorder."[46] The latter is only an intriguing speculation but the former seems reasonable given Gray's brutal father and severely abused mother, and his being plunged at age nine from what euphemistically has been called "the dispiriting atmosphere of his home" into the "alarming" and "bewildering confusion of a great public school," where his only solace lay in "shrinking from contact with the herd" into the camaraderie of the Quadruple Alliance.[47] While Ketton-Cremer thoroughly romanticizes, not to say sanitizes, Gray's Eton years as "unquestionably the happiest he was ever to know" (3), the available evidence (though scant) suggests rather that such a judgment is more applicable to Walpole than to Gray, whose Eton College Ode (Ketton-Cremer's main "evidence") is, as we shall see, hardly a sentimental exercise in nostalgia/melancholy.

In a relatively recent essay on Gray's letters, Robert Snyder says that "we may never know the precise causes of Gray's depression" but he suspects, and then "proves," that "it was linked closely to his cultural inheritance and to his perception of the dominant values of his time," neither of which unfortunately is sufficiently established to be a compelling reason. But he does say, helpfully if not with striking originality, that Gray's letters reflect a tension between "the world of affairs as the arena for self-realization" and "the sacrifice of self-possession which it seems to entail." Concomitant with that, Gray is said to have yearned "for direct human contact which yet frustrates itself through a wary diffidence of being realized,"[48] a remarkably fuzzy idea that, despite Snyder's avoidance of the issue, does make sense with respect to Gray's homosexual/ homoerotic (or even merely homosocial) desires—especially as they are evidenced in his intercourse with Richard West and his plangent recollections of him even long after his death. It is only in those terms, as developed so tellingly by Hagstrum, that one just might accede to Snyder's judgment of Gray's "melancholy" as "a variant mode of eighteenth-century sensibility."[49]

All this, I suppose, sounds suspiciously like the prelude to a psychobiography, and I am not unwilling that what follows be received as something *like* a psychobiography. I have eschewed, however, an elaborate skein of theoretical underpinnings from Freud or Foucault or Lacan or Irigaray or Kristeva—or from other related, off-quoted authorities—in my pursuit of what I have called Gray's "agon." If certain of these underpinnings surface here and there, in general intricate psychoanalytic theories and criticism would, I believe, unnecessarily cloud my intention to illuminate not so much Gray's life as Gray's life *in* his poetry, not so much Gray as man but Gray as poet seeing himself as a man, not so much Gray's psyche as his imaginative reflections and representations of that psyche in the poetry, of which it is fundamentally constitutive. In short, I essay not so much a biography as a poetic autobiography, his "secret life" (as it were) shorn of the melodramatization inherent in that phrase.

What I have in mind is something like the distinction drawn by James Olney between "autobiography simplex" and "autobiography duplex." "One might say," he writes, "that autobiography is simple when . . . one can detach the style from the substance and can handle and dissect it to see what it reveals about its maker." Rather than seeing that style "as turn[ing] back on itself with self-criticism, there is the felt assumption . . . that this is the way the thing is said, that there is no other way."[50] All the debate about, the excuses and apologia for, and the attempts to explain away Gray's famous "artifice" seem to me to be of this order, to point toward and to justify the prevailing conclusions about his "sensibility" and even his "preromanticism" (whether in old-fashioned literary-historical terms or in Marshall Brown's attempted rejuvenation of that now widely derided term).[51] In contrast, the act of duplex autobiography, "both as creation and as recreation constitute[s] a bringing to consciousness of the nature of one's own existence, transforming the mere fact of existence into a realized quality and a possible meaning," a "definition of the writer's self . . . in the present, at the time of writing," an awareness "of himself describing himself in the past" coupled with an awareness "that this awareness is his present view on reality" (Olney, 44). And, one might add, his present view on his "real" self, both the then-ness and now-ness of what Hagstrum has called (to me unarguably) Thomas Gray Agonistes, about whom we know so little, in a poetic era that we still find ungrasp-able, not to say uncharacterizable.

One final note. In 1979 Paul de Man argued that "the autobiographical project may itself produce and determine the life and that whatever the writer *does* is in fact governed by the technical demands of self-portraiture and thus determined, in all its aspects, by the resources of his medium."[52] My point in the following pages is that rather than writing a *Prelude* or some other poetic (or prose) form of autobiography, Gray set out to write a poetry that at once would determine and reflect the life of *a* poet—a project in which his editor and biographer, William Mason, eagerly and (un)scrupulously conspired. The latter's biography, in fact, as well as his cavalier and even ruthless editing of the poems and letters, powerfully govern our reading of the poetry as that of a gentleman scholar and man of letters par excellence. The portraiture we have received, then, in large measure is determined by the technical resources of Mason's media, not Gray's. Gray therefore opted for the only alternative available to him as poet to give us his self, what I have called the insistent yet hidden, oc-cluded, disguised, and secret subtext that to date has been as largely un-recognizable as the poems have become widely recognized and signally memorable. If, as de Man noted, "autobiographical discourse [is] a dis-course of self-restoration" (74), what Gray restores via his subtext (*pace* de Man's claim for prosopopoeia) is a self whose name, in his milieu, can be made "intelligible and memorable" only as a face without a name.[53] De Man's autobiography thus is the one which Mason governs by his editorial depredations, the one Gray's poems only ostensibly convey to us, the one that is a deliberate disfigurement "to the precise extent that it restores" again and again to our readerly consciousnesses the Gray we (and Mason) know and love. Even more crucially, that bio-/autobiography "veils a dis-placement of the mind of which it is itself [in this case but a witting partner in] the cause" (de Man, 81), even as that mind reveals itself to us, movingly and powerfully, in its subtextual restoration of its buried self.

Rather than clinically psychobiographize, then, my approach to Gray and his poetry will be seen to verge on seeing the poems as what John

H. Gagnon and William Simon call "intrapsychic scripts," and the letters (particularly those to and from West) as "interpersonal scripts." At the most personal level of their subtextuality, the poems consist of "private fantasies that reorganize reality in ways to satisfy the individual's 'many-layered and sometimes multi-voiced wishes.' As an individual plays them out in imagination, intrapsychic scripts seem to come from the deepest self" even as "cultural scripting is at work, particularly as an individual gives play to conflicting desires and to wishes that cannot readily be accommodated in cultural scenarios or in interpersonal scripts." These quotations are from Bruce Smith's remarkable *Homosexual Desire in Shakespeare's England,* where the concluding remark rests solidly on his underlying conviction that, as "Latin is a male code-language" so "only poetic discourse," not moral or legal or medical, "can address homosexual desire." [54] I would differ from Smith only on the issue of interpersonal scripts, since my argument will be, as indicated above, that the Gray-West correspondence is in fact an interpsychic scripting of their deepest selves, their mutual homosexual desires and the fears deriving therefrom, replete with precisely the same private fantasies Gray's poetry dramatically plays out in his poetic imagination.

The Miltonic
Background

In order to gain a purchase on the interlocking double narrative of personal histories that Gray's poetry enacts, it is necessary to address the origins and precise nature of his engagement with Milton's ghost.[1] More accurately, we need to try to determine how Gray perceived his relationship to his illustrious predecessor in the progress of poesy, for his awe (adoration *and* fear) of Milton is only partially grounded in the familiar terms of the early eighteenth-century's intensely self-conscious post-Miltonism. It is hardly necessary to document the fact that the entire century was profoundly influenced by Milton's achievement, and if the power of his precedent as poet and as man showed little signs of waning throughout the nineteenth century (indeed until the generation of Eliot and Pound spoke out loud and bold),[2] it is also true that anxieties about that achievement and precedent progressively waned with, or were submerged by, the growing power and status of (especially) Wordsworth's poetry.[3]

Before Gray appeared on the scene, Milton's preeminence (except for Shakespeare) among English poets had for several decades been firmly established by critics, editors, and poets alike, despite the hostility provoked in some quarters by his political and religious opinions. He had been eulogized (though less frequently, and never habitually, imitated or borrowed from) in prose and verse by Dryden, but Pope's substantial borrowings date from the pastorals and extend through *The Dunciad*. Although neither of these two giants can be charged with being Milton-haunted, or even with being in any real sense "Miltonic" poets (witness Dryden's idiosyncratic lower-than-"middle-flight" opera, *The State of Innocence*), the vast majority of their lesser contemporaries in the first three decades of the century (except, perhaps, for Thomson) were prompted into more or less flaccid imitations. Usually these took the form of translations, ersatz panegyrics, dutiful (mostly religious) moralizings, or second-to-tenth-rate burlesques—more often than not cast in unrhymed couplets or gussied up to masquerade as blank verse. *Miltonic*, then, meant less sublimity and daring than it did the salient features of a poetic style and diction that at least seemed more readily imitable.[4] On those occasions when *Miltonic* did mean to some poets sublime soaring, the results were generally akin to Sir Richard Blackmore's infamous and unintentional parodies, which in turn were parodied by others—the insufferable epics *Prince Arthur, King Arthur, Eliza,* and *Alfred,* all appearing between 1695 and 1723.

In criticism the picture is somewhat different. Writing in the midst of the ancients-moderns debate, John Dennis attacked not only the "gaudiness and inane phraseology" Wordsworth pilloried in his immediate predecessors and contemporaries but the artistic poverty, grossness of sentiment, and inappropriateness of language that the poetry of the day—especially in 1700 with Dryden dead—wallowed in. Since for him poetry of a high order springs from the deepest and loftiest passions of our nature, according to Dennis any reformation of its debased state must take the form of sacred themes dealt with poetically in such a way as to reinstill in the human breast the inspiring influence of elevated religious feeling. It is in this, Dennis argues, that the ancient poets excel the moderns. But if their enthusiasm derived from religion, and pagan religions have long since been proved false, clearly a truer modern inspiration, as well as a truer sublimity, must derive from the Christian religion. As Thomas Greene puts it, "From Petrarch's youth to Milton's age Europe awaited the poet and the poem which would demonstrate the equality of the modern age to antiquity. . . . At issue . . . was the imaginative richness of the Christian religion."[5] But Dennis went even beyond "equality": his English Milton surpassed not only all English poets but the ancients as well. Before he completed his formulation of these central critical tenets in expansive, detailed, and endlessly repetitive form in *The Grounds of Criticism in Poetry* (1704, intended as the first portion of his abortive *A Criticism upon our most celebrated English Poets Deceas'd*), Dennis in 1692 called Milton "one of the most sublime" English poets, and in 1696 "the sublimest of all our Poets." By 1704 *Paradise Lost* was not only "the very best of our Epick poems" but "the most lofty . . . that has been produc'd by the Mind of Man." And as late as 1725 Dennis's Milton was still "the Immortal Authour of the sublimest Poem that ever was writt in the world"[6] (he had little to say of *Paradise Regained* or *Samson Agonistes*), in its force, sublimity, elevation, and terrible majesty surpassing even Homer and Virgil.

That Gray early in his life read Dennis with some care is certain, as we shall see shortly, and Milton's already awesome presence in Gray's studious mind was clearly intensified by the critic's powerful testimony. But even if, as Raymond D. Havens argues (not entirely accurately), "the first great protagonist of *Paradise Lost* was not Addison but the forgotten John Dennis,"[7] Addison's eloquent, widely read *Spectator* papers on *Paradise Lost* echo, extend, and popularly disseminate Dennis's panegyrics. Like Dennis he does not argue that modern poets should imitate Milton if they aspire to be what Blake called "true poets," but Addison's meticulous book-by-book tour through *Paradise Lost* in eighteen separate papers (six of which range beyond that poem) reflects both his assumption of a wide audience knowledgeable about Milton's great poem but also, therefore, one that would readily appreciate his analyses of those particular "Beauties" constitutive of its greatness, incomparable sublimity, and majesty— in conception, language, sentiment, description, and character portrayal. Whether Addison actually widened Milton's readership in England is open to question; nor was that his aim. Rather, free of Dennis's single-minded concentration on the intrinsic sublimity of Milton's Christian subject but still sensitive to the reigning critical dicta respecting epic, Addison established the particular grounds for an intelligent and deeper enjoyment of *Paradise Lost* by readers already prepared to enjoy it. There is little doubt that Gray was one of these.

While Addison's impact cannot be overestimated, Edward Bysshe's amazingly popular *Art of English Poetry* (1702; ten editions in all) not only reflected but helped to form the reading taste of the times. In his "Rules for Making English Verse" and in more than half of his 384-page "Collection of the most Natural, Agreeable, and Noble *Thoughts* . . ." Bysshe quotes nearly eight hundred lines from Milton, all from *Paradise Lost*, thereby implicitly arguing a Miltonic readership even more populous than Dennis, perhaps even Addison, had assumed.[8] On the other hand, Bysshe's Milton quotations, most of which are the same passages cited by Dennis and Addison, probably would have impressed the scholarly Gray less (had he actually read Bysshe) than the more authoritative judgments of the two powerful early-century critics. In any case, and however startling to twentieth-century readers, it is little wonder that between 1705 and 1800 there were over 100 editions or publications of *Paradise Lost*.

For all this public adulation, however, and despite the equally demon-strable fact that not all early post-Miltonic poetry was weakly and pas-sively imitative, before 1732 or so several negative elements in Milton's achievement and precedent were not infrequently cited, not least (aside from his political, social, and religious views) the fact that his verse, lan-guage, and literary form were deleterious, even stultifying, to the poetry of his successors. After 1732, despite continuing suspicion of Milton the man, as anti-Royalist, antiprelatical blasphemer, and arch antitraditionalist in general, Milton as poet began to become "a universal standard of excel-lence, an expression of authority, a pattern for imitation, and a source for poetical license."[9] And even with nagging uncertainties about his personal views, by 1753 he was taken to Britain's bosom in terms succinctly sum-marized in that year by Theophilus Cibber:

> The British Nation, which has produced the greatest men in every profession, before the appearance of Milton could not enter into any competition with antiquity, with regard to the sublime excellences of poetry. . . . The ancients . . . stood unrivalled by all succeeding times, and in epic poetry, which is justly esteemed the highest effort of genius, Homer had no rival. When Milton appeared, the pride of Greece was humbled . . . , and since Paradise Lost is ours[,] it would, perhaps, be an injury to our national fame to yield the palm to any state, whether ancient or modern.[10]

Cibber's views articulate sharply what Arthur Johnston suggests more broadly (in terms one need not agree with to assent to his fundamental point) in his essay on "Poetry and Criticism after 1740": "In one respect the period 1740–1780 is engaged on a quest for a lost literary culture, which was found in the Elizabethan age, when national credulity, chas-tened by reason, had produced a sort of civilized superstition, and left a set of traditions fanciful enough for poetic decoration, and yet not too violent and chimerical for common sense."[11] Roger Lonsdale, however, seems to me to come even closer to the truth by arguing that "what was happening to English poetry in the 1740s, as one sees the younger poets moving, for example, away from the inevitable influence of Pope to persis-tent echoing of the diction and phrasing of Spenser, Shakespeare, and Milton, . . . [is] a reorientation of poetry . . . to the pre-Restoration native tradition."[12] Moreover, this "reorientation" seriously called into question the hoary doctrine of obligatory imitation of the ancients so dear to the hearts of late-seventeenth- and early-eighteenth-century critics and poets alike—even while that fundamental critical and creative principle continued to sustain itself throughout much of the rest of the century.

Much more might be cited here to remind us of just how glorious Milton's reception was in the early decades of the eighteenth century, but I should like to focus on a less frequently acknowledged aspect of that reception, one that is crucial to understanding Gray's perception of Milton's legacy. If Milton was rarely envisioned as Satanic in the sense of Blake's enlistment of him in "the devils party," there were some sputtering disputes about who was the hero of *Paradise Lost* ever since Dryden raised the question. To the extent that Milton was associatable with Satan, his political and religious "rebelliousness" was usually to blame, a "misfortune" (as Andrew Marvell called it in his defense of him) attributable to his "living in a tumultuous time," his being "toss'd on the wrong side," and his writing "*Flagrante bello* certain dangerous Treatises."[13] On the other hand it is also Marvell who initially provides the terms defining the reverse side of Gray's hardly unusual awe at Milton's achievement and stature, his acute sense of Milton's presumptuousness and transgressiveness in writing *Paradise Lost.*

Marvell confesses an initial fear, in his "On Paradise Lost" (prefixed to the 1674 edition of Milton's poem),

> That he would ruine (for I saw him strong)
> The sacred Truths to Fable and old Song
> (So *Sampson* groap'd the Temples Posts in spight)
> The World o'rewhelming to revenge his sight.

This fear is compounded by a second, as Marvell continued to read the poem: that Milton would be unable, though "bold," to succeed in "his vast Design" of "Heav'n, Hell, Earth, Chaos, All," that indeed he might "perplex the things he would explain, / And what was easie . . . render vain." Both fears allayed by his full reading, Marvell then asserts "that no room is here for Writers left, / But to detect their Ignorance or Theft," and that the poem's reigning majesty, even when it dares to treat "things divine," preserves Milton (as well as his readers) as "inviolate." And, finally, Marvell attributes Milton's achievement ("above humane flight soar[ing] aloft") to "Just Heav'n" which, to "requite" him, "like Tiresias . . . / Rewards with Prophesie thy loss of sight."

There is little doubt that Gray knew Marvell's poem, and even less (I believe) that he read himself into Marvell's lines, specifically his own

gnawing sense of transgressiveness in attempting to soar aloft above hu-
man flight. The familiar portrait of Milton in *The Progress of Poesy* presents
him as

> he, that rode sublime
> Upon the seraph-wings of Ecstasy,
> The secrets of the abyss to spy.
> He passed the flaming bounds of place and time:
> The living throne, the sapphire blaze,
> Where angels tremble while they gaze,
> He saw; but blasted with excess of light,
> Closed his eyes in endless night.

The transposition here of Marvell's terms is instructive, as are Gray's obvi-
ous omissions. Whereas Marvell's "aloft" becomes Gray's more generic
"sublime," Gray's allusion is far more pointedly to Christ's cherubic char-
iot ("He on the wings of Cherub rode sublime," *PL* 6. 771), thus reflecting
his sense that Milton's usurpation of the Son's power was the root cause
of the Father's divine punishment of everduring dark. Marvell, of course,
says no such thing. Rather, with a nod to his own account of Samson's
avenging his blindness, Marvell transforms Milton's into a heavenly re-
quital, the reward of prophetic insight that enabled the in-spiration of
Paradise Lost.

Yet Gray's deepest fears are also reflected in Marvell's prophecy that
after Milton "no room is . . . for Writers left"—precisely the argument of
one of the closest eighteenth-century imitations of Marvell's poem, the
reclusive Sneyd Davies' long *Rhapsody to Milton*. A few samples may suf-
fice to show Davies' language as uncannily apt to Gray's sense of his own
predicament:

> Soul of the Muses! Thou supreme of Verse!
> Unskill'd and Novice in the sacred Art
> May I unblam'd approach thee? May I crave
> Thy Blessing, Sire harmonious! amply pleas'd
> Shou'd'st thou vouchsafe to own me for thy Son.

This remarkable appropriation of the invocation to Book 3 of *Paradise Lost*,
a passage Gray himself alludes to frequently, explicitly articulates what
Gray dared express only to himself and was constrained to suggest only
obliquely in the near-subliminal subtext of much of his poetry. Where

Milton, in hailing that "holy Light, offspring of Heav'n first-born" even "Before the sun," expresses his temerity with "May I express thee un-blamed?", Davies boldly places Milton himself in the role of divine muse, "holy light," coeternal with the Eternal, as indeed a poetic God-the-Father ("Sire harmonious") of whom he aspires to be vouchsafed the son if (again in Milton's terms) Milton will be well pleased with Davies' prayer—albeit a son expressed humbly by Davies as "dwindled from the mighty Size, / And Stature; much more from the Parent's Mind."

Davies then goes on to survey briefly the awesomeness of Milton's "Heav'nly Notions," "the Burden of [his] Thought," his language that makes "all other Verse / . . . trifling (not excepting *Greece* and *Rome*)," his "Eagle's Flight" and "Dove-like" poising in "th' unconscious Sky," the "Scene of *Eden*," the "bolder Page" of the war in heaven, and Milton's Hell that "Copied by other Hand whate'er, will lose / It's Terrors; and thy Paradise it's Sweets / Soil'd by rude Touch." It is enough, then, "to admire, / Silent admire" and be content to feel. Even though the poem proposes that one *might* aspire to resemble ("tho' in inferior Strain") rather than rival Milton, Davies concludes with an unqualified prophecy of an inveterately and abysmally failed progeny of would-be imitators:

> Ah me! I fear,
> And see, and feel the Reason; Faulters why
> The Muse this Moment, wearied, flags and pants
> Despairing? Such a Distance hast thou got
> From thy first start, and left Pursuit behind:
> On the Top Brow of Fame, in laure!'d Chair
> Seated, and thence to look down on Mortal Toil,
> That climbing emulous would pace in vain
> Thy footsteps, trackless thro' Excess of Light.[14]

What can be seen from this skeletal history of eighteenth-century criticism of Milton, and more generally in all compilations of Milton criticism from the poet's death to the rise of the Romantics (and their taking Satan to their own revolutionary bosoms), is the seeming absence (except in Marvell and Davies) of any substantive anticipation of Gray's belief that his model predecessor had Satanically and fatefully transgressed human bounds. Hints may be found here and there but with few exceptions they are limited to debates over Milton's supposed Arianism or Socinianism. A sampling of these will suggest how muted the charges of transgression are, especially when compared to Gray's readings. A letter to the *Gentleman's*

Magazine of April 1738, cribbing directly from *Spectator* 315, argues that "*Milton*'s Majesty forsakes him ... where the Divine Persons are introduced as Speakers. One may ... observe that the Author proceeds with a kind of fear and trembling, whilst he describes the Sentiments of the Almighty." William Wilkie's preface to his *The Epigoniad* (Edinburgh, 1757) levies a charge of "impiety" against Milton for representing the deity in "the form and condition of a man," contriving "for him a particular character, and method of acting, agreeable to the prejudices of weak and ignorant mortals." Although Christ himself did that "in the early ages of the church, it would be indecent in any man to use the same freedom, and do that for God, which he only has a right to do for himself." Dealing with the Father, Son, and life in heaven "according to the narrowness of human prejudice" is "inconsistent with truth, and the exalted ideas which we ought to entertain of divine things." It is a charge repeated ad nauseam throughout most of the century.[15]

Far more interesting than these, and not entirely unusual, is a dialogic essay by Daniel Webb in *Remarks on the Beauties of Poetry* (1762) on the "purpose of imagery," illustrated by two passages on Satan (1. 589–91; 10. 441–50). The dialogue concludes that "the principal beauties in *Paradise Lost* have been naturally thrown on the person of Satan," for unlike the "one blaze" of "permanent and unchangeable glory" that is the Godhead, "fallen Greatness ... , interrupted splendor ... , a superior nature sunk and disgraced, but emerging at intervals from its degradation" is "so truly poetic" that "the senses are hurried away beyond the reach of reflection." The respondent to this argument characterizes it as "the best apology I ever heard for a diabolical greatness."[16] Even Johnson, whose criticism of Milton oscillates in time between dislike of him as a man and admiration for much of his achievement, pooh-poohs Dryden's snide remark about Milton's flats among his elevations: "Milton, when he has expatiated in the sky, may be allowed sometimes to revisit earth; for what other author ever soared so high, or sustained his flight so long?" Philip Neve, later in the century (*Cursory Remarks on Some of the Ancient English Poets, Particularly Milton*, 1789), goes this familiar locution and conception one better: "*Shakespeare*, though the first scholar in the volume of mankind, rises 'above the wheeling poles,' but in glances and flashes of sublimity; *Tasso* up to the heavens 'presumes'; but *Milton* 'into the heaven of heavens,' [soars] and dwells there. He inhabits, as it were, the court of the Deity."[17] To that extraordinary note I shall but append a rather wonderful poetic

version of Neve's domiciling of Milton. It is by Blake's sometime friend
and enemy William Hayley:

> Apart, and on a sacred hill retir'd,
> Beyond all mortal inspiration fir'd,
> The mighty MILTON sits—an host around
> Of list'ning Angels guard the holy ground;
> Amaz'd they see a human form aspire
> To grasp with daring hand a Seraph's lyre,
> Inly irradiate with celestial beams,
> Attempt those high, those soul-subduing themes,
> (Which humbler Denizens of Heaven decline)
> And celebrate, with sanctity divine,
> The starry field from warring Angels won,
> And God triumphant in his Victor Son.
>
> .   .   .   .
>
> With such pure joy as our Forefather knew
> When Raphael, heavenly guest, first met his view,
> And our glad Sire, within his blissful bower,
> Drank the pure converse of th' aetherial Power,
> Round the blest Bard his raptur'd audience throng
> And felt their souls imparadis'd in song.[18]

Of course, Gray could not have read Hayley, nor need we assume that
he saw the other texts I have cited (Dennis, Addison, and possibly Davies
aside), but Hayley's sense of Milton's aspiration "Beyond all mortal inspi-
ration," his "daring" and high attempt, and his godlike success in "impara-
dising" even the souls of angels, all sound notes reminiscent of the pas-
sage from Gray's *Progress of Poesy* I have cited before. What is largely
absent in all these criticisms, however, is any sense of Milton's *satanic*
transgressiveness, of his presumptuously, invasively gazing upon "The liv-
ing throne, the sapphire-blaze" where even "angels tremble" at the sight,
and of having his eyes "blasted with excess of light" in punishment there-
fore. In his notes to *The Progress* in the 1768 edition of his poems, Gray
cites as the source for his implicit reordering of events in Milton's life the
Odyssey's account in Book 8 of the Muse's blinding of Demodocus and
her granting him in exchange the power of sweet song. Since the idea of
punishment or retributive requital is no part of the Muse's act (indeed
she loves Demodocus intensely), Gray's pointing to this source seems an
intentional obscuring of the implications of his own lines, a tactic habitu-

ally employed in his lifelong poetic and autobiographical relation with
Milton as both poet and man. Moreover, it also reflects his conflicted sense
that Milton had dared too much (thereby becoming a reflection of, alter-
nately, his own Satan, Eve, and Adam), even though the extraordinary
success of that daring made him the epitome of the great poet, and *Para-
dise Lost* the epitome of the great poem, the greatest the world had ever
seen. Indeed, as acute a reader of Milton as he was, Gray could not but
recognize the telltale evidence of Milton's own sense of Satanlike trans-
gression, of poetic presumption beyond the limits of sublunary human
imagination and aspiration—as well as, perhaps, evidence of a kind of
subliminally confessed guilt (or at least incipient guilt) deriving from that
presumption.

Even more important for this study, Gray, I believe, increasingly saw in
Paradise Lost a specular image of himself, of his own agon that was being
played out in his poetry but only rarely illuminated there by the sort of
spotlight Milton shines upon himself and his own mind. Let me put the
matter, the essence of that agon, more bluntly. Gray came to regard his
own aspiration to emulate Milton as precisely the same kind of "Satanlike
transgression" of holy ground, the same "poetic presumption beyond the
limits of human imagination and aspiration," and the same guilt deriving
from that transgressive presumption that he regarded as being enacted in
Paradise Lost: as God and heaven were to Milton, so Milton and poetic
immortality were to Gray; as *Paradise Lost* was to Milton, so Gray's poetry
was to him. Although there is no evidence that Gray read Jonathan Rich-
ardson's 1734 *Explanatory Notes and Remarks on Milton's Paradise Lost* (al-
though Richardson did paint Gray's portrait when Gray was about fifteen),
the painter/critic's formulation of Milton's achievement is apt here. He
suggests "that *Paradise Lost* be treated like Scripture, like the revealed
Word of God . . . , not simply as a classic, but as a sacred classic text, a
Psalms rendered more sublime by its Christian subject."[19] And since it
was "Scripture," and Milton therefore "God," Gray's intense sense of what
he himself was "daring" in his poetic career—and therefore in virtually all
his intersections, biographical and poetic, with Milton's poem and life—is
self-protectively submerged beneath the decorous language and atmo-
sphere of his so-called sensibility.

We need, then, to recall here those famous and oft-commented-upon
passages in *Paradise Lost* where Milton speaks out about himself and his
own epic enterprise, passages to which Gray returns repeatedly in his po-

etry and, clearly, in his most intensely self-scrutinizing moments as well.
I refer, of course, to the invocations to Books 1, 3, 7, and 9). While there
is little point here in my entering into the theological, psychobiographical,
political, and poetic complexities of the abundant critical interpretations
these invocations have provoked, I do need to examine some of Milton's
language to suggest not only the obvious—that like many modern critics
Gray read them as accurately reflecting Milton's state of mind in compos-
ing *Paradise Lost*—but the less obvious point that Gray saw in them an
articulation of his own state of mind in his efforts to emulate the master.

To begin at the beginning, the invocation of the "Heav'nly Muse" in
Book 1 leads to an extraordinary set of conflations or multiple identifica-
tions. If the conventionally feminine associations a reader attaches to the
muse of a male poet obtain, they are all but vitiated immediately by Mil-
ton's evocation of Moses's direct theophanies on Mount Horeb and Sinai,
hearing the voice of God and thereby being literally in-spired to inscribe
God's word in the Bible's sacred text. Milton then extends the Muse's
signification to the temple of Jerusalem and thence to the son's ministry
and miracles, specifically his healing of the congenitally blind man with
moistened clay and the man's subsequent washing away of both clay and
blindness "in the pool of Siloam" (John 9:1–11).[20] And, finally, it is that
entire complex of inspirations which Milton reverently and with "upright
heart and pure" calls upon to aid his "advent'rous song, / That with no
middle flight intends to soar / Above th' Aonian mount [i.e., above those
"flights" empowered merely by Helicon's muses], while it pursues /
Things unattempted yet in prose or rhyme." While it is patently impossi-
ble to know Gray's precise response to this virtuoso invocation (not yet
complete where I've left it, of course), it is also impossible that he was
unaware of Milton's self-conscious trepidation and presumption in these
first sixteen lines.[21] Milton will be the new Moses, inspired directly by
God, but at the same time he will be somehow superior to Moses in the
adventuresomeness of his flight *above* and beyond the Muses' sanction,
implicitly above Horeb and Sinai in pursuit of that which has *never* been
done by mortal man.

The full power of the word "advent'rous" here must detain us, for its
implications are inherent in Gray's veneration and fear of Milton's model.
For both poets it becomes progressively in *Paradise Lost* a word and idea
that hovers round Satan. For example, in Book 2 Beelzebub's proposal,
inspired by Satan himself, to appoint someone to "tempt with wand'ring

feet" the infinite abyss "or spread his airy flight / Upborne with indefatiga-
ble wings / Over the vast abrupt" (404–5, 407–9) becomes "th' adventure"
(474). Satan becomes to the fallen host "their great adventurer" (10. 440),
and to himself, "returned / Successful beyond hope" from his journey, he
is the conquering (or about-to-conquer) hero who "by my adventure hard /
With peril great achieved" (10. 462–63, 468–69). In Satan's absence the
efforts of the fallen angels to find some "easier habitation" by exploring
the horrors of hell are also described as adventures, the wandering host
themselves as "th' advent'rous bands" (2. 570, 615). Sin and Death's at-
tempt to find a path from hell to the new world is "Advent'rous work"
(10. 255). When in Book 6 Milton uses the same adjective to characterize
the mobilized heavenly armies' preparations to do "advent'rous deeds /
Under their godlike leaders, in the cause / Of God and his Messiah" (66–
68), the effect of the repetition, sandwiched between the plural occur-
rences of the word in Books 2 and 10, has an oddly disconcerting reso-
nance. And finally, the adventurousness of Satan and his cohorts and of
their respective journeys and deeds Milton dramatically transfers to the
fallen Eve in such a way as to evoke, if distantly, his own invocation to
Book 1. "Bold deed thou hast presumed, advent'rous Eve," says Adam,
"And peril great provoked, who thus hast dared" (9. 921–22)—her bold-
ness at once Satanic and implicitly analogous to Milton's assumption of
Godlike powers in the exordium to Book 1.

Similarly, consider Milton's word "unattempted" ("Things unat-
tempted yet in prose or rhyme"), which retrospectively can be seen/heard
as consorting with "tempted." That Milton was fully aware of the lexical
relationship of these words goes without saying. The opening of Book 10
is but one of many instances where they are used interchangeably: God
"Hindered not Satan to attempt the mind / Of man" and, Milton says,
Adam and Eve "ought to have still remembered" God's "high injunction
not to taste that fruit, / Whoever tempted" (5–15). Less noticeable but no
less pertinent is an instance in *Paradise Regained:* just as Milton earlier
announced that his "advent'rous song" with "no middle flight" will "soar"
even as it "pursues" things "unattempted yet," here the "Tempter" "with
these words his temptation pursue[s]" (2. 404–5). Two more "attempts"
from Milton's two later epics will suggest the remarkable range of the
resonances that emerge from these usages. In his colloquy with Harapha,
Samson refers to himself as "thy appellant, / Though by his blindness
maimed for high attempt" (1220–21), and in *Paradise Regained* Satan
tempts Christ with

> wherefore deprive
> All earth her wonder at thy acts, thyself
> The fame and glory, glory the reward
> That sole excites to high attempts the flame
> Of most erected spirits, most tempered pure
> Ethereal, who all pleasures else despise,
> All treasures and all gain esteem as dross,
> And dignities and powers, all but the highest?
>
> (3. 23–30)

Did Gray tune in to all these disturbing resonances? Probably not—or almost certainly not to the point I have argued. But if we recall his praise of Milton's exquisite ear, it would be absurd to suggest that Gray's ear, fully capable of relishing Milton's sonorousness, was incapable of registering at least some.

But even if it cannot be claimed confidently that he made all *my* connections, it is hard to imagine the final nine to ten lines of the opening of *Paradise Lost* not registering clearly for Gray Milton's sense of his transgressiveness as well as their mirroring of Gray's own self-conscious anxiety about daring too much. For these lines Milton invokes God's creative power and wisdom to instruct him—in one sense a modest enough beseechment; but immediately he then equates his own hoped- and prayed-for creative powers with the creative, inseminating power of Divinity sitting "Dove-like brooding on the vast abyss" and making it pregnant—if not exactly Coleridge's "finite act of creation in the infinite I AM," then certainly the dove's descent at Jesus's baptism and the Spirit which "moved upon the face of the waters" in Genesis 1:2.[22]

To as attentive a reader as Gray, even clearer than the implications of this remarkable proem, however, is the retrospective power it garners from its relationships to the famous, even more intensely personal/autobiographical invocation of Book 3. Like the originary creative power of God which "from the first / Wast present" (to whom Milton prayed in Book 1 so that "what in me is dark" be illumined), the "Eternal coeternal beam" of "holy Light" is apostrophized in Book 3 as the power invested in "the rising world of waters dark and deep" of Genesis 1 that was "Won from the void and formless infinite" by God's "increate" creativity. Here, then, is Milton's own already demonstrated (in Books 1 and 2) creative power to illumine what was but darkness, to win from the "void of light" (1. 181), the "void of pain" (2. 219), the "void profound" (2. 438), and the "void immense" (2. 829) of hell the "rising world" of his poem—and to "win" as well the risen world *in* the poem, now newly created and toward which Satan is flying. That is to say, recalling his prayer for the Heavenly Muse to aid his adventurous song in soaring to hitherto unattempted heights, Milton now asserts his internalization of that power to essay suprahuman, supraHeliconian flight with even "bolder wing," rising now out of "Chaos and eternal Night" even as his poem too rises as "The rising world . . . / Won from the void and formless infinite."

The presumptuousness of Milton's language is inescapable, especially since he then goes on to metamorphose that daring into self-conscious transgression by echoing, in his own bold flight "Through utter and through middle darkness borne,"[23] the terms of Satan's prior flight in Book 2. "With thoughts inflamed of highest design" (recall Milton's "highth of this great argument" in 1. 24), Satan "Puts on swift wings, and toward the gates of hell / Explores his solitary flight," "soars / Up to the fiery concave tow'ring high" in quest of the world of light above the "spacious empire" of Chaos and Ancient Night (630–32, 634–35, 974). "With fresh alacrity and force renewed" by Chaos's encouragement ("go and speed"), Satan then

> Springs upward like a pyramid of fire
> Into the wild expanse, and through the shock
> Of fighting elements, on all sides round
> Environed, *wins his* way. . . .
> (1012–16; my italics)

"Harder beset" than other "heroes" like Jason and Ulysses but with the same "difficulty and labor" (1016, 1021) that Milton himself overcame in his "hard and rare" ascent (3. 21), Satan approaches "at last the sacred influence / Of light" (the "Bright effluence of bright essence increate" of 3. 5) shooting from the "walls of heav'n / . . . far into the bosom of dim Night / A glimmering dawn" (2. 1034–37).

Although Milton's language in lines 13–21 of Book 3's exordium is, as I have already suggested, in its simplest sense a reference to his poetic achievement in Books 1 and 2 as well as a prospectus for the events of Books 3–6, its first-person syntax and metaphorical account of his completing the books on hell and darkness—taken together now with his asserted intent to survey the precincts of light on earth and in heaven—powerfully speak to Satan's actual *physical*, not imaginative, experience, descent, and reascent. Indeed, in his words to Eternal Light, "Thee I revisit now with bolder wing," Milton himself alludes not merely to his poetic emergence from his account of Eternal Night and hell but also to Satan's even bolder, more transgressive *re*-visiting of the precincts of light from which he had fallen. For it is Satan, far more insistently than Milton, who has now "Escaped the Stygian pool, though long detained / In that obscure sojourn" (3. 13–15).

I offer this "satanic" reading of Book 3's opening passage,[24] however, not so much to suggest that it is the only one but rather to underscore those powerful, overt suggestions of *poetic* transgressiveness that Gray internalized in his own poetic enterprise. From the beginning he aspired to soar with bolder wing into a Miltonically ruled literary universe, his career-long poetic efforts self-consciously risking whatever consequences might ensue from appearing Satanically ambitious. Having argued that analogy, I nevertheless decline to join Bloom's devil's party and elevate Milton's Satan to the "archetype of the modern poet" and his God to "ancestral poet." Nor do I wish to appear, by reasoning and comparing on my own Mount Niphrates, as a Satan become weak and ending up in *Paradise Regained* as what Bloom calls "the archetype of the modern critic at his weakest."[25] Both such extremities seem but to hyperbolize the (finally) amusing argument long ago about who was the "hero" of *Paradise Lost:* Dryden was for Satan; earlier on, Addison (in his poem "An Account of the Greatest English Poets," 1694) seemed to be as well, only to shift in the *Spectator* papers to the Messiah; and Dennis sort of opts for Dryden's view but muddies that position by arguing for "two Actions" in the poem, the one that Satan wins, and the one (the war in heaven) that the Messiah wins. And Richardson stalwartly opted for Adam. I have no idea which of these candidates Gray opted for—unless it was Milton himself, who, as William Riggs argues, in his own recognition of "the audacity of his . . . high poetic aspirations," succeeded after prolonged struggle in distinguishing them "clearly from the kind of aspiring he sees as satanic."[26] That is a distinction I believe Gray, finally, was unable to make, either in his own reading of *Paradise Lost* or his own efforts to emulate, in *some* fashion, that high achievement.

One possible index to that inability, or rather to Gray's progressively debilitating sense of his inability on both counts, may be found, as a matter of fact, in the very proem to Book 3 of *Paradise Lost* that I have been exfoliating—in particular Milton's repetition of the word "revisit" in lines 13 and 21. Milton initially says he will "revisit [the "holy Light"] with bolder wing" than Books 1 and 2 required, but he then asserts (not pleads or hopes or aspires) that he will "revisit [it] safe." As resonant as "adventurous," this last word connotes a physical perilousness now overcome. In fact, "safe" is a word that insistently punctuates Milton's portraiture of the fallen angels and their plight as well as his portraiture of Satan. For example, in Satan's first speech after the grand debate, he poses the central question in lines instinct with self-nomination as well as proleptic with respect to Book 3's opening lines:

> Who shall tempt with wand'ring feet
> The dark unbottomed infinite abyss
> And through the palpable obscure find out
> His uncouth way, or spread his airy flight
> Upborne with indefatigable wings
> Over the vast abrupt.....
> ...what strength, what art can then
> Suffice, or what evasion bear him safe
> Through the strict senteries and stations thick
> Of angel's watching round?
>
> (2. 404–13)

Such a "dreadful journey" Milton describes as "The perilous attempt" (420), but Satan in his "imperial sov'ranty, adorned / With splendor, armed with power," scoffs at all difficulty and danger that might deter him "from attempting." Safety is not at issue; pursuit of the "bold design" is. Still, the idea of safety does arise prominently almost immediately. Milton identifies Satan's bold design as public-spirited self-sacrifice, a remnant of prelapsarian virtue: toward Satan the fallen host bend

> With awful reverence prone; and as a god
> Extol him equal to the Highest in heav'n.
> Nor failed they to express how much they praised,
> That for the general safety he despised
> His own.....
>
> (2. 477–82)

For Milton, of course, "safety" *is* an issue, *especially* in the context of *his* self-conscious pursuit of a bold design. And so it is for Gray. Ultimately so fearful of his "satanic" despising of safety in pursuit of his bold design, Gray must settle, in *The Progress of Poesy*, for precisely that "middle flight" Milton eschews, even as that decision is the more tortured by his recollection that, led by Urania, Milton had both "presumed" (even if only an "earthly guest") to enter "the heav'n of heav'ns" and yet had been "with like safety guided down." So protectively clad, Milton from Book 7 on can

"More safe . . . sing" even with "mortal voice" the Divine Creation as well as the Fall (7. 12–24)—what Hunter describes as Milton's "full assurance of illumination." [27]

One final comment on Book 3's invocation is in order here, to briefly undergird, prior to more detailed examination of it below, the centrality of Gray's *Progress* poem to his—and my—entire enterprise. The sequence of Milton's opening fifty-five lines, coupled with his immediately consecutive "portrait" of God in "the pure empyrean . . . / High throned above all highth," [28] strikingly resembles the sequence of Gray's famous Milton portrait. He is first seen riding "sublime / Upon the seraph-wings of Ecstasy" but, rather startlingly, not to soar into the empyrean but rather to "spy" the "secrets of the abyss" as Satan does in Book 4 ("To wing the desolate abyss, and spy / This new-created world," 936–37). Then "Milton" soars beyond "the flaming bounds of space and time" and sees "The living throne, the sapphire-blaze"—Gray's reference here, of course, being to Ezekiel (as he duly noted in the 1768 edition), to *Paradise Lost* 6. 750–59 (carefully unnoted), and (also unnoted) to Satan's vision of the far-off "empyreal heaven" with its "battlements . . . / Of living sapphire" as he nears "This pendent world" (2. 1049–54). And it is at the height of this moment of seeing God (3. 56 ff) that Gray's Milton, "blasted with excess of light," is sentenced, as it were, to having his eyes "Closed . . . in endless night." For Gray, Dryden's "less presumptuous" flight provokes no such retribution for the rhymed "achievement" of *The Age of Innocence*. Nor, of course, does Gray's—unless we imagine that "retribution" as self-inflicted, later metaphorized in the Bard's plunge into "endless night."

The utter and irreparable collapse of the progress of poesy here could not be more complete, or more devastating. For all the bravado and panache of having Dryden's poetic chariot drawn "o'er the fields of glory" by "Two coursers of ethereal race" (a phrase stolen from Virgil via Pope's *Iliad*, as Lonsdale notes) "With necks in thunder clothed, and long-resounding pace," the lines reflect Gray's acute sense that the ostensible immediate heir to Milton's mantle flopped badly in that role, his earth-bound couplets (the "Two coursers") clothed with little thunder and galloping even less resoundingly well below "th' Aonian mount." Perhaps in some sense this monumental failure was Dryden's requital for lack of presumption (albeit, paradoxically, he did presume to enter Milton's poetic cosmos), a fate, one would think, far direr than an endless night or "ever-during dark" replete with the hope, at least, of an inward-shining "celestial Light" irradiating "the mind through all her powers."

But, as I shall argue below, *The Progress of Poesy* waffles uncertainly between the two risks, the two utterly irreconcilable fates. Even if Gray *seems* to call for a worthier heir to Milton than Dryden proved to be, or even if what he does call for in the downward spiral of the poem's final twelve lines *seems* to be a Miltonic heir to Dryden (some "*daring* spirit" capable of waking the "lyre divine" that Dryden's hands explored in the preceding lines), such "daring" apparently will be insufficient to enable the heir to poesy's supreme mantle to sail "with supreme dominion / Through the azure deep of air" as Pindar did with *his* "pride and ample pinion." Thus the poem ends with a "mount[ing]" without seraph-wings (or any other kind of pinion) or car or coursers on some vaguely terrestrial "distant way."

More of this in due course, but here we must turn to Milton's third great invocation, in Book 7. At once reflecting the success of his earlier beseechments of the Heavenly Muse to inspire and guide his song, as well as replete with a continued if less overt sense of possible personal danger in completing the second half of his suprahuman enterprise, Milton here for the first time names Urania. Conflating Horace's invocation to Calliope to "descend from the skies . . . / And sing your flute a lingering melody" (*Odes* 3:4, 1–2) and Matthew 3:16 ("he saw the Spirit of God descending like a dove, and lighting upon him")—and thereby incorporating his own invocation to Book 1—Milton implores Urania to "Descend from heav'n" as the specifically Christian Muse, distinct from those of Olympus and co-eternal now with "eternal Wisdom," both "heav'nly born, / Before the hills appeared or fountain flowed" (1–10). Following her voice, Milton is thus empowered to claim that "above th' Olympian hill" he soars (as he *has* soared) precisely as he "intended" in Book 1's invocation, even above "the flight of Pegasean wing." In his new-won conviction of divine in-spiration and his sublime achievement in Books 1–6, Milton in retrospect can present his earlier presumption as now authorized by Urania:

> Up led by thee
> Into the heav'n of heav'ns I have presumed,
> An earthly guest, and drawn empyreal air
>
> (12–14)

—air (breath in-spired) tempered by Urania's ministration or mediation since, as Hunter reminds us, "no direct theophany" was available to Milton "comparable to that of Moses." [29]

Milton's soaring thus far, then, has been in safety, his prayer now being for Urania to "with like safety" guide him down and

> Return me to my native element,
> Lest from this flying steed unreined (as once
> Bellerophon, though from a lower clime)
> Dismounted, on th' Aleian field I fall,
> Erroneous there to wander and forlorn.
>   (15–20)

Gray may or may not have recognized these final lines as an echo of the "adventurous bands" of fallen angels in Book 2 who, "roving on / In confused march forlorn,"

> With shudd'ring horror pale, and eyes aghast,
> Viewed first their lamentable lot, and found
> No rest.
>   (2. 614–18)

But he certainly knew well the Bellerophon story in the *Iliad* (from which Milton draws his own language) as well as Pindar's *Isthmian Ode* 7. As the latter puts it, in Abraham Moore's strikingly apt translation,

> Man is too brief long aims to reach:
> Presumptuous hope, that fain would stretch
> To heaven's high throne her daring view,
> Is but the winged steed that threw
> Bellerophon, what time his frenzied pride
> Aspired to tread th' eternal domes above,
> And sit amongst the peers of Jove.[30]

Even more luminous and moving to Gray, however, would have been the climactic "I fall" of Milton's line 19 and line 20's immediately consequent perversion of the proem to Book 3 ("Yet not the more / Cease I to wander where the Muses haunt") into "Erroneous" and "forlorn" wandering.[31] J. B. Broadbent's rationalizing gloss on the Bellerophon passage seems awkwardly defensive, as if no suggestions of Milton's self-doubts occur earlier in the poem: "It can only be because the invocation intrudes into the poem's structure the poet's anxiety about the presumptuous heroics of Book VI and the cosmography of Books VII and VIII. Bellerophon insures Milton against the sin of Adam and Eve, curiosity."[32] More than curiosity is at issue here. For all the confidence and élan of the present-tense "I soar" and of reaching beyond even "Pegasean wing," and despite the quiet assurance of Urania's safely guiding his return down to his "native element" and enabling him to sing "More safe," Milton's powerful insistence is upon his having fallen,

> fall'n on evil days,
> On evil days though fall'n, and evil tongues;
> In darkness, and with dangers compassed round,
> And solitude.

The echo here of Sin's speech in Book 2 may well be read as devastatingly self-incriminatory, for Sin presents herself as "Inhabitant of heav'n and heav'nly-born," yet doomed to

> perpetual agony and pain,
> With terrors and with clamors compassed round.
>   (861–62)

Milton then concludes this remarkable revelation of still-gnawing inner fears of enacting the very fall he has already chronicled in Satan's history (and is about to recount in Adam and Eve's) by recalling Orpheus's fate at the hands of "that wild rout" whose "barbarous dissonance" and "savage clamor drowned / Both harp and voice." And, he adds, after one of the most poignant pauses in all of *Paradise Lost*, "nor could the Muse defend / Her son."

The final two lines of this exordium, even given their consolatory efficacy, cannot erase completely the fear of retribution, both divine and human, that hovers in Milton's consciousness as both man and poet. "So fail not thou who thee implores" is in its very imprecision and all-inclusiveness a plea not so much for inspiration as for the very protection ("For *thou* art *heav'nly*"—my italics) that Orpheus's pagan muse ("she an empty dream") could not provide—protection, exculpation, redemption, salvation, poetic success, and "safety." It is with considerable courage, then, that Milton embarks on this lower poetic flight "Within the visible diurnal sphere" through the "Half yet [remaining] unsung," for the flat presumptive (or assumptive) declaration of the multiple Muses' presence and voice divine still leading him ("Say, goddess, what ensued") virtually belies the necessity for imploring her two lines earlier not to fail him.

Supreme confidence amidst such evil days and potentially self-destructive fears, however, finally does become explicit only in the poem's final invocation, which both echoes and reverses the imploring of Book 7:

> my celestial patroness . . . deigns
> Her nightly visitation unimplored,
> And dictates to me slumb'ring, or inspires
> Easy my unpremeditated verse.

At this point, Hunter argues, the poem "abdicates . . . its generic requirement of external support" in favor of "a mood of peaceful acknowledgment that Grace has been freely and fully extended"—and as fully internalized—for the completion of the poem. Milton's "if" ("If answerable style I can obtain"), Hunter adds, "is conditional only in the most nominal sense."[33] How Gray might have responded to this optimism and confidence we have no way of knowing, though one might surmise that he saw it either as continued and egregious arrogance, presumption, and transgression, or as evidence of that supreme self-possession, self-knowledge, and divine empowerment which loomed so awfully and intimidatingly in his consciousness of Milton's achievement and model—and in his own deepest poetic longings. Or, of course, both. Suffice it to say that Gray's acute insight into Milton's explorations of his inner dilemma complicated considerably his entire view of Milton. On the one hand, unquestionably he saw in Milton's achievement what Dennis, Addison, Dryden, and others saw, the Godlike English poet who not only demonstrated at long last the equality of modern poetry to that of antiquity, but epitomized all notions of what the greatest poet in the history of the world should be and do. On the other hand, Gray recognized more than any of his predecessors or contemporaries (including Collins)[34] that such an achievement was realizable only through some form of the very satanic ambition and transgression *Paradise Lost* was dedicated to undermine.

If indeed Milton was what Dennis and other critics claimed, then "imitating" him in the rich Augustan sense became not merely as acceptable and desirable as imitating the ancients but even more so, since Milton was the epitome of native English genius, learned as well as inspired, the inventor of the modern epic, the expander (and even creator) of poetic language, and above all the first achiever since Moses of the true sublime. *How*, not whether, to imitate him became the problem. Except in rare instances (*Absalom and Achitophel* and *The Dunciad*, for example), as I indi-

cated earlier, Miltonic imitation quickly became the easier and more com-
fortable attempt to adopt his style, diction, syntax, and imagery. To be
Miltonic was to don the master's clothes, not to emulate his spirit. Edward
Young was right: "He that imitates the divine *Iliad*, does not imitate
Homer. . . . Imitate not the *Composition*, but the *Man*." [35] Though Young's
language may strike our modern ears as somewhat quaint, it nevertheless
eloquently proverbialized a commonplace fully applicable to the host of
poets in the mid and late century who turned eagerly to *L'Allegro* and *Il
Penseroso* for their Miltonic models, confessing thereby their inability (or
disinclination, even fear) to "Tread in his steps to the sole Fountain of
Immortality" and drink at "the true Helicon." [36] Whereas Young himself
in *Night Thoughts* and Thomson in *The Seasons* dared, in their own ways, to
sip from that fount, even those monumental poetic efforts reflect Young's
oft-quoted idea that "illustrious Examples [of "unprecedented births"]
engross, prejudice, and *intimidate.* They *engross* our attention, and so prevent
a due inspection of ourselves; they *prejudice* our Judgment in favour of
their abilities, and so lessen the sense of our own; and they *intimidate* us
with the splendor of their Renown, and thus under Diffidence bury our
strength." [37] Burying strengths under diffidence is a shrewd perception,
characterizing as it does all those who dared few grand conceptions for
which they sought an answerable style, but who settled instead for mim-
icking that part of Milton's canon that neither engrosses nor prejudices
nor intimidates. In so doing they deluded themselves into believing they
had become (and hence were content to become) what Young calls "noble
Collateral[s]" rather than the humbled Milton wanna-bes their pensero-
soistic imitations confessed them to be.

In one sense it might be argued that Pope's importation of *Paradise
Lost*'s sublimity into the *Dunciad*'s epic structure and machinery paradoxi-
cally situated Milton's achievement and overarching presence in the world
of letters at the causal core of the Fall of poetry and the triumph of Dull-
ness and Darkness—*Paradise Lost* turned upside down and inside out, as
it were. If there is at least a kernel of truth in such a supposition, it is
little wonder that Thomson's orderly, good universe, even given the often
splendid Miltonic flavor of his blank verse, essays but a grander, larger-
scale version of the mid and late century's umpteen imitations of what I
called above Milton's manner.

The problem Gray faced, then (and it is a tribute to him that he per-
ceived it so clearly), was the task of somehow imitating Milton the poet
without actually being conventionally "Miltonic." What he essays instead

is a kind of entrance into Milton's consciousness, into the recesses of his mind with all its hopes and fears, joys and sorrows, conflicts and resolutions, triumphs and defeats, heights and depths. That is to say, in his moments of creation Gray silently invokes Milton's Uranian aid in *his* adventurous song, one that for a time, at least, aspired to soar with no middle flight even if not "Above th' Aonian mount" nor in pursuit of "Things unattempted yet in prose or rhyme." And, intensely conscious of his intrusion into the mind and heart of one imbued with celestial fire, he might well have prayed, "Pleased / With thy celestial song" I have "presumed, / An earthly guest" to be "Up led by thee / Into the heav'n of heav'ns" of your sublime poetic universe; now "with like safety" guide me down and

> Return me to my native element,
> Lest from this flying steed unreined . . .
> . . . .
> Dismounted, on th' Aleian field I fall,
> Erroneous there to wander and forlorn.

More surely he believed that "more Safe [he would] sing with mortal voice" "Standing [here] on earth," "narrower bound / Within the visible diurnal sphere," "not rapt above the pole"—hoping, no doubt, that with Milton "govern[ing] . . . his song" he would "fit audience find, though few."

No such self-conscious obeisance and beseechment, of course, were ever articulated by Gray, in the letters or in contemporary accounts of him; the deepest inner sanctums of his lonely musings remain to us as mute as the *Elegy*'s dead. Nevertheless, as I shall try to demonstrate, my lapse into fantasy here is no mere overstatement of Milton's role in Gray's evolving sense of vocation and the shape of his poetic career. Added to this there is abundant evidence in the poetry of his mounting awareness of looming failure in his heroic attempt not merely to emulate but to be—at least in some sense accommodatable to the changing aesthetic norms of his day—Milton's heir. Before turning to the poetic specifics of that attempt, however, we need to turn to the second major narrative of Gray's subtextual autobiography, his relationship with Richard West.

Gray, West, and
Epistolary Encoding

It must be said at the outset that the number, range, and variety of anxieties I have charted in my survey of the "satanic" Milton's presence in *Paradise Lost* (and in a strain of Milton criticism up to Gray's day) have no counterparts in Gray's letters, even when Gray does make one of his rare comments about Milton. But given the ubiquity of Miltonic references in Gray's poetry, that very absence is as eloquent a testimony of Gray's self-consciousness about Milton's impact on him as is Gray's studied reluctance to acknowledge those poetic debts in his 1768 notes. For Milton is there from the very beginning, in his juvenile (Gray was not yet eighteen) "Lines Spoken by the Ghost of John Dennis at the Devil Tavern," and he is still there in that strange performance, the *Ode for Music,* two years before he died. Not often in the very early poetry but ubiquitous soon thereafter, and insistently present in the letters (often as heavily veiled as the Milton poetic allusions), is a moving history of Gray's relationship with Richard West. His correspondence with Horace Walpole is even more extensive, of course, but those letters evince a strikingly different flavor, content, and tone, with little evidence of attachment beyond friendship and mutual intellectual and gossipy interests. While Gray's extensive correspondence with a wide variety of contemporaries warrants much further study in its own right, that task obviously cannot be mine here, though I will have something to say of his letters to Walpole and Ashton and several of theirs to him and to West.

Often as artfully crafted as his poetry, Gray's letters to West, and often West's letters to Gray, bespeak a friendship that in its passionate intensity went beyond the epistolary language of male friendship common in eighteenth-century England. This is not to say, however, that the sort of desperate protestations of love Gray would blurt out in his letters to Charles-Victor Bonstetten are also apparent in the Gray-West correspondence. On the contrary, Gray's and West's love for each other is more often than not disguised or encoded in various ways to effect a surface complimentariness that was not only permissible but widely employed in letters of conventional homosociality. The distinction I am attempting to draw here is obviously fraught with difficulties of various kinds, but as I indicated in my introduction I do not intend to enter the lists for or against the many scholars now intensively investigating homosexuality in far more complex and accomplished fashion than I am capable of—or disposed to—mustering. As Ronald Sharp modestly allows in his book on *Friendship and Literature,* "strong handshaking, friendly slapping on the behind, or vigorous backslapping . . . may be sexual displacements, but . . . the more important point is that they are also forms for the expression of friendship." [1] Sharp's "may," of course, is crucial, and it may serve here to define the fine line I propose to tread in the Gray-West relationship—one that eschews unverifiable pronouncement but attempts to highlight what Hagstrum has argued so firmly and gracefully in his essay "Gray's Sensibility." More sweepingly than I will argue, he sees in Gray's letters to both Walpole and West, from their Eton days on, "verbal love-play," double entendre, and parody.[2] While, as I have already indicated, Gray's relationship with Walpole was considerably different from that with West, as this book's title indicates, I fully agree with Hagstrum's bottom line: "The true man was Gray Agonistes" (7).

At the outset, then, it may be useful to note what the Gray-West letters are not. They are not, as Cecil Emden suggests, merely a reflection of Gray's "reliance on friendship, his clubbability, tolerance, kindliness, and his capacity to amuse, both himself and his friends." They are not (though Gray's letters to other correspondents may well be), as Tillotson says, "a closely knitted monologue of personal comments on persons and things, the evidence that life is continuing for Gray and that Gray is continuing to meet it with day-to-day wakefulness" as well as with whimsicality. And they are not, as Ian Jack argues, evidence that the "learning of Gray was an iceberg of which ten-tenths remained below the surface." [3] Nevertheless, what Emden, Tillotson, Jack, and a handful of others have to say of Gray's letters is precisely what he does parade before his correspondents—and implicitly before the public he knew would eventually see his letters—as a protective coating for very nearly ten-tenths of his inner life, though there are, even before the Bonstetten affair, a few moments and glimpses of that inner life, Gray's and West's, that is more habitually deflected by both men in one way or another.

The first West-to-Gray letter extant, that of 14 November 1735, is one of those moments.[4] He opens by chiding his friend for not answering his last letter (presumably the one in Latin West mentioned to Walpole the previous July). The language, even in its unremarkable conventionality, bespeaks a moving woundedness: "You use me very cruelly." But then there is this passage, pointedly unhyperbolic, begun with graceful compliment ("the pleasure of seeing your handwriting," which falls short of the pleasure of "hearing you") but moving quickly to fond recollection of their earlier times together:

> Really and sincerely I wonder at you, that you thought it not worth while to answer my last letter. I hope this will have better success in behalf of your quondam school-fellow; in behalf of one who has walked hand in hand with you, like the two children in the wood,
>
> > Through many a flowery path and shelly grot,
> > Where learning lull'd us in her private maze.
>
> The very thought, you see, tips my pen with poetry, and brings Eton to my view.[5]

In his answer about a month later Gray apologizes, with appropriate compliment to match West's, and explains his brevity on grounds of the "hurry" he is "in to get to a place [London] where I expect to meet with no other pleasure than the sight of you." The compliment is then somewhat oddly compromised by Gray's setting it against his preceding confession of a neglect of "duty," a charge modulated several lines later into "ingratitude," not mere "indolence." But in fact the main body of the letter is devoted to precisely such indolence, his days and years, Gray writes, going "round and round like a blind horse in the mill . . . fancying he makes a progress" but knowing "that having made four-and-twenty steps more, I shall be just where I was." As if to bring himself back to West's recollection of their walking "hand in hand" like children in the wood, Gray then turns his language to accents clearly intended to match West's vision of their past, even as the warmth of his own affection is artfully masked via a theatrical metaphor. Confessing "the vanity" of the "undeserving" to "wish somebody had a regard for" him, Gray is "pleased," he says, "that you care about me. You need not doubt, therefore, of having a first row in the front box of my little heart." And if that is "asking you to an old play, indeed," perhaps West "will be candid enough to excuse the whole piece for the sake of a few tolerable lines." Verbal love-play? Double entendre? Parody? All these characterizations seem too strong, too decisive for now. But the studied evasion of the psychic and emotional "truth" of West's unguarded, innocently expressed vision of their past hand-in-hand togetherness is nevertheless a muted prelude to Gray's sense of homosexually centered passions neither fully understood nor mastered—nor finally, in his love for Bonstetten, suppressed.[6]

In another letter from West, of 22 December 1736 (*CTG*, 57–58), amid mistaken thoughts that Gray was about to leave Cambridge for the Inns of Court and West's attempt to dissuade him from abandoning poetry for the "disgusting sober follies of the common law," we have this seemingly unguarded moment: "In one of these hours I hope, dear sir, you will sometimes think of me, write to me, and know me yours," as if closing the letter. The plaintiveness of "sometimes" and the repetitive you-me couplings are but accentuated by the feigned epistolary correctness of "dear sir" and "know me yours." Moreover, West is *not* closing the letter at all, for it goes on for another paragraph, to which is prefixed, in Greek, "speak it forth, hide it not in thy mind, that we both may know it." Why Greek? A little scholarly squib? Or is the Greek itself both a speaking forth *and* a hiding of the thought from prying eyes? West's own translation, which immediately follows, is, to say the least, disarming, for it clearly flattens the intensity and specificity of the Homeric original (*Iliad* 1. 363) into "that is, write freely to me and openly, as I do to you." What "it" is that Gray should speak forth, of course, is unclear, though presumably West's enclosure in this letter was intended as "proof" of *his* writing openly to Gray. That enclosure was a translation of one of Tibullus's love elegies.[7] But Mason, who first printed this letter in his *Memoirs of [Gray's] Life and Writings*, omitted the elegy, and Toynbee and Whibley merely note that it "apparently has not been preserved" (*CTG*, 58 n). Mason's watchdog bowdlerizing even led him to cut out (or to urge Walpole to cut out) such innocuousness as Gray's frequent salutations to Walpole as "My dearest Celadon," his grounds being that they were "infantine beginnings . . . hardly fit for schoolboys, and yet will not be considered as written by a schoolboy" (*CTG*, 1 n).

Similar tiptoeing around the nature of the Quadruple Alliance's interrelationships is also evident in Toynbee's introduction to his *Correspondence of Gray, Walpole, West, and Ashton.* For example, after quoting Walpole's assertion that Gray's, Ashton's, and his own "feigned names" at Eton were adopted so "that they might correspond with the greater freedom," Toynbee dodges the obvious question, freedom from what, or for what? What he does offer some pages later is a carefully modulated statement that the early (1734–38) letters between Gray and Walpole, which he prints (or prints in full) for the first time, "are of especial interest . . . in that they throw quite new light on the early relations between Gray and Walpole, which prove to have been of a far more intimate character than had hitherto been suspected" (Toynbee, xvii, xxxii). On the excision of the "puerile" salutations Toynbee argues that Walpole "throughout his life was haunted by the dread of ridicule" and thus "anxious to suppress" the salutations (and sometimes the closings) lest they "should expose him to the banter of acquaintances" (Toynbee, xxxii n). Despite the firmness of his assignment of responsibility for excisions in the letters, the fact is that Mason, not Walpole, was the prime mover in the matter. And that matter is of sufficient moment, and pertinence to my argument about the Gray-West relationship, for me to turn from the correspondence for a moment to address it.

Whibley's fine introduction to the standard edition of Gray's correspondence deals in some detail with Mason's modification, corruption, and falsification of the texts of the letters, for many of which Mason's are the only texts known to be extant. In various ways he tried to conceal these depredations, by promising his readers that he will present Gray in no light other "than that of Scholar and Poet." Freeing him thereby (one assumes) of human frailties, of mortal pulse or passion, Mason presents Gray as "maintaining a blameless decorum" (*CTG*, xiv). Even more devastating than these evasive tactics, however, are the countless instances of Mason's seeing to it that original letters lent him were destroyed, urging others (like Walpole) to join him in the holocaust, and levying righteous indignation on those (like Thomas Wharton) who did not burn Gray's letters to them as Mason had instructed. In fact Mason was brazen enough to "sanction" the burning of originals in the service of protecting his own editorial integrity. In a letter to Norton Nicholls of 31 January 1775 he writes:

> Mr Mason returns many thanks to Mr Niccols for the use he has permitted him to make of these Letters. He will find that much liberty has been taken in transposing parts of them &c for the press, and will see the reason for it, it were however to be wished that the origi-

nals might be so disposed of as not to impeach the Editors fidelity, but this he leaves to Mr Niccols discretion, for People of common sense will think the Liberty he has used very Venial.

(CTG, xv)

Somewhere in his conflagrational purification rites, Mason burned *all* of the letters between Gray and West that one way or another came into his hands.

But there is another offense Mason is guilty of that deserves separate noting. In late December 1738 or early January 1739 West sent to Gray a letter that included, or possibly consisted entirely of, an "Imitation of Horace Lib: I: Ep: 2" *(CTG,* 95–99). Mason did not print it and the original has disappeared. We can only guess, then, at the contents of the letter, but the Horace "translation" survived because Gray took the trouble to transcribe it in his commonplace book. If Gray replied to the letter, that is not extant either. His silence would have been unusual in this case because he and West habitually exchanged translations as well as other poetry to which each responded with critiques, brief judgments, or other comment. And Gray did not depart for his trip to France and Italy with Walpole until several months later, 29 March 1739. His ostensible "silence," then, extends to his first extant letter to West from abroad, dated April 12. The dating complications occasioned by the switch from Old Style to New Style on the Continent (though not yet in England) aside, Mason (perhaps sensing his readers' puzzlement at this extended silence) appended a note on chronology in his *Memoirs:*

> Mr. West spent the greatest part of the winter [of 1738–39] with his mother and sister at Epsom, during which time a letter or two passed between the two friends [Gray and West]. But these I think it unnecessary to insert, as I have already given sufficient specimens of the blossoms of their Genius.
>
> *(CTG,* 95 n)

There is little doubt in my mind (nor in Whibley's) that Gray not only replied to West's Horatian verse letter but more than likely replied in kind, as was his wont. In this instance, moreover, he surely would have acknowledged in some fashion the moral lessons West's redaction of Horace focuses on. Mason no doubt frowned severely on West's Horace (if not Gray's probable response as well) as far too revelatory of "breathing, human passion" (to borrow Keats's language) and fed both to the fire. And given his editorial principles, he was right to frown, for despite West's discreet packaging of personal discourse in an ostensible translation of a carefully identified original, the between-the-lines is not difficult to read.

In the original, Horace addresses Lollius Maximus,[8] who is in Rome giving speeches "on themes out of Homer," providing the occasion for Horace to advise his friend on the basis of what Homer exemplifies as "noble or base." The latter is in the *Iliad;* the noble correctives, in the *Odyssey,* by means of which Horace catechizes Lollius in terms of Odysseus's "useful example." None of this West makes use of in his "translation," although he does draw an analogy between Lollius's absent speechifying and Gray's thought of abandoning Cambridge to study law. But West does emulate Horace's citation of Homeric moral exempla in his own reading of moral exempla in *Paradise Lost* in order to present Gray with what he calls his "moralizeing *[sic]* Song." However, the heart of what he calls that "Tale disastrous," as well as of "that other Tale" *(Paradise Regained),* is so tritely moralized as to invite Gray's closer scrutiny, for West was never given to celebrating such truisms as "trust in God, & obey God's Laws." His self-styled "Sermon" now over, West jollies it with a verbal nudge—

> I perceive, you nod.
> You think me mighty wise, & mighty odd:
> Your lips, I see, half verge upon a Smile—

to prompt Gray, in effect, to read between his "odd" lines. That is to say, West's sudden shift from comic doggerel to formal address ("Dear Sir"), designedly prepares Gray, at the time preparing to go abroad with Walpole, for the heart of the matter:

> Dear Sir, observe the Horace in my Style.
> Just such to Lollius, his misguided Friend,
> He knew with decent Liberty to send
> Beneath the Critique dext'rous to convey
> Advice conceal'd, in the best-natured Way
> But You're no Lollius, and no Horace I.

West's "dextrousness" lies in his refusing to offer such "sage Maxims" as "Satan, my friend, may lead the best astray" in favor of saying outright, "All men are Adam, & all women Eve," "all corrupted, much I fear."

Somewhere between outrightness and advice dexterously concealed (the latter apparent nowhere in Horace) is the implication of Gray as "no Lollius" and West as "no Horace" (Walpole?). That is to say, West regards Gray as not susceptible to the human follies Horace implies Lollius may well be and therefore he need not act as moral advisor to Gray by emulating Horace's delivery of prudential lesson for Lollius's "profit." On the surface, then, West seems to be denying the very analogy he has developed, but by introducing Adam and Eve into it he, in effect, translates Horace's (and his own) advice-giving into precisely what he earlier said he won't say, that Satan will lead even "the best astray"—and therefore Gray is meant to understand that Milton's/West's "advice" is, more effectively than Horace's, to forestall Gray's "fall" or disagrace at the hands of a "satanic" Horace, Walpole.

While much of West's poem more of less follows the second half of Horace's original, that very faithfulness may well be an effort to disguise West's apparent concern about the hazards of Gray's closeness with Walpole in a part of the world widely regarded as (to borrow Byron's phrase) "sin's long labyrinth." It would also, of course, guard against consquences should the letter be opened by someone or, more possibly, against Walpole's fully understanding what it all meant should he be given access to it (he and Gray often shared their letters on the tour). Thus, perhaps to forestall gossip about fellow travelers of the same sex, West's actual advice to Gray is couched in generalities: "Make honest Things, & Studies all thy Care," for "At sight of Industry Vice flies away." Horace's language, which West obviously counted on Gray's knowing, is far more specific:

> unless you exert your
> Mind in the study of noble and serious matters, your sleepless
> Nights will be tortured by cravings of envy or amorous passion.[9]

Even such loose translation is interrupted continually by West, however, with more radical redactions such as that of Horace's penultimate lines:

> Drink up instruction. Drink now, and to higher things open your senses.
> Earliest use of the wine jar imparts the bouquet that is longest Lasting.

West rather curiously biblicizes the passage:

> First cleanse the Vessel, e're *[sic]* the Wine you pour;
> T'will else be Vinegar, & Wine no more.

And then, even more mysteriously than his earlier reference to "advice concealed," West writes, "Obvious to Sense the Allegory lies." Obvious perhaps to Gray, but what we are left with is only what appears to be West's translation of the "allegory":

> Would you be happy, be but only wise.
> Reject all Pleasures of the Sense: they're vain.
> Each Hour of Pleasure has it's Hour of Pain.
> Bound thy mad Wishes. . . .

Not exactly Horace's "Spurn all delights" but more or less linguistically familial. Not so, however, with

> Sore shall He smart & most severely pay,
> Who lets his Passion o'er his Reason sway—

the closest Horatian antecedent to these lines being "any joy that is purchased with pain will be harmful," or possibly Horace's advice to hold one's "temper," bending it to one's will lest it "bend *you.*"

Finally, there is no Horatian precedent at all for West's closing verse paragraph, which reads in part:

> Now, Boy, 's the time. my gentle Boy, draw nigh:
> Come with thy blushing Front, & open Eye
> Now, while thy Breast is, as the Current, clear,
> Unruffled, unpolluted, & sincere:
> Now fair & honest all thy Hours employ,
> For know, the Man is grafted on the Boy.

Gray, of course, was no boy (he was twenty-eight), West no paternal guardian (he was twenty-three), but the advice seems clear enough: don't succumb to either European vice or to Walpole's dazzlingly fashionable blandishments. Or if that be overdecoding, perhaps simply: return to me the same person I remember from Eton's boyhood days when we wandered hand in hand like the children of the wood. "Thus ends," West says, his "moralizeing Song," and he jokes about having to forgive Pope for stealing the phrase. Was Mason's mind working somewhat along the lines of mine to prompt him to destroy the letter and the translation? Possibly—perhaps even probably. Whatever Mason's reasons, Gray's copying of the poem into his commonplace book seems to have less to do with its intrinsic merits (it is exceedingly uneven in quality) than with the fact that it is West's voice speaking to him over the miles in accents unmistakably flavored with "powerful feelings," however unspontaneous they are made to appear in the habiliments of a Horatian epistle.

In contrast to these disguises, subterfuges, verbal displacements, and encodings, the letters to which Mason apparently had no access provide a compelling body of evidence of the sort of homoerotic language and Hagstrumian "sensibility" that surely would have prompted his ruthless editorial excisions, rewritings, and destructions. Among these are the disappointingly few exchanged by West and the least-known fourth member of the Quadruple Alliance, Thomas Ashton. Toynbee is unique (so far as I know) in remarking that "intimate relations . . . are known to have subsisted between" Walpole and Ashton (Toynbee, xix), a "fact" silently excluded from the standard edition of the letters. Whether Toynbee was literally correct or not, there are certain letters from Ashton to West that contain an openness of warmth that bears comparison to that evident in a number of West's letters to Gray. For example, Ashton often closes his letters to West with "I love you and long to see you" and "I am yours—entirely" (Toynbee, 1: 88, 46), but those aside as perhaps expressions of warm sincerity, we have this extraordinary, and still inexplicable, long letter from Ashton to West of 7 July 1737 (Toynbee, 1: 143–46), from which I quote but a part:

> It will surprize you to see one so regardless of fame and so desirous of Love, as I have always been, now, without any Provocation, give up the thing I love, in order to master that which I sincerely despise. . . .
>
> If I alone were concerned in their [his "Enemies," as earlier sentences make clear] reflexions the noise of Calumny should lull me to sleep. but I must ward off a blow, which I regard not, rather than you should be wounded thro' my Side. 'Tis not to justify myself but your friendship for me, that I . . . [write] this simple, serious letter.

He goes on, then, to pursue the "fact" of his being "extremely hated" and avoided:

> Why I am avoided, it is incumbent on them to shew, who do avoid
> me. . . . That such a constant Watch over a Mans actions, should
> never yet discover are [clearly a slip or misprint for "one"] par-
> ticular on which to fasten infamy, is a convincing proof that I
> have done Nothing infamous. Most of my accusers one [for "are"]
> those to whom I never spoke, not one of them who ever knew
> me. . . . Ask their authority, they had it from ———— and he
> from ———— and so on, in infinite Succession [the blanks are
> Ashton's].

What these accusations or infamy were about we will never know, but
Ashton's confiding in West this way provides an entrée into the heart of
an even deeper mystery—this one involving West, who did reply to the
letter just cited with what he described to Walpole as "a long serious let-
ter" (Toynbee, 1: 146). Sadly, it has been lost or destroyed. In fact, al-
though Ashton wrote several times to West over the next four to five
months, none from West to Ashton during that time have survived—thus
making the "deeper mystery" even more intriguing.

I refer here to a letter from Ashton to West of 6 December 1737,
(Toynbee, 1: 166–67), one that focuses upon West's "enemies," not Ash-
ton's: "With respect to the little insults that have been levelled at you, I
would not have you perceive 'em. Tis the completest revenge in Nature
to let a Man see, that you won't believe him to be your Enemy." Nowhere,
in any letter or elsewhere, is there a record of West's ever mentioning such
insults to Ashton (or to anyone else, for that matter), or of his responding
to this particular letter. One possible explanation for these "insults" levied
at West is the widespread gossip in both Cambridge and Oxford circles
about the intensity of the friendships within the Quadruple Alliance, per-
haps even about some occasional public or semipublic display of such
(though West and Gray brazenly hand in hand seems out of the question).
It was precisely such talk (or perhaps just general knowledge) of the na-
ture of these relationships that Mason feared as destructive of Gray's im-
age as "Scholar and Poet" of "blameless decorum." On the other hand, it
may well be that Ashton's public actions with respect to both West and
Gray were somehow less discreet than we know (he was not thought of as
especially clever or engaging), at least in certain quarters. That would
account in some measure for Ashton's repeated epistolary concern for his
own, and for West's, reputation. For example this letter written sometime
in 1739–40:

Altho' I rejoice that 'tis now in my Power to assist you, it grieves me
that you have need of such assistance. You have honord me with the
name of friend, and I will endeavor to endue myself with the nature
of one. In consequence whereof I lye under indisputable Obliga-
tions to detect & defeat, as much as in me lyes, all conspiracies,
Plots & Combinations whatever, or however laid against your Person
or Character. . . . Alas Zephyrille. what Asylum has Life for virtue,
when well doing exposes us to danger & Desert is the Pander to our
destruction? Be not secure, for you are not safe. Know then that your
Continency has objected you to the Resentment of a troop of Amazo-
nian Spinsters inhabiting in the Confines of St. Ann's Westminster.
You have the alternative of losing your Chastity or your Life.
(Toynbee, 1:316–19)

Toynbee's comment is simply that "there is nothing in the correspon-
dence to throw light on this somewhat clumsy badinage of Ashton's as to
West's being threatened with the fate of Abelard." [10] Perhaps that *is* all
that can be said firmly, though in the context of the other letters from
Ashton examined above it seems not dismissible as merely "badinage,"
especially given Ashton's reference to West's continency and the re-
sponses to that apparently well-known (and talked-about?) reputation by
women of the town.

I have detoured here into Ashton's letters not because he is a major
player in my double narrative of Gray's life and career, but rather to bring
closer to bear on my account of the Gray-West relationship what G. S.
Rousseau calls "the landscape of homosexuality in the Enlightenment."
A striking increase in, and the greater severity of punishments for, sodomy
in the early eighteenth century bred an understandable, palpable fear,
even of mere gossip, in all those who engaged in "romantically idealized
same-gender friendships," even those who were "at best . . . homopla-
tonic." [11] Such a fear is reflected in a common epistolary language of eu-
phemistic encodings, including flowery rhetoric verging on the mock-sub-
lime, the use of fictional "pet names," and the general burying of
passionate attachment that goes beyond warm friendship in the rush of
gossip and/or in deliberately obfuscating circumlocution and other modes
of displacement or deflection. It is in this discursive context that the Gray-
West relationship and correspondence functioned, and the apparent one-
sidedness of the Ashton-West "affair" (Ashton consistently playing the
more aggressive role) thus provides an instructive context for studying
West and Gray's. There the greater mutuality of passionate attraction led

on the one hand to West's more Ashton-like openness of expression and on the other to Gray's studied caution in his letters, a caution that progressively moves beyond mere uneasiness about the risks of public exposure (even among friends) as his homoerotic ardor intensifies. And so I turn back now to the epistolary and poetic history of the Gray-West relationship in the years prior to the first of Gray's odes, the one on the spring in 1742, and to its eerie contemporaneousness with West's death.

On 4 July 1734 Gray was admitted at Peterhouse as a pensioner, taking up residence there on 9 October; early in the summer of 1735 West went up to Oxford. Ashton was already at King's College, but Walpole did not make his appearance at Cambridge until the middle of March 1735. With the Quadruple Alliance having now become a triple alliance, West understandably felt both isolated and forlorn—perhaps even rejected—not only from his Etonian circle of friends but, by extension, from everything their closely interrelated lives at Eton had made glad. Apparently out of sheer loneliness and dispiritedness West initiated a renewal of friendship with Gray via a letter to him in Latin (not extant) of late June 1735 or so, but even four or five months later we find him still wondering (in a letter to Walpole), "Is Orosmades [Gray] defunct? Does Almanzor [Ashton] exist? Is the divine Plato [still unidentified; perhaps William Cole] alive? What sort of a thing is Tydeus [another contemporary Etonian, also unidentified]?" [12] West's irritation at Gray's seeming abandonment of him could hardly have been assuaged when Gray does finally break his silence in response to West's "You use me very cruelly" letter, for "the general tone" of that letter, as Ketton-Cremer accurately observes, "lacks some of the warmth and intimacy with which Gray would have addressed Walpole in similar circumstances," [13] and there is no question that through the end of 1735 "Walpole was the ascendant star of Gray's firmament." Very possibly this was due to Gray's being flattered by attention paid him by one who "moved in the world with the effortless assurance that befitted a son of the great Minister" (Ketton-Cremer, 15). Gray's "advantages," such as they were, excluded all that Walpole had. His self-consciousness over his inferior social, not to mention financial, status even prompts him, in a letter of 28 March 1736 (corrected in *CTG*, on solid grounds, to 1738), to apologize to Walpole for having no "materials but myself to entertain you with. love, & brown Sugar must be a poor regale for one of your Gout, & alas! you know I am by trade a Grocer" (*CTG*, 84). Mason glosses this last word as "a man who deals only in coarse and ordinary wares" and is interpreted by him to mean that Gray is pleading the "plain sincerity of his own friendship, undisguised by flattery." In fact there is flattery aplenty throughout Gray's correspondence with Walpole, as Toynbee and Whibley appreciate in a note (*CTG*, 80). All in all, my own sense of the enduring Walpole-Gray relationship, interrupted only by their mysterious falling out during the European tour, is that it reflects something like "hero-worship" on Gray's part (substituting perhaps for the painful lack of any real relationship between Gray and his irascible father) and, on Walpole's part, a genuine appreciation for and love of Gray's wit, genius, and humor.

On 8 May 1736, Gray does finally resume regular writing to West. That letter, the first as far as we know since December 1735, includes a translation from Statius that I shall comment on in due time, but more importantly it exhibits a warmth of affection for West that is the more surprising for Gray's long epistolary silence. If, indeed, Mason had not in effect created that silence, had there been during those months something like a lovers' quarrel? If so, it was obviously exacerbated by Walpole's flattering attention to Gray during those months. Moreover, Gray's 8 May letter was seriously garbled by Mason and originally printed only in part[14]—possibly to disguise Gray's efforts therein to heal whatever breach there may have been, visible still in the "indiscreet" emotion of his wistful imagining of Walpole's arrival at West's door: "I hope too, I shall shortly see you; . . . my dear West, I more than ever regret you; it would be the greatest of pleasures to me, to know wh^t you do, wh^t you read, how you spend your time, &c: &c: & to tell you wh^t I do not do, not read, & how I do not, &c: &c: for almost all the employment of my hours may be best explained by Negatives" (*CTG*, 39). While the "nothingness" and melancholy of this letter are not uncommon in Gray's correspondence virtually throughout his life, other, familial circumstances may have contributed to his so ardently desiring to see West: his confusion and anger at news of his father's increasing brutality to his mother and her seeking judicial counsel amid his vows to even "ruin himself to undo her, and his only son" (Ketton-Cremer, 17). If such circumstances more logically seem provocations to seek out the stability of a Walpole rather than a West (whose isolation was as intensely felt as his own), clearly Gray was beginning to see his own life (and perhaps his dormant poetical career still not clearly envisioned) as akin to, even replicating, that of West, whom Ketton-Cremer describes as "the gentle scholar, the shy recluse, fostering in retirement his little flame of poetry" (16). Moreover, given the situation at home, Gray needed the warmth and closeness (unavailable for different reasons from Walpole or Ashton) of a friend to whom he could, after his own fashion, unburden himself.

Three months later, Gray went to visit his mother's eldest sister and her husband in Burnham, Buckinghamshire, but he wrote no letters from there to West (again so far as we know) but did write Walpole several times. Clearly puzzled, even vexed, by Gray's latest silence (it will last until December 1736), West writes to Walpole on August 20 canceling his trip to Cambridge and adds in a postscript, "Gray at Burnham, and not see Eton?" And then he appends his own distant prospect of Eton College, *Ode: To Mary Magdalene*. For its rather remarkable anticipation of Gray's poem, and its relative obscurity, I quote the poem in full without further comment here, since I shall return to it later in my discussion of the Eton College Ode:

> Saint of this learned awful grove,
> While slow along thy walks I rove,
> The pleasing scene, which all that see
>   Admire, is lost to me.
>
> The thought, which still my breast invades,
> Nigh yonder springs, nigh yonder shades,
> Still, as I pass, the memory brings
>   Of sweeter shades and springs.
>
> Lost and inwrapt in thought profound,
> Absent I tread Etonian ground;
> Then starting from the dear mistake,
>   As disenchanted, wake.
>
> What though from sorrow free, at best
> I'm thus but negatively blest:
> Yet still, I find, true joy I miss;
>   True joy's a social bliss.
>
> Oh! how I long again with those,
> Whom first my boyish heart had chose,
> Together through the friendly shade
>   To stray, as once I stray'd!
>
> Their presence would the scene endear,
> Like paradise would all appear,
> More sweet around the flowers would blow,
>   More soft the waters flow.
>   (Toynbee, 1:99–102)

In addition to my earlier speculations about the possible causes of Gray's infrequent writing to West, it may also be in part attributable to his making many new friends at Cambridge, among the most faithful of whom were Thomas Wharton and Rev. James Brown, both of Pembroke. Even so, on one of the rare occasions that Gray and West met (about mid-October 1736) during their long epistolary separation, it was, in Gray's account to Walpole on 27 October, obviously unsatisfactory. Some something was missing:

> West sup'd with me the night before I came out of town; we both fancied at first, we had a great many things to say to one another; but when it came to the push, I found, I had forgot all I intended to say, & he stood upon Punctilio's and would not speak first, & so we parted. (CTG, 55)

The language here resonates with something like the aftermath of a lover's quarrel, as well as the awkwardness bred of long physical/geographical separation and epistolary silence. What precisely "happened" we have no way of knowing, but it seems not entirely coincidental that West's Mary Magdalene Ode resonates similarly with the aura of loss and absence—especially more telling since for West, as we shall see, Eton was not merely the Quadruple Alliance but more especially Gray, the place where he and Gray walked "hand in hand . . . like the two children in the wood" or, in the words of *Mary Magdalene*, "together through the friendly shade / To stray, as once [we] stray'd."

Somewhere between October and December 1736 West apparently re-initiated his correspondence with Gray, for in December Gray seems to be responding to an increasingly persistent account of West's precarious health:

> If the default of your spirits and nerves be nothing but the effect of the hyp [slang for hypochondria], I have no more to say. . . . I too in no small degree own her sway. . . . But if it be a real distemper, pray take more care of your health, if not for your own at least for our sakes, and do not be so soon weary of this little world: I do not know what refined friendships you may have contracted in the other, but . . . among your terrestrial familiars . . . , though I say it that should not say it, there positively is not one that has a greater esteem for you. (CTG, 56–57)

That may be as close as Gray will allow himself to venture in a "love letter," but the curious "I say it that should not say it" is more patently Gray's apology for "deserting" West, especially at a time when West's health was visibly failing. Ketton-Cremer ventures the guess that Gray, in referring to his own submission to the hyp, is actually exaggerating "his low spirits for the sake of West, whose depression was darker and more constant" (23). While that seems an unlikely strategy to cheer up a dying man gripped by forces far more dire than the hyp, Ketton-Cremer is surely correct to say that "West sought the comfort and reassurance of their [Gray's and Walpole's] letters with pathetic eagerness and treasured the memory" of what were but very occasional meetings with the other members of the quadrumvirate.

That Gray's renewed attentiveness, concern, and love had a powerful effect on West is attested to movingly in *Ad Amicos*, a poem he sent to Gray in July 1737 (*CTG*, 61–64). Though I shall comment more extensively on this remarkable verse-letter later, a portion of it is relevant to this different context:

> But why repine, does life deserve my sigh?
> Few will lament my loss whene'er I die.
> . . . .
> For me, whene'er all-conquering Death shall spread
> His wings around my unrepining head,
> I care not; though this face be seen no more,
> The world will pass as chearful as before,
> . . . .
> Unknown and silent will depart my breath,
> Nor Nature e'er take notice of my death.

By December this mood deepens into West's anguished complaint that his "health and nerves and spirits are . . . the very worst." We might recall here West's plea the previous December (*CTG*, 58) for Gray to "speak it forth, hide it not in thy mind, that we both may know it," and his enclosure in that letter of the "translation" of Tibullus's love elegy Mason obviously destroyed. For Tibullus frequently set his elegies in the context of his dreams of an idealized past without conflicts or ills, and equally often in the context of the threatening imminence of death. "His death will be dreadful," however, only "if it happens far away from Delia, if she is not present to cry and participate in his burial."[15] In West's *Ad Amicos* these are the concluding lines:

> Yet some there are (ere spent my vital days)
> Within whose breasts my tomb I wish to raise.
> Lov'd in my life, lamented in my end,
> Their praise would crown me as their precepts mend:
> To them may these fond lines my name endear,
> Not from the Poet but the Friend sincere.

For the plurals here, one must (I believe) read "Gray," to whom the poem, and the letter in which it appears, are addressed.

Of the Latin love elegists that Georg Luck has surveyed admirably, Tibullus, while not the most consummate artist of them all, was unique in several respects. In fact, West's distinguishing Tibullus from Ovid (the former "more elegant" and "natural," the latter excelling him "only in wit"—*CTG*, 55) anticipates Luck's point that Tibullus "avoids emphasis, the striking phrase, Propertius' kind of realism, Ovid's kind of brilliance. . . . [He] aims at vividness without effect, at the phrase that is not startling but haunts the mind."[16] Ovid himself, as West no doubt recalled, describes Tibullus's poetry as "elegant" *("cultus Tibulle")*. More importantly, however, Tibullus was often "haunted by an ever present sense of loss, of having been robbed of some irretrievable happiness," an attitude or state of mind characteristically expressed in "precious unspoken subtleties," "by the discreet gesture, the *sotto voce* of his appeal."[17] Luck's language here splendidly defines not only West's life and poetry but Gray's as well—for it is the latter, of course, who *was*, unforgettably, robbed of such happiness by West's premature death.

Additionally pertinent to my comparison is the fact that Tibullus wrote not only of his love for Delia but also for the boy Marathus. The poem that introduces this "affair" ("Sic umbrosa tibi contingant tecta") is usually classified as a literary exercise in the genre of Priapic poems, a judgment based almost solely on Tibullus's confessing to Delia in two subsequent elegies (1.5 and 1.6) that "Sic umbrosa" was such an exercise. But in Elegies 1.8 and 1.9 he returns seriously to Marathus. In any case, one must wonder whether West's Tibullus translation echoed, adapted, or even translated such lines as these from the Priapic poem:

> "Trust to no gentle band of boys," [Priapus] told me.
> "They give you too much reason to grow fond—
> one by his skill at reading will attract you;
> one, swimming strongly in a quiet pond;
> one by his young and touching self-assurance,
> and one, perhaps, still shy enough to blush. . . ."

It is a pleasant fiction to find here in the first, third, and fourth of these "boys" something approaching West's longings for a rebirth of the Quadruple Alliance, with Walpole, Gray, and Ashton "fitting" one or the other of Tibullus's character vignettes. Priapus's advice finally is that since "Love gains by what love yields," Tibullus should go where Marathus goes, do what he does, and share his every activity, so that "His guard once down, . . . the long-dreamed-of kisses" may be taken. The lore of other love poets make your own, the poem concludes, for "verse keep[s] these things [i.e., such dreams] alive."[18]

In another passage (this one from Elegy 1.8) the speaker is some version of Tibullus himself, and the lines (out of context) rather hauntingly evoke the illness-plagued, isolated West, who had accused Gray of using him cruelly by his silence:

> Marathus loves you. Why be cruel to him?
> who deserves cruelty except the old?
> If he looks jaundiced, love has made him ill—
> no cause to shun him, or reproach, or scold.
> Hear how he weeps for her who will not hear—[19]

With these Tibullan verses in mind, it seems more than merely coincidental that some four months before the *Ad Amicos* letter one of West's letter to Walpole is cast in language that is at least reminiscent of Tibullus's:

> It seems so long to me since I heard from Cambridge [it was actually less than two months], that I have been reflecting with myself what I could have done to lose any of my friends there. The uncertainty of my silly health might have made me the duller companion, as you know very well; for which reason, fate took care to remove me out of your way.[20]

"Cambridge" here in effect "means" Gray, and "any" at the end of the first sentence has all the poignant force of "all"—though it may also be a surrogate for Gray, of course, since the last sentence is but a fantasy of his actually being or having been at Cambridge.

When Walpole sent him Gray's tripos verses "Luna est habitabilis" and Jacob Bryant's "Planetae sunt habitabiles," West's spirits seemed to rise and he responded in fanciful kind (Toynbee, 1: 132–39). Yet even so, the vanished, irretrievable past, both the metaphorical past into which West has thrust the present of his friends at Cambridge and the ever-fading past

of Eton days, asserts itself powerfully as a fantasy- or dream-shatterer.
Playfully mimicking and parodying both Latin exercises, West says that
he was led to "dream . . . concerning the luna territory" where, upon his
arrival, the king of this "land of Galilaeo" showed him a "cabinet of *Lost
Things upon Earth.*" As in *The Rape of the Lock,* from which West cribs,
he then lists twenty items ranging from the serious ("Honour, Sincerity,
Hospitality, Friendship") to the silly, but the entire list stops with "Most
of the Eton play exercises, etc., etc., etc." While the infinity of the repeti-
tive etceteras is painful enough, West's final paragraph is even more so.
Finding the king's "curiosities" to be for sale, he says, "You may be sure,
for the honour of our school, I should have bought up at any rate the
things specified in the last article; but I must own I was so surprised to
see it that the sudden anguish it put me in, made me awake."[21] "The
things specified" are precisely the etceteras of West's dreams—Eton,
friends, an idyllic past, love for Gray—all the more anguish-producing for
the impossibility of their realization.

Ad Amicos is a dream/anguish poem—powerful in its simplicity, even in
its sporadic ineptness—and the first major testament of the depth of
West's love for Gray. West clearly knew that Gray would recognize how
little of the Tibullus elegy he was "translating," that in fact this "more
melancholy epistle of his own" *was* his own—personal, intimate, and even
astonishingly open in its own way. I give *Ad Amicos* here in its entirety:

> Yes, happy youths, on Camus' sedgy side,
> You feel each joy that friendship can divide;
> Each realm of science and of art explore,
> And with the antient blend the modern lore.
> Studious alone to learn whate'er may tend
> To raise the genius or the heart to mend;
> Now pleas'd along the cloyster'd walk you rove,
> And trace the verdant mazes of the grove,
> Where social oft, and oft alone, ye chuse
> To catch the zephyr and to court the muse.
> Mean time at me (while all devoid of art
> These lines give back the image of my heart)
> At me the pow'r that comes or soon or late,
> Or aims, or seems to aim, the dart of fate;
> From you remote, methinks, alone I stand
> Like some sad exile in a desert land;
> Around no friends their lenient care to join
> In mutual warmth, and mix their heart with mine.[22]
> Or real pains, or those which fancy raise,

For ever blot the sunshine of my days;
To sickness still, and still to grief a prey,
Health turns from me her rosy face away.
    Just heav'n! What sin, ere life begins to bloom,
Devotes my head untimely to the tomb;
Did e'er this hand against a brother's life
Drug the dire bowl or point the murd'rous knife?
Did e'er this tongue the slanderer's tale proclaim,
Or madly violate my Maker's name?
Did e'er this heart betray a friend or foe,
Or know a thought but all the world might know? [23]
As yet just started from the lists of time,
My growing years have scarcely told their prime;
Useless, as yet, through life I've idly run,
No pleasures tasted, and few duties done.
Ah, who, ere autumn's mellowing suns appear,
Would pluck the promise of the vernal year;
Or, ere the grapes their purple hue betray,
Tear the crude cluster from the mourning spray.
Stern Power of Fate, whose ebon sceptre rules
The Stygian deserts and Cimmerian pools,
Forbear, nor rashly smite my youthful heart,
A victim yet unworthy of thy dart;
Ah, stay till age shall blast my withering face,
Shake in my head, and falter in my pace;
Then aim the shaft, then meditate the blow,
And to the dead my willing shade shall go.

At this, almost the exact center of West's poem, "he quits Tibullus," Mason says (*CTG*, 62 N). In truth, though, West's first verse paragraph has little precedent in Tibullus except for the Latin poet's final lines, which echo hauntingly in West's articulation of his own "exile" and his anticipation of a lonely death. Here is Tibullus:

> Enjoy our Tuscan lakes, the naiad-haunted,
> their ripples parting lightly to the oar.
> Love life, and do not let me be forgotten
> if Fate decrees I share in it no more.
>   (Carrier, 89)

West's intensification of this last line and his appropriation of Milton's *L'Allegro* ("Stygian cave forlorn," "ebon shades," and "dark Cimmerian desert") portend a near despair at the looming of almost certain death.

West's second verse paragraph, on the other hand, does rest firmly on the Tibullan original, but Mason attributes the first ten lines of West's third verse paragraph solely to Pope's letter of 15 July 1712 to Richard Steele about health and sickness, youth and age. It is certainly true that Pope's idea that "Sickness is a sort of early old age" which "teaches us a diffidence in our earthly state, and inspires us with the thoughts of a future, better than a thousand volumes of philosophers and divines,"[24] is precisely the basis for West's valiant attempt to rationalize his present illness and probable early death. Indeed, he echoes Pope's words in crucial places as if the letter were before him as he composed. His paragraph begins,

> How weak is Man to Reason's judging eye!
> Born in this moment, in the next we die;
> Part mortal clay, and part ethereal fire,
> Too proud to creep, too humble to aspire.
> In vain our plans of happiness we raise,
> Pain is our lot, and patience is our praise;
> Wealth, lineage, honours, conquest, or a throne,
> Are what the wise would fear to call their own.

Pope writes that "the attractions of the World have not dazzled me very much" and that he has "a full conviction of the emptiness of all sorts of ambition, and the unsatisfactory nature of all human pleasures." West's

> Health is at best a vain precarious thing,
> And fair-fac'd youth is ever on the wing

echoes Pope's "a smart fit of sickness tells me this scurvy tenement of my body will fall in a little time, [and] I am . . . unconcerned." And, continuing the above lines, West writes,

> 'Tis like the stream, beside whose wat'ry bed
> Some blooming plant exalts his flowry head,
> Nurs'd by the wave the spreading branches rise,
> Shade all the ground and flourish to the skies;
> The waves the while beneath in secret flow,
> And undermine the hollow bank below;
> Wide and more wide the waters urge their way,
> Bare all the roots and on their fibres prey.
> Too late the plant bewails his foolish pride,
> And sinks, untimely, in the whelming tide.

And here is Pope: "Youth at the very best is but a betrayer of human life in a gentler and smoother manner than age: 'tis like a stream that nourishes a plant upon a bank, and causes it to flourish and blossom to the sight, but at the same time is undermining it at the root in secret."

West's intensifications of Pope are apparent, but he also expands on his source in unPopean ways. In place of Pope's simpler, less dire phrasing in the last sentence above, West writes, "Wide and more wide the waters *urge* their way, / Bare all the roots and *on their fibres prey*" (my emphasis); and his final moral (only barely implicit in Pope) and doomsday vision evoke Milton far more powerfully (he knew Milton as intimately as Gray): "Too late the plant bewails his foolish pride, / And sinks, untimely, in the whelming tide." West's identifying himself with Lycidas could not be clearer to Gray, since Milton's line "For Lycidas is dead, dead ere his prime" West had already echoed in an earlier line ("My growing years have scarcely told their prime"). In effect, West's self now sinks in the same "whelming tide" Milton imagines as Lycidas's fate ("Where thou perhaps under the whelming tide / Visit'st the bottom of the monstrous world"), but for West no dolphins appear to waft *his* "helpless," youthful self. Nor is there any consolation, no day-star "sink[ing] . . . in the ocean bed" and "yet anon repair[ing] his drooping head," no Lycidean reenactment of this diurnal round and, though "sunk low," mounting high into "the blest kingdoms meek of joy and love." Instead, West's "day-star" after his death will merely "Bright as before . . . appear" along with the verdant fields, clear skies, and cheerful world.

He does find "consolation," however, in Pope's philosophizing.

> But why repine, does life deserve my sigh?
> Few will lament my loss whene'er I die.
> For those the wretches I despise or hate,
> I neither envy nor regard their fate.
> For me, whene'er all-conquering Death shall spread
> His wings around my unrepining head,
> I care not.

Pope tells Steele that "so excessively weak as I now am, I may say . . . that I am not at all uneasy at the thought, that many men, whom I never had any esteem for, are likely to enjoy this world after me." And where West writes,

> though this face be seen no more,
> The world will pass as chearful as before,
> Bright as before the day-star will appear,
> The fields as verdant, and the skies as clear,

Pope's lines read, "The morning after my exit, the sun will rise as bright as ever, the flowers smell as sweet, the plants spring as green, the world will proceed in its old course."

Ad Amicos then concludes thus:

> Nor storms nor comets will my doom declare,
> Nor signs on earth, nor portents in the air;
> Unknown and silent will depart my breath,
> Nor Nature e'er take notice of my death.
> Yet some there are (ere spent my vital days)
> Within whose breasts my tomb I wish to raise.
> Lov'd in my life, lamented in my end,
> Their praise would crown me as their precepts mend:
> To them may these fond lines my name endear,
> Not from the Poet but the Friend sincere.

Nothing in Pope's letter or in the Tibullus original prompts or even suggests this consolation. *Lycidas* and, perhaps surprisingly, *Paradise Lost* have shifted the register of West's elegy—with a brief, affecting assist from a lovely echo of the close of Horace's ode 2.6, beginning "Septimi, Gadis aditure mecum." There, looking forward to spending his declining years in "the lonely Galaesus valley" which "charms [him] more than all other earthly / Places," Horace writes,

> There for you and me is a home and happy
> Citadel, and there you may shed the tear you
> Owe the yet-warm funeral ashes of your
>   Friend and your poet.[25]

But the Horatian echo is all but buried in West's tissue of Lycidean allusions even beyond those already cited. They appear as early as the second verse paragraph, immediately following the almost inaudible echo of "For Lycidas is dead, dead ere his prime." In fact, what West does in this paragraph reinforces that echo with a rather daring appropriation of Milton's introduction to the line:

> I come to pluck your berries harsh and crude,
> And with forced fingers rude
> Shatter your leaves before the mellowing year.

What is startling in West's "version" is its transformation of Milton as ele-
gist into Death itself—or (in West's phrase) into the "Stern Power of Fate"
with its "ebon sceptre":

> Ah, who, ere autumn's mellowing suns appear,
> Would pluck the promise of the vernal year;
> Or, ere the grapes their purple hue betray,
> Tear the crude cluster from the mourning spray.

Similarly, in his closing verse paragraph, West again adapts *Lycidas* to his
own autoelegiac purposes. Where Milton offers us the traditional pastoral
procession of mourners, West prophesies that "Few will lament my loss
whene'er I die,"

> Unknown and silent will depart my breath,
> Nor Nature e'er take notice of my death.

Instead of "the heavy change" at Lycidas's death, and "the woods and
desert caves, / With wild thyme and the gadding vine o'ergrown" mourn-
ing that change as "universal nature did lament" Orpheus's death, at
West's death there will be no "signs on earth, nor portents in the air";

> The world will pass as chearful as before,
> Bright as before the day-star will appear,
> The fields as verdant, and the skies as clear.

Yet, remarkably, for all the depressive darkness of West's view of himself,
standing alone "Like some sad exile in a desert land" (while Gray roves
"the cloyster'd walk" of Cambridge "To catch the zephyrs" [West's pet-
name, of course]), dying "Unknown and silent," and having tasted "No
pleasures . . . and few duties done," the poem's coda aspires to rescue it
from utter despair. But even those lines, in their awkward attempt at a
modest gracefulness, offer only a fond hope that "these fond lines" may
endear West's name to "some," the vague plural bearing the full freight of
Milton's singular "some gentle Muse" (i.e., poet/friend) who will "favor

[his] destined urn" with a few "lucky words." The implicit singular, as I suggested earlier, is Gray, in whose breast West wishes to raise his tomb:

> Lov'd in my life, lamented in my end,
> [Gray's] praise would crown me as [his] precepts mend.

Finally, with these insistent Miltonic resonances and West's obvious capitalizations on his friend's intimate knowledge of Milton's poetry, we can appreciate more fully Gray's remarkable later Miltonic revision of one of West's Miltonic lines. Six lines before the end of *Ad Amicos* West's parenthesis originally read "ere sunk in endless night," a phrase that will reappear as the final line of *The Bard* some twenty years later, a poem whose composition rather oddly sent Gray back to *Ad Amicos* to make "corrections" in it sometime during 1747. Thus borrowing West's parenthetical phrase for his own poem, Gray substitutes in *Ad Amicos* "ere spent my vital days," which, to my ear at least, chimes well with Milton's "When I consider how my light is spent, / Ere half my days. . . ." Had West lived to see the change, he might well have approved, for his own second verse paragraph in *Ad Amicos* seems a reminiscence of Milton's sonnet. "Useless, as yet, through life I've idly run," for example, may lean on Milton's "one talent which is death to hide / Lodged within [him] useless"; and for Milton's lament that half his days have been spent, West substitutes his "growing years" that have "scarcely told their prime," during which he has done but "few duties."

But whether or not West consciously alluded to Milton's sonnet, Gray, amid his own career anxieties, could not but see himself in West's lines and thus make the same specular connection with Milton's self-portrait. Gray was only twenty-one at this time, whereas Milton was forty-three when he wrote the sonnet. And, unlike Milton, Gray had written nothing of any consequence, apparently had neither plans nor ambitions to do so, and must have been at least moderately abashed at West's achievement in *Ad Amicos*. Perhaps this is why, in his next letter to West (*CTG*, 66), written in low spirits (because, he says, of his hearing of Walpole's mother's death), he is far more depressed than that event alone would have occasioned: "After a month's expectation of you, and a fortnight's despair," he begins, "I am come to town [London], and to better hopes of seeing you." But, after thanking West for "the produce of [*his*] melancholy" (*Ad Amicos*), he then goes on to confess his own deeper funk.

Low spirits are my true and faithful companions; they get up with
me, go to bed with me, make journeys and returns as I do; nay, and
pay visits, and will even affect to be jocose, and force a feeble laugh
with me; but most commonly we sit alone together, and are the pret-
tiest insipid company in the world. . . . Would I could turn them to
the same use that you have done, and make an Apollo of them. If
they could write such verses with me, not hartshorn, nor spirit of
amber, nor all that furnishes the closet of an apothecary's widow,
should persuade me to part with them.

Despite Walpole and Ashton's presence at Cambridge, such a debilitating
sense of isolation and dark melancholy fully answers to West's in *Ad
Amicos*—even without the superaddition of chronic illness and looming
death. Gray's own affected jocosity paradoxically intensifies the central
burden of the letter's confession: he can write nothing, but West, even
with Death's dart poised and even on its inevitable trajectory, writes as
both Milton and Lycidas in the guise of Tibullus. Is that why Gray appar-
ently took almost fifty days to even respond to West's letter and poem?
West apparently wrote him again in October or November of 1737 but
received no answer—to that or to another letter early in December—until
22 January 1738. The first of these West letters has not surfaced, possibly
destroyed by Mason, and the other suffers from what is known to be a
garbled, even partially forged Mason transcription.

Whether or not, at this stage of Gray's life and his love for West, *Ad
Amicos* with its stirring Miltonisms, passionate feelings for Gray, and fore-
cast of West's death somehow conspired to galvanize Gray into poetic ex-
pression of his own conflicted emotions—about himself, his abortive ca-
reer, and West—the *Ad Amicos* letter is unquestionably a turning point in
Gray's life. For, aside from his letter to West of 22 August 1737 quoted
above, no letters by Gray to West are extant until in January 1738 he
responds in kind to West's poem with a Latin prose epistle, *Glaucias Fa-
vonio suo S*, and a Latin letter of June 1738 that includes Gray's poem *Ad
C. Favonium Aristium*. These are the only letters from Gray to West (except
the one of August 22) between his receipt of *Ad Amicos* in early July 1737
and 29 August 1738—a gap so extensive that one must assume Mason's
destruction of letters he regarded as morally damaging. Perhaps, indeed,
those "lost" letters had something to do with Ashton's "mystery" letters.
In any case, given West's congenital frailties, the thought of his possible
early death could not have escaped Gray, and in the last six months or so
of 1737 that possibility approached probability. The complex nature of

that heavy change in Gray's life and career must now, therefore, prompt our attention to the letters of 1738 to early 1742, prior to the extraordinary coincidence of West's death and Gray's sudden burst into a career—not only as Miltonic poet but as sustainer and continuer, as it were, of West's career. And what I hope thereby will become clear is the emergence at this critical stage of Gray's life of the gradual, intricate interfoliation of the dual narratives and twin anxieties I outlined in my first chapter.

Gray, West, Walpole, and the Letters

Sometime early in November 1737, after a long separation, Gray sought out West in Oxford and they had one of their rare dinners together. Amid his usual chattiness to Walpole, in mid-November Gray added some chit-chat about that dinner: West "entertain'd [him] with all the product of his brain, Verses upon Stow, Translations of Catullus, & Homer, Epick Epigrams, & Odes upon the New-Year, Wild Ducks, & Petits Pates: we are to write each other every post, if not oftener" (*CTG*, 69). What he does not speak of is West's serious illness in July, his receipt of *Ad Amicos*, or his own obvious concern about West's health. Instead he focuses on himself and his own plight, his continued poetic inactivity, just as he had in his August 22 letter to West ("Would I could turn [my "Low spirits"] to . . . use, and make an Apollo of them"). The Walpole letter as a whole, then, is precisely the sort of "feeble laugh" he told West his low spirits forced out of him when they "affect[ed] to be jocose" (*CTG*, 66). And if, indeed, West said nothing to Gray at dinner about Ashton's 7 July 1737 letter about "warding off a blow . . . rather than you [West] should be wounded thro' my Side," we might at least wonder why—perhaps especially since Walpole, Gray, and West are silent on the matter in the letters that have survived.

In any case, that tantalizing mystery aside, West's recollection of his dinner with Gray differed sharply from the latter's. For him—and seemingly more than for Gray—the brief evening brought them closer together. In addition to the rare pleasure of seeing and talking with him, and the concomitant prompting of fond memories of their past together, West now confesses even more openly than before his deep feelings for Gray: "The slight shadow of you which I had in town, has only served to endear you to me the more. The moments I past with you made a strong impression upon me." It may be only a coincidence that West here uses the word "endear" precisely as he did in *Ad Amicos* ("may these fond lines my name endear" to you), but just as the poem and the entire July 4 letter were prompted by his illness, so too this letter turns immediately, after its affectionate opening, to his health: "My health and nerves and spirits are, thank my stars, the very worst, I think, in Oxford. Four-and-twenty hours of pure unalloy'd health together, are as unknown to me as the 400,000 characters in the Chinese vocabulary." [1] West then appends an even more painful translation than the Tibullus-inspired *Ad Amicos:* a Latin version of a Greek epigram by Posidippus or Callimachus—which I give here in W. R. Paton's translation in the Loeb Classical Library:

> The dumb image of himself attracted Archianax the three year old boy, as he was playing by the well. His mother dragged him all dripping from the water, asking herself if any life was left in him. The child defiled not with death the dwelling of the Nymphs, but fell asleep on his mother's knees, and slumbers sound. [2]

In contrast, West's Latin (which Gray transcribed in his copy of the 1566 *Anthologia Graeca*) has the boy being overwhelmed in a stream, his mother pulling his dying body from the cold water and vainly trying to revive him in her embrace. But the boy finally becomes inert, closing his eyes forever ("aeternum lumina composuit")—yet another terrifying vision, it seems, of West's own "version" of Lycidean death (*CTG,* 70–71 and nn. 6 and 7).

Returning now to the narrative begun in my previous chapter: when Gray resumes his correspondence with West, it is with a chatty Latin prose epistle (*CTG,* 77–78)—in response to West's request for physicianly expressions of friendship—presenting himself as a ministrant to West's ills of both mind and body, even as he confesses his inability to provide (in person or in prose or verse) unmixed merriment, witty conversation, and laughter. But there is more here than mere chattiness, including an inexplicable lamentation over having been bereft ("orbarer") of many delights in a single month—followed immediately by a quotation from Lucretius:

> Medio de fonte leporum
> Surgit amari aliquid.

Gray then goes on to contrast his own poetic insignificance and unproductivity with West's aspirations and progress toward Olympus, urging him,

"amabo te," to exercise, walk the fields, take to the open air. And he con-
cludes with something of West's characteristic plaintiveness, as well as his
greater openness: "vale, & me ut soles, ama." West's thank-you letter a
month later, available unfortunately only in Mason's transcript, has neither
salutation nor farewell, and Mason's note to it is disingenuous to say the
least: "This was written in French, but as I doubted whether it would
stand the test of polite criticism so well as the preceding [Gray's Latin
letter] would, I chose to translate so much of it as I thought necessary in
order to preserve the chain of correspondence" (*CTG*, 78 n).

If there were more letters exchanged by West and Gray between Febru-
ary and the end of August 1738—and it is unlikely there were none—only
one has survived, by Gray to West in June. But it is in this meantime that
West left Oxford planning to take up residence and the law at the Inner
Temple, apparently in concert with what he assumed would be Gray's
departure from Cambridge for the same purpose. Gray, however, re-
mained in Cambridge until mid-September, and although he never did
take up residence in the Temple, he wrote West the June letter noted
above, available only in Mason's transcription. It opens without salutation,
with a Latin poem that, in his Commonplace Book transcription of it, he
called *Ad C. Favonium Aristium* (*CTG*, 85–87), the "C." for "Gaius." The
title, then (which Mason also omits), as well as the poem's first line, wittily
reflect the site of the two friends' proposed reunion, the "barbaric temple"
of the law. It is at least possible that the title may also be intended to
connect West/Favonius with Gaius, the eminent second-century Roman
jurist, although both Gray and West were sufficiently versed in things Ro-
man to know that both Gaius and Gaia were names commonly used for
husband and wife, bridegroom and bride. Whether that neat double en-
tendre is there or not, what is clear is that Gray is deliberately recalling
West's *Ad Amicos* in several ways: West's vision of wandering carefree in
"the verdant mazes of the grove" and courting the muse become Gray's
second stanza; West's evoking of Eton's idyllic friendships and imagining
Gray "catch[ing] the zephyr" as he used to do are reflected in Gray's pre-
senting himself as luxuriating in "the brighter season of Favonius" and of
"cloudless skies" (West, we recall, characterized himself as the victim of
real or imagined pains that "for ever blot the sunshine of [his] days," dying
even as the day-star reappears and skies are clear). Moreover, West's focus
on early death at the hands of the "Stern Power of Fate" Gray remarkably
transforms into an affecting blessing: "if *kindly* fate would permit me,

sinking low in like fashion" (in his imagined idyllium), "to hide [himself] in peaceful death."

This quite extraordinary evocation of West's allusions to and personalization of *Lycidas* must be seen, then, as Gray's loving elegiac consolation, not for himself, of course, as West had done, but for his beloved friend, who he clearly believed was dying. In this light, the opening stanzas of *Ad C. Favonium Aristium* reveal the reason for his allusion to the opening of Horace's ode beginning "Septimi, Gadis aditure mecum et," precisely the ode whose closing stanza West evoked at the end of *Ad Amicos*. Here again are Horace's lines:

> There for you and me is a home and happy
> Citadel, and there you may shed the tear you
> Owe the yet-warm funeral ashes of your
> Friend and your poet.[3]

"There" is the "lovely Galaesus valley" that "charms [him] more than all other earthly / Places," like Gray's paradisal landscape. And Gray *does* shed that tear—in the exquisite Alcaic fragment that he appends to the Latin elegy: "O Fountain of tears which have their sacred sources in the sensitive soul! Four times blessed he who has felt thee, holy Nymph, bubbling up from the depths of his heart."[4]

West's response to this and Gray's previous letter was from Epsom, where he was staying with his mother and sister after leaving Oxford.[5] Gray's two letters, he writes, could not have come more apropos: I was without any books to divert me, and they supplied the want of every thing; I made them my classics in the Country, they were my Horace and Tibullus." That is to say, you were my Horace and Tibullus, or, to put it in the vernacular, "I got the message"—of their idyllic past together, of the irretrievability of that receding past, of their enduring, ripening love, all emblemized in Horace's odes on friendship and love and Tibullus's love elegies. (Clearly these were West's and Gray's favorite Latin poets.) Once again, we do not know if we have all of this letter (it lacks both salutation and closing, for example) or if what we have is precisely what West wrote, for it derives only from Mason's *Memoirs*. But Mason does include West's Latin *Elegia*, preceded by its introduction: "we shall see one another, I hope, to-morrow." Such a meeting, if indeed it took place, would have been their last prior to Gray's trip abroad with Walpole.

While West's poem is framed gracefully, if conventionally, in praise of country meadows, streams, and groves, with appropriate dryads and "the divine Amaryllis," it is also an elegy for the absence of the very love that the poem asserts as inflaming the groves and "liv[ing] in the deep valleys," where "under every bough many a bird rejoices in tremulous concert"; "even the hard trees enjoy marriage with one another in the forests," and the rocks are inspired by Venus. But absent from this loving and lovely landscape is Gray, whom West addresses by name in his second couplet. "I embrace you, Gray, and with my whole heart I long for you, Oh longing of mine already too long enduring."

> Harder than stones and harder than oak is he who forbids love, heart and sole. Not into his hands would I wish to place a holy pledge, not to him open my inmost heart; he knows not friendships who knows not tender loves. Ah! if there be no Venus, the country pleases me not at all. Although the fates bid me, located in a foreign land, draw out my days far from my native country, if the only beloved face only be present, I would not cry against the great gods with complaining voice.

Although West closes his poem with the conventional wish to be in his mistress's arms and there forget his cares, Gray could not have misconstrued the intense personalness at the heart of this love elegy for mere convention. Nor would he have been unaffected by West's hypothetical placing of himself abroad as a reminder of Gray's soon-to-begin grand tour with Walpole—without West's "beloved face ... present" except as he will imagine it visible in the pastoral countrysides of Europe.

Given West's recurring bouts of illness, the last line of his *Elegia* is especially affecting despite the subterfuge of wishing to lie in the "sweet lap" of his mistress, forgetting his cares: "I should pray to die within those dear arms." A year later, with Gray literally "in a foreign land," West sends him another Latin poem in Sapphics, again dwelling on his "ill breast" and "increasingly, ah too threatening cares," but adding a fond wish to see his "comrade Gray returned here, taking pleasure together with me in the shade." Finally, nearing his death, West on 4 April 1742 devotes a Latin ode entirely to his cough, his "ceaseless struggling," distorted face, "panting voice," and irksome sleeplessness"; and he concludes with a recall of his *Elegia*'s reference to Gray's "beloved face": "Nor if you were here with me, pleasant companion, would your words help, nor would your sweet voice suffice to assuage this suffering, or your beloved face." [6]

If Gray responded to the *Elegia* letter (he doesn't mention it in his letter of December 1738—though that date is conjectural) we have no evidence of that, nor is there extant a follow-up letter from West to Gray before the ostensible "Imitation of Horace. Lib. I: Ep: 2" (circa January 1739) already commented upon. That there were some other letters Mason himself acknowledges in his usual unhelpful way: between September 1738 and March 1739, he writes, "a letter or two more passed between the two friends. But these I think it unnecessary to insert, as I have already given sufficient specimens of the blossoms of their Genius" (*CTG*, 95 n). Their loss is particularly vexing for several reasons: (1) the increasing warmth and frequency of the correspondence at this time, especially the encodings of powerful feeling in their exchange of poems (recall West's Horatian imitation, "Beneath the Critique dext'rous to convey / Advice conceal'd," immediately after his rehearsal of Satan's temptation and Adam's fall in *Paradise Lost*); (2) the precarious but imprecisely known status of West's health at this time;[7] and (3) the reasons behind Gray's seemingly paradoxical decision to abandon West and England for Walpole and the Continent. As Ketton-Cremer writes, "Gray had probably seen more of West [he also exchanged more letters with him] . . . during the past year, than he had done since they were at Eton together"(26)—though his concluding delicacy ("an increasingly sympathy had developed between them") patently understates, even obscures, the case.

Gray's departure does seem odd, to say the least. Ketton-Cremer's speculations about Gray's reasons seem to me self-contradictory. On the one hand, he characterizes Gray, like West, as "of retiring disposition . . . [and] low spirits, awkward in social life, unfitted to jostle successfully in the robust and noisy world"(26). Moreover, "temperamentally unsuited to Walpole's . . . world," he "saw clearly . . . that he would never make one of that circle, acquire its deceptively easy manners, or gain the approval of its lovely and intimidating women" (27). Thus, while he "continued to be deeply attracted" (the adverb seems excessive) to Walpole, "the days of sentimental hero-worship," Gray must have known, "were gone for ever" (28). So why go? Not, I think, because he was so attracted to Walpole's life of "elegance and refinement" that he couldn't resist—although it certainly may be argued that Gray, who certainly had some measure of "wistful admiration for the graces of life" and "people gifted . . . with personal charm, self-confidence, the *bel air*" (Ketton-Cremer, 27), couldn't resist even a mini grand tour (as indeed it was originally planned) completely at Walpole's expense. A more likely reason, I suggest, was Gray's "subjecting himself, and in a lesser degree his friends," not "to a dispassionate, humorous and sometimes quite ruthless analysis" (Ketton-Cremer, 26–27), but rather to an honest (perhaps even ruthless) appraisal of his own homoerotic feelings for West and their possible frightening consequences (to West and himself) in an age militantly antipathetic to homosexual love. A break at this critical stage may well have seemed to Gray both wise and prudent, a sort of stock-taking. Such a conjecture gains some measure of certainty from the fact that the tour was to consist of "some months in France"—with a "possible" visit to Geneva (Ketton-Cremer, 25). In any case, whatever Gray's reasons were, Ketton-Cremer's assertion that "Gray's contentment" on leaving England "was almost without a cloud," even though he "perceive[d] the flaws" in Walpole's character, is open to serious question.

Still, to give the biographer's general sensibleness its due, even though Gray's anxiety about his deepening affection for West might well have been such a "cloud," it is still possible that (1) Walpole was not someone he, in his lesser social station, could refuse, that (2) his writing nothing to speak of demanded a change of scene, and that (3) he thought West's health, iffy though it seemed to be, might well do without Gray's presence and personal ministrations for the brief time he'd be away.[8] Yet, if this last were really true, it seems utterly inconceivable that they extended their tour to almost two and a half years—despite the fact that for the last year and a half of it Gray's and Walpole's relationship grew progressively strained, even to embittered enmity in their famous quarrel in May 1741. Moreover, despite Ketton-Cremer's caution against taking at face value Walpole's own retrospective judgment that even before they got to Calais "Gray was dissatisfied, for I was a boy, and he, though infinitely more a man, was not enough so to make allowances," that judgment seems to me closer to fact. While Gray may not have been averse to occasional social whirlings, the opportunities for antiquity exploration, sightseeing, the ballet, and opera were more to his taste than Walpole's avid pursuit of the bon ton, the salons, and Parisian high play.

Gray's grumblings, never loud but notably persistent, punctuate his letters to both Ashton and to West. For example, he mentions to Ashton that they might go to Rheims for "a Month or two" but then adds: "This is our present design & very often little hankerings break out, so that I am not sure, we shall not come back [to Paris] tomorrow" (*CTG*, 105). Again to Ashton he complains of his being "confined to the narrow bounds of the history of We, quatenus We. . . . Our tete a tete conversations . . . consist less in words, than in looks & signs, & to give you a notion of them, I ought to send you our pictures; tho' we should find it difficult to set for 'em in such attitudes, as we very naturally fall into, when alone together" (*CTG*, 109). Finally, Walpole himself seems equally perturbed with Gray. Writing to Mason in 1773, he recalls that one of Gray's mid-1739 letters in French to West revealed "how easily [a miswriting for *early?*] I [i.e., Walpole] had disgusted him" (*CTG*, 111 n). Gray's accelerating troubles with Walpole, whatever their cause, were certainly exacerbated by his sense of being trapped in the relationship with Walpole not only because the latter underwrote all of the expenses but because he made a will prior to their departure that left everything he then possessed to Gray—both these pressures underscored by Walpole's unilateral decision making about where they would go and how long they would stay. Virtually the only outlet Gray had for his frustrations was writing letters, especially to his mother and to West. To the former he wrote eleven, which were almost entirely accounts of the tour itself: travelogues, exploration of antiquities, and the like. The letters to and from West are, as one might expect, a more complicated matter that deserves attention here.

Between 12 April 1739 and 21 April 1741 Gray wrote at least eighteen letters to West, whereas only eight from West to Gray are definitely known to have been written. In view of Mason's version of a paper shredder working at full throttle, Gray's eighteen are clearly far from all, and West's eight are most likely an even smaller fraction of what he wrote.[9] Moreover, of these eight, four are not extant and one is to Gray *and* Walpole (which Mason did not have access to), but there are partial transcripts by Mason of three originals now lost. Given Gray's far more numerous letters to West, the dates of West's extant four (or parts of four) are instructive, when read in the context of the only complaint Gray made to West about not writing often enough.[10] Those dates are 24 September 1739 (the letter to Gray and Walpole), 28 September 1739, April 1740 (Mason prints only West's second *Elegia* but scrupulously notes that "the letter which accompanied this little elegy is not extant"), and 5 June 1740 (*CTG*, 119–21, 151–52, 164–65). Of the letters we know Mason destroyed, one from West to Gray he adjudged "too bizarre for the Public" (*CTG*, 137). He apparently destroyed Gray's answer as well, in part at Walpole's prompting. In fact, throughout his correspondence with Walpole, Mason persistently defers to Walpole's sensibilities with respect to the Gray-West correspondence as well as, for more obvious reasons, to Walpole's letters to Gray—often acceding to Walpole's advice about what to revise or omit from Mason's *Memoirs*, or even to burn. Walpole writes to Mason on 17 April 1774, echoing Mason's own oft-iterated editorial principle, "You know my idea was that your work should consecrate [Gray's] name." [11] These depredations and decimation of the Gray-West correspondence during the Walpole tour Mason explains away in a note to his printing of Gray's 12 January 1741 letter to Philip Gray: "Between the date of this and the foregoing letter [also to Philip Gray] the reader will perceive an interval of full three months: as Mr. Gray saw no new places during this period, his letters were chiefly of news and common occurrences, and are therefore omitted" (*CTG*, 179 n). Finally, in contrast to the above history of the Gray-West correspondence, the Yale *Walpole Correspondence* prints (or accounts for) fifteen letters from West to Walpole between 4 April 1739 and 22 June 1741, and twenty from Walpole to West.

The pitiful remnants of the West-Gray correspondence over this two-and-a-half-year separation yield but a small, tantalizing taste of what the actual body of that correspondence many have contained, for they all reflect one way or another the passionate affection the two friends had developed in the months prior to Gray's departure—albeit, as usual, veiled or encoded in some fashion, only on occasion approaching unguarded verbalization. The earliest exhibit here is West's translation of Propertius's Elegy 17 (book 2), sent to Gray at Rheims in June 1739. The Propertian original is an invocation to Bacchus to cure the poet's love "malady" that "keeps its old fire alive" in his bones, for sober nights, he complains, always rack lovers on their lonely beds, and hope and fear distract their minds. "Do thou only release me from my cruel slavery," Propertius concludes, "and overcome this troubled head with sleep." [12] West's version stilts this lovesickness into such lines as:

> Thine great Lyaeus is the power confest
> To chase our sorrows, & restore our rest:
> 'Tis thine, each joy attendant on the bowl,
> Thine each gay Lenitive that glads the Soul.
> God of the rosey cheek, & laughing eye,
> To thee from Cynthia and from love I fly:
> If every Ariadne was thy Care,
> Now shew thy pity, & accept my prayer. [13]

Even though West clearly counted on Gray's bringing Propertius's explicitness and passion to bear on his own blander language, as if not fully confident of that, he translates Propertius's similarly bland conclusion

("Do thou only release me from my cruel slavery, and overcome this trou-
bled head with sleep") into a plea for "A slight reward" from Bacchus for
the poet's self-dedication to sounding the god's glories "in no common
verse":

> 'Tis but to ease my bosom of its pain
> And never may I feel the pangs of love again.

Though the letter that included West's translation is no longer extant, the
poem happily was transcribed by Gray in his commonplace book with a
note: "Fav[onius]: June 1739" (*CTG*, 111).

If Gray acknowledged, or responded to, West's Propertian elegy, that
letter has not survived (though Gray did send a translation of Propertius
to West in April 1742, a poem to be commented on below). West's letter
to Gray of 28 September 1739 seems to suggest that Gray had written him
to say (among other sentiments we can only imagine) something like
"Wish you were here," for Mason's "version" of it begins *in medias res:* "If
wishes could turn to realities, I would fling down my law books, and sup
with you to-night. . . . I cannot help indulging a few natural desires; as for
example, to take a walk with you on the banks of the Rhone, and to be
climbing up mount Fourviere:

> "Jam mens praetrepidans avet vagari:
> Jam laeti studio pedes vigescunt."
> [My mind is really anxious to be going,
> my feet are dancing with anticipation!]

The innocuousness of these lines from Catullus belies West's clear as-
sumption that they would trigger Gray's extraordinary verbal memory to
recall Catullus's lines from the same poem:

> So it's good-bye now to those dear companions
> who set out from a distant home together,
> whom varied roads now carry back diversely.[14]

Gray, Eton, separation, ardent wish-fulfillment, all the themes West has
centered upon before, overtly and covertly, are here. It is hardly surpris-
ing, then, that he closes this letter with the brief Latin poem I commented
upon earlier, to Gray as Glaucias the physician, addressing more power-

fully, and sadly, the same themes, shadowed with thoughts of his own death (*CTG*, 120–21).

In the next letter to West that survived, dated 16 November 1739, Gray seems intent on responding in kind to the Catullan/West poetry of desire, as well as on recalling West's reference to Gray's "beloved face" in the *Elegia* of September 1738:

> If I do not mistake, I saw you . . . every now and then at a distance among the trees; il me semble, que j'ai vu ce chien de visage la quelque part. You seemed to call to me from the other side of the precipice, but the noise of the river below was so great, that I really could not distinguish what you said; it seemed to have a cadence like verse.
>
> (*CTG*, 128)

The allegory here matches West's despairing sense of separation/distance/loss and the plaintiveness of wish-fulfillment. Given the explicit longing of this letter, the one Gray writes to West five days later, available only in Mason's transcript, has clearly been sanitized into the traveloguish detail Gray habitually wrote to his mother. Between late April 1740 and the end of September, however, several significant letters (or parts of letters) between Gray and West have survived, beginning with Gray's of May 1740, which opens with a love-poem addendum to his prose longings of 16 November 1739: *Ad C: Favonium Zephyrinum.*[15]

Whereas in the November letter Gray imagined seeing West's face everywhere and hearing him call to his beloved from every precipice, here he imagines him whiling away his time amid the gentle breezes of the West wind "forgetful of his friend."[16] What he hears now is only his own voice calling "the name of Favonius," which is echoed by "lofty Tibur" and reechoed by "the cliffs dear to the Latin Naiads." Then "a miracle": hearing Gray/Zephyrus sing, "the grove became silent, and the sacred springs; and to this very day . . . the rocks . . . keep repeating the soft strains." And Gray concludes his tender love elegy by imagining that "under every leaf in the dark grove cling dreams inspired by Phoebus, and stream and breezes [Zephyrus] speak more melodiously than any virtuoso"—this last a melancholy echo of some lines in *The Aeneid*: "In the midst an elm, shadowy and vast, spreads her boughs and aged arms, the home which, men say, false Dreams hold here and there, clinging under every leaf" (6. 282–83, noted in *CTG*, 159 n).

No responding letter by West is extant, only the melancholy, confused, and even despairing letter of 5 June 1740 (*CTG*, 164–65), in which, very much like Gray, he laments the directionlessness and purposelessness of his life and his vain groping about for a career. But then, abruptly, he addresses Gray in terms Mason seems rather remarkably to have left intact:

> Dear Gray! consider me in the condition of one that has lived these two years without any person that he can speak freely to. I know it is very seldom that people trouble themselves with the sentiments of those they converse with; so they can chat about trifles, they never care whether your heart aches or no. Are you one of these? I think not. But what right have I to ask you this question? Have we known one another enough, that I should expect or demand sincerity from you? Yes, Gray, I hope we have; and I have not quite such a mean opinion of myself, as to think I do not deserve it.

Mason comments specifically on this passage as follows: "this letter was written apparently in much agitation of mind, which Mr. West endeavours to conceal by an unusual carelessness of manner." I see little of that manner myself unless Mason is, in effect, explaining away West's candor here as carelessness. What is in evidence, of course, is considerable mental and emotional stress as well as West's deep anxiety about his relationship with Gray, despite its being precisely the loving, caring one he desperately needs. The operative (but not necessarily the sole) occasion for this near desperation was surely, as Toynbee and Whibley point out, his mother's alleged "liaison" with her deceased husband's secretary, an affair Gray later described to Norton Nicholls as robbing West of "his peace of mind, his health" and being therefore the root cause of West's fatal bout of consumption.[17] The full text of his comments to Nicholls (available in *CTG*, 1300) bespeaks the depth of Gray's rage at the news as well as of his sense of West's critical need not only for a friend but someone to love, to trust, to confide in, to be with, to sustain him in the loneliness of an exile within.

Gray's response to this "agitation of mind" (*CTG*, 167–70) was prompt, lengthy, and more open than had been his usual wont:

> I have not a thought, or even a weakness, I desire to conceal from you; and consequently on my side deserve to be treated with the same openness of heart [a phrasing that echoes West's earlier *Elegia*]. . . as mutual wants are the ties of general society, so are mu-

tual weaknesses of private friendships, supposing them mixt with
some proportion of good qualities; for where one may not sometimes
blame, one does not much care ever to praise.

More "open" to be sure, but not yet approaching the unabashed candor
of Gray's later-life love letters to Bonstetten—an affair, as we shall see,
that rather eerily seems an unrestrained replay of Gray's relationship with
West and its being cut off so cruelly by the latter's tragically early death.
What seems clear here, nevertheless, is that Gray felt miffed by West's
seeming uncertainty about the depth of Gray's feelings for him. While he
may have thought he was not concealing his concern and love from West,
his congenital reserve (and possibly his fear of public exposure) con-
strained him from baring his heart about "mutual wants" or "mutual
weakness"—and certainly about "mutual desire," erotic or platonic. The
lines I have quoted are obviously not "I love you," but may be as close to
such a confession as Gray could manage to venture outside the protection
and obfuscation of the translational and allusionary encodings punctuating
his correspondence with West.

The rest of this same letter, fully four-fifths of it, Gray devotes to advis-
ing West about choosing a career, the law or any other—obviously in re-
sponse to West's confessed ignorance not only of his "own interest" but
even of his "own inclination." If the advice is sensible and must have
comforted West in some measure, the giving of it is noteworthy in another
way. In the course of marshaling his thoughts toward alleviating West's
aimlessness and uncertainty, Gray surely recognized once again his own
aimlessness and uncertainty, drifting around Europe in lieu of pursuing
any career, perhaps least of all poetry. "Our inclinations," he tells West,
"are more than we imagine in our own power; reason and resolution deter-
mine them, and support under difficulties." He then distinguishes sharply
between a public life that requires one to be "serviceable to the rest of
mankind" and a private one that involves "a reasonable pride" rather than
"ambition," one that demands "the cultivation of [one's] own mind" and
yields but "a private happiness." As if catching himself in mid-thought,
Gray then adds: "I am sensible there is nothing stronger against what I
would persuade you to, than my own practice; which may make you imag-
ine I think not as I speak. Alas! it is not so; but I do not act what I think."
Gray is not quite twenty-four, and poetry is as yet almost solely a product
of his scholarly bent, neither vocation nor profession, indeed a kind of
pedantry. It was precisely those aspects of his character, and specifically

his penchant for botanizing on antiquities, that perpetually irritated Walpole as the two moved inexorably toward their personal rupture.

The implicit self-analysis of this letter is followed by an even severer self-appraisal two weeks later, when Gray (in his share of a Walpole-Gray letter to West) wryly capitalizes on Walpole's opening dissertation on coins and medals by adding, "I have struck a medal upon myself: the device is thus O, and the motto *Nihilissimo*, which I take in the most concise manner to contain a full account of my person, sentiments, occupations, and late glorious successes." Of the two final extant letters Gray wrote West from abroad (that we know of) the first, dated 21 April 1741 (*CTG*, 181–83), gives a somewhat fuller account of his "sentiments," erstwhile reserve, and scholarly subterfuges, and in the course of it he seems on the verge of unraveling that reserve at the prospect of soon being reunited with West:

> You are the principal pleasure I have to hope for in my own country. Try at least to make me imagine myself not indifferent to you; for I must own I have the vanity of desiring to be esteemed by somebody, and would choose that somebody should be one whom I esteem as much as I do you. As I am recommending myself to your love, me thinks I ought to send you my picture.

This last, I believe, is intended to show West how he had changed in two years while remaining very much the same: dull, largely silent, thinking (doing what resembles thinking), suffering "a want of love for general society." But "On the good side you may add a sensibility for what others feel, and indulgence of their faults or weaknesses, a love of truth, and a detestation of every thing else." While these sentiments reprise his earlier letter of self-analysis in response to West's seeming uncertainty about Gray's feelings for him, they are now accompanied by firmer, more pointed declarations of love, thinly disguised as "esteem." In fact, in response to West's answer to this letter (which is "lost") Gray himself makes precisely this translation, undisguised: "It [West's letter] assured me, very strongly, of your esteem, which is to me the thing"—and then he cites Guillaume-Hyacinthe Bougeant's 1739 *Amusement philosophique sur le Langage des Betes*, which he had sent West in May of that year:

> Bougeant . . . fancies that your birds, who continually repeat the same note, say only in plain terms, "Je vous aime, ma chere; ma chere, je vous aime;" and that those of greater genius indeed, with

> various trills, run divisions on the subject; but that the fon[t], from
> whence it all proceeds, is "toujours je vous aime." Now you may, as
> you find yourself dull or in humour, either take me for a chaffinch or
> nightingale; sing your plain song, or show your skill in music, but in
> the bottom let there be, toujours, toujours de l'Amitié.
>
> (CTG, 177–78).

This little allegory is as stunning a confession of his love for West as Gray
ever essayed, and one must wonder how it got by Mason's prudish eye.
Because Bougeant was a Jesuit? It is also, of course, a letter that testifies
to Gray's reading of West's letters and poems as his singing, "in plain
terms" or in "various trills" and "divisions on the subject," *his* love for
Gray.

Similarly undisguised is the poem Gray includes in the letter about his
and West's mutual "esteem" noted above. The poem, he says, is "a pretty
little Sonnet" by Buondelmonte (more properly Buondelmonti), which he
translates into Latin from the original Italian (given in the letter). In J. R.
Hendrickson's translation the Latin "imitation" reads:

> Sometimes Cupid [*Amor* in both the Italian and the Latin] sports
> veiled in the cloak of friendship and disguises his presence under
> garments all in decent array. Presently he puts on a cloak of anger
> and assumes a threatening expression; then his look of hatred swiftly
> melts into tears. Fly from him when he is in a sportive mood, nei-
> ther put any trust in him, whether he weeps or rages: his face may
> change, but he is always the same god.

The Italian, which Gray of course could also read, seems to me more
pointedly apropos to his relationship with West:

> Often Love laughs and hides
> Under the form of friendship:
> Then he mixes and confuses himself
> With disdain and with malice.
> He transforms himself into Pity;
> He seems a toy and he seems an annoyance;
> But in his various aspects
> He is always the same Love.[18]

Neither Gray's all-too-obvious shift of "Amor" to "Deus" nor his caution-
ary "Fly from him" (*fuge*) is in the Italian original, which stresses the

sameness of "Amor" in all his guises—including that "D'amistà."

Seemingly unrelated to these sentiments, Gray writes that he is enclosing "a metaphysical poem . . . in Latin too to increase the absurdity," the first fifty-three lines of *De Principiis Cogitandi*. More or less a Lucretian "translation" of Locke's *Human Understanding*, it presents itself as an unpromising dry-as-dust scholarly enterprise; but that impression is immediately leavened by a dedication "Ad Favonium" coupled with an ostensible invocation to Locke himself ("the great Priest of Truth" to whom "the hearts of men are open, and the secret places of the lofty Mind"). This immediately becomes an address to Favonius, West. He is beseeched to lend an attentive, sympathetic ear, for this work is "for you," to whom it owes its origin and whatsoever is "joyful and lovable" in it. The poem is an odd performance, to say the least, and one must wonder why Gray even thought to undertake it. The temptation now is to read the much later (1742) threnody on West's death that Gray called "Liber Secundus" back into the apparently complete Book 1—especially since the whole was, as Gray says, "for" West. Without entirely resisting that temptation, I would point out that, even without the aid of the fragment of Book 2, Gray's second verse paragraph focuses on himself as poet, emulating, though with possibly fancied trepidation, West's achievement in the portion of his *Pausanias* that he had sent Gray earlier in 1741. "These first-beginnings, though small," he says, will give rise to no slight activities [the whole of the *De Principiis?* other poems?]. Then he goes on, "Whenever anything joyful and lovable is conceived [are we, or West, really to equate this with discoursing in Latin on Locke?], it owes its origin to these first-beginnings . . . [which must] work together in harmony and favour the result. From this source [joyfulness and lovableness?] arise the varied arts of life and milder practice, and *the sweet bond of friendship*."[19] Nothing of this, of course, has anything to do with Locke, and although Gray does finally invoke a kind of generic muse at the end of this first verse paragraph, both the muse and (in some sense) the "subject" of his poem are patently Richard West.

Even so, it would be absurd to regard *De Principiis* as a love poem, though it does tremble repeatedly on the verge of impassioned communication: for example, the limitlessness of the sense of touch "takes the leading part," asserts "wider sway," "has its dwelling deep in the marrow of the bones and throughout the vicera," and diffuses "its being in the warp and woof of the skin."[20] But far more overtly sexual, one might say libidinally overwrought, than lines like these is Gray's account of the other

senses: "quivering lips," "shapes of loveliness and comely motions,"
"shafts of radiance," the "insatiable appetite" of eyes "taking delight in
gazing," "the moist expanses of the tongue," and the sense of smell "seiz-
[ing] upon . . . the fragrances that the dewy kisses of Flora impart when,
at the hour of twilight, she shyly responds to the prayers of Zephyr [West's
pseudonym] and sighs with gentle love." And, after a hortatory parenthe-
sis in its penultimate verse paragraph ("lend favoring ears to my words"),
the "book" concludes with sensations that "feed the eyes" and "tiny bod-
ies" that "seethe and boil among themselves with vibrating pulsation,
with the result that the vibration . . . is able to slip through the vibrating
doors of the eager sense of hearing and begets sound. Meanwhile, in close
array, vibrating bodies, with no intermediary, directly invade the delicate
fibres of the nerves and, unassisted, set up a motion that produces sensa-
tion throughout the vitals."

   None of this, of course, is Lucretian, nor is it linguistically "Lockean."
In fact, it more nearly reminds one of something like Erasmus Darwin's
Loves of the Plants. Perhaps Gray's consciousness of his own repressed,
however here *ex*pressed, sexuality is what leads him to twitter nervously
to West about the whole performance in the enclosing letter:

> Poems and Metaphysics (say you, with your spectacles on) are incon-
> sistent things. A metaphysical poem is a contradiction in terms. It is
> true, but I will go on. It is Latin too to increase the absurdity. It will,
> I suppose, put you in mind of the man who wrote a treatise of Can-
> non Law in Hexameters.

No, it won't. Though West actually may never have seen more than the
fifty-three lines Gray sent in the letter, even that would have reminded
him vividly of his scholarly, melancholy, nihilissimo friend earnestly trying
to write the only kind of love letter he could manage—or perhaps *dared*
to try to manage at all in a society where such "Love! sweet Love! was
thought a crime," as Blake put it in "A Little Girl Lost" *(Songs of Experi-
ence)*. And, as Gray and West both knew, "Mà nel suo diverso aspetto /
Sempr' egli è l'istesso Amor."

   And so we have arrived at the eve of 1742, the first of Gray's two ver-
sions of an annus mirabilis, inaugurated in early June with the writing of
his *Ode on the Spring*, virtually coincident with West's death. We know
about, or actually have, six letters from Gray to West between September
1741 and June 1742 when he arrived back in London, and five from West

to Gray during the same period, but I reserve comment on these until I address the full context of Gray's composition of the Spring Ode and his forwarding it to West, not knowing that his friend had already died. To the first major phase of Gray's poetic career, then, I now turn to trace its painfully slow dawning, paradoxically energized by the trauma of West's death and with it the death of love and the mythical idyll of their past together—virtually all cast in Miltonic terms.

The Poems (I)

Although, as may already be obvious, Milton appears but little in Gray's correspondence, his life and his poetry were very much present in Gray's imagination from the beginning, even in what appears to be his first effort at poetry in English, the generally ignored "Lines Spoken by the Ghost of John Dennis at the Devil Tavern," written when he was not quite eighteen. While a certain logic would dictate my beginning at that beginning, considerations other than simple chronology prompt me to begin at the pinnacle of Gray's agonistic relationship with Milton: *The Bard,* that powerful and ultimately heart-wrenching prelude to the end of his repressed (or displaced) subtextual autobiography of his poetic self. It is in that poem, of course, that the famous lines on Milton discussed in some detail in chapter 1 occur: "A voice as of the cherub-choir / Gales from blooming Eden bear," and so on. But there is considerably more to this minicharacterization of Milton and his achievement, especially in *Paradise Lost,* than was appropriate to an introductory chapter. I turn to the passage again, then, and to its expansive contextualization in *The Bard,* which, I hope to demonstrate, was both a climactic and a pivotal point in Gray's career. The time is 1755–1757, almost fifteen years after West's death, though West is still very much alive in Gray's mind during his protracted struggle to complete the poem.

I begin by noting the absence of Milton's name in *The Bard,* a habitual evasion except for, somewhat oddly, the circa 1752 *Stanzas to Mr. [Richard] Bentley* (which also names Dryden, Pope, and Shakespeare). In *The Bard,* that evasiveness may be attributable to the realization that the disembodied "voice" Gray (and/or the Bard-speaker) hears is the one an earthbound Milton implores the "Sphere-born harmonious sisters, Voice and Verse" to vouchsafe him, the one that can sing

> That undisturb'd song of pure concent,
> Aye sung before the sapphire-colored throne
> To him that sits thereon,
> With saintly shout and solemn jubilee,
> Where the bright Seraphim in burning row
> Their loud uplifted angel-trumpets blow,
> And the Cherubic host in thousand quires
> Touch their immortal harps of golden wires.
>   (Milton, *At a Solemn Music*)

Moreover, although Gray himself in the 1768 edition of his poems identifies the "voice" he hears as Milton's, the phrase "blooming Eden" is from Young's *Night Thoughts;*[1] and the lines that immediately follow the "voice" speak of "distant warblings" that "lessen on [his] ear" and "lost in long futurity expire," phrases that Gray himself glosses as "The succession of Poets after Milton's time" (Lonsdale, 199 n). This rather startling prophetic look into the future as if it were but a continuation of the post-Miltonic past now being swept into silence[2] functions as a prelude to the final lines of *The Bard*, where the voice that speaks them and all the poem's preceding lines is swallowed up in the bard's plunge "Deep in the roaring tide . . . to endless night."[3]

But in between that spectacular act and the expiration of "distant warblings" Gray returns to *A Solemn Music* and thus positions himself as the subject of the Bard's final prophecy:

> Fond impious man, think'st thou yon sanguine cloud,
> Raised by thy breath, has quenched the orb of day?
> Tomorrow he repairs the golden flood,
> And warms the nations with redoubled ray.
> Enough for me: with joy I see
> The different doom our fates assign.
> Be thine despair and sceptred care;
> To triumph, and to die, are mine.

If, in reading these lines, we recall Milton's beseeching of "Voice and Verse" ("Blest pair of Sirens" who are "pledges of heav'n's joy"), we find that prayer to be for their "mixed power" to empower him "on earth with undiscording voice / [To] rightly answer" the "melodious noise" of saintly and cherubic heavenly song—

As once we did, till disproportioned sin
Jarred against Nature's chime, and with harsh din
Broke the fair music that all creatures made
To their great Lord . . .
                          . . . whilst they stood
In first obedience and their state of good.
O may we soon again renew that song,
And keep in time with heav'n, till God ere long
To his celestial consort us unite,
To live with him, and sing in endless morn of light.

To be sure, the Bard's condemnation of impious man's presumptuousness
does not quite square with Milton's idea of disproportioned sin breaking
prelapsarian music's heavenly harmony into fragmented din, but in the
early eighteenth century there is a Latin poem that strikingly resembles
Milton's and does square with Gray's "version." The poem is Hieronymus
Vida's "Hymnus xv" in his *Poemata* of 1732, cited first by John Mitford,
Gray's early-nineteenth-century editor:

> Impious man [*Impie*], why dost thou rage?. . . Thinkest thou that
> thou canst hide the splendid flames of the golden-tressed heaven,
> and quench ["extinguere"] the sun himself? Thou wilt, perhaps,
> avail to raise by the breath a dark mist, and curtain with momentary
> cloud his encumbered rays. Yet his light shall burst forth; forth with
> the reddening gleam his torch shall burst, and scatter all the rack
> with a flood of golden fires ["auriflua"].[4]

Despite Lonsdale's subtle adjustments of the Latin to bring his translation
closer to how he thought Gray might have read Vida, and despite the
unignorable similarities between Gray's lines and Vida's ("adjusted" or
not), it is still difficult to assume that Gray expected his readers to catch
the echoes. Or, of course, as was often his wont, he didn't care. In any
case, whatever echoes *we* may now catch at Mitford's and Lonsdale's prod-
ding are thoroughly subsumed by Gray's (not much more recognizable)
Miltonic contextualization of the entire fourteen-line conclusion to *The
Bard*. That contextualization is constructed out of a remarkable conver-
gence in his imagination of *Lycidas*, *At a Solemn Music*, *Paradise Lost*, and
the memory of West's death—salted with the intensity of Gray's own
sense of having arrived at what I called earlier the pinnacle of his Miltonic
agon. For his career-long effort to emulate, if not triumph over, Milton's
precedent, even now in the waning 1750s at age forty, had produced not

only no "voice as of the cherub-choir" but one already dwindling into "distant warblings" on the verge of the very extinction the Bard enacts.

I return, then, yet again to *At a Solemn Music* and the impiousness of man that Milton cites as the agent of celestial harmony's disintegration. Gray's own implicit indictment of himself (through the Bard's language) as impious constitutes a rather daring redaction of Milton's conception into a confession of his own punishable trespass into the Edenic/celestial regions of Milton's song/voice. To put it bluntly, his (Gray's) voice, as stolidly earthbound as he, can neither "undiscordingly" nor "rightly" answer Milton's "melodious noise." Tragically unable to "renew that song, / And keep in tune with" Milton, he remains excluded from "*his* [Milton's, not God's] celestial consort" and thus not only does not "sing in endless morn of light" but indeed sings no more at all. As the Bard he famously said he felt himself to be, Gray undoes Milton's final line of *Solemn Music* into the utter silence of endless night to which he now consigns his own poetic career.

But what of *Lycidas* here? The possibility of Vida's influence aside, Gray clearly imports into his final nine lines Milton's

> So sinks the day-star in the ocean bed,
> And yet anon repairs his drooping head,
> And tricks his beams, and with new-spangled ore
> Flames in the forehead of the morning sky.

But what is pointedly ignored by Gray is the analogical functioning of this conceit: "So Lycidas sunk low, but mounted high" to be united by God (in the words of *At a Solemn Music*) "To his celestial consort" and "live with him, and sing in endless morn of night." Milton's own echo in *Lycidas* of these lines has of course been noted before, Lycidas hearing

> the unexpressive nuptial song
> In the blest kingdoms meek of joy and love.
> There entertain him all the saints above,
> In solemn troops and sweet societies
> That sing, and singing in their glory move.

In addition, given Milton's thrice-repeated word "sunk" to describe Lycidas's fate, Gray's initial version of his last line may be seen as deemphasizing the willfulness of the Bard's suicidal leap in favor of some other "fatal and perfidious" agency that, as in *Lycidas*, "sunk so low that sacred head of thine." That earlier version is "Deep in the roaring tide he sunk to endless night," where, again like Lycidas, the Bard too "under the whelming tide / Visit'st the bottom of the monstrous world."

It is here that Gray's love for West and the indelible memory of his youthful death play their parts in this extraordinary final passage. In the parable he took from Pope's letter to Steele, West in *Ad Amicos* twenty years earlier metaphorized "fair-fac'd youth" as a blooming plant nourished by the stream but soon undermined by the water; and

> Too late the plant bewails his foolish pride,
> And sinks, untimely, in the whelming tide.
> (*CTG*, 63)

Moreover, as I noted in my analysis of *Ad Amicos*, West's final six lines invoke "some[one] . . . (ere spent my vital days) / Within whose breast my tomb I wish to raise," that parenthesis originally having been "ere sunk in endless night" until Gray himself revised it. *The Bard*, then, is for Gray not a tragic fulfillment of West's prophecy of his own imminent death but rather a prophecy of Gray's metaphorically dying West's death before becoming a great poet—mournfully as if he (Gray) were still young. The Bard thus enacts in his plunge the willful sinking of Gray himself into the depths of eternal night and silence from which "his drooping head" will never be repaired nor his voice speak, much less sing. And there are none "Within whose breasts [his]tomb" he can raise, none whose "praise [will] crown [him] as their precepts mend," none to whom these lines his "name [will endear]," none who is "the Friend sincere" *(Ad Amicos)*. Not only are these lines a reversal of West's, but they are an even more spectacular reversal of the overall movement of Milton's entire poem from death to eternal life: Gray's is from life to death—*his* "sable shroud" (*Lycidas*, 22) now literally that of "some mute inglorious Milton."

What Gray essays at the end of *The Bard*, in other words, is nothing less than the deaths (literal or figurative) of the Bard and Gray as well as of West and Milton himself, all refigured here in varying degrees as Edward King. With respect to the latter pair, "Lycidas is dead"

> and hath not left his peer.
> Who would not sing for Lycidas? He knew
> Himself to sing, and build the lofty rhyme.
> He must not float upon his wat'ry bier

Unwept, and welter to the parching wind,
Without the meed of some melodious tear.
. . . .
For we were nursed upon the self-same hill [cf. line 11
        of *Eton College*],
Fed the same flock, by fountain, shade, and rill.
   Together both, ere the high lawns appeared
Under the opening eyelids of the morn,
We drove afield, and both together heard
What time the gray-fly winds her sultry horn
. . . .
   But O the heavy change, now thou art gone,
Now thou are gone, and never must return!

Then Gray himself, ventriloquistically on himself, and on West's death:

   Alas! what boots it with uncessant care
To tend the homely slighted shepherd's trade,
And strictly meditate the thankless Muse?
. . . .
Fame is the spur that the clear spirit doth raise
(That last infirmity of noble mind)
To scorn delights, and live laborious days;
But the fair guerdon when we hope to find,
And think to burst out into sudden blaze,
Comes the blind Fury with th' abhorrèd shears
And slits the thin-spun life.

What is missing, of course, in Gray's "Lycidas" with respect to Milton's death is the un-Bardic triumph of Milton's elegy. Although, like Lycidas to Milton, Milton will never be "dead" to Gray, henceforth in Gray's career he will no longer be "the Genius of the shore"—nor in his "large recompense" will he "be good" to Gray, who will continue to "wander," lost in *his* "perilous flood" with only a monumentally abortive later foray into the "fresh woods, and pastures new" of Norse and Welsh myth. West, on the other hand, to the end of Gray's life will be "mounted high" in Gray's memory, *that* "blest [kingdom] meek of joy and love" that is their past together, their Eton, their walking hand in hand like the children of the wood, their Eden.

For all the above, a kind of coda to this depressing story is necessary in order to flesh out my earlier claim that *Paradise Lost* also plays a role in *The Bard*, one that reflects what I have called more than once Gray's progressively debilitating sense of his poetic transgressiveness onto Milton's hallowed ground. I begin with the ostensible tenor and mode of the third epode I have been reading and rereading. By tenor and mode I mean Gray's historical grounding of the Bard's prophecy and the curious response he has him offer to his presumably self-consolatory statement about the sun's repairing itself on each tomorrow. "Enough for me," he says. To what, we may ask, does "Enough" refer? That the sun also rises? That somehow, inexplicably, it rerises "with redoubled ray"? That it warms presumably *all* "nations"? That nature, history, life all go on, despite impious man's benighted, perverse efforts to stall their progress? The simplest answer I can muster to the first of these questions derives from Gray's commonplace book sketch of what he calls the "original argument" of the poem. As Gray projects it, the Bard's prophecy proper (though the entire poem save the final two lines is the prophecy in toto) inheres in the eight lines prior to his plunge. In *that* context the "Fond impious man" is Edward I, the "sanguine cloud" the slaughter at his command of all the Welsh bards. The lines on the sun's self-repairing, then, extend Milton's metaphor in *Lycidas* to the deathlessness of what Gray calls in the commonplace book "the noble ardour of poetic genius in this island"—to which he adds immediately, "men shall never be wanting to celebrate true virtue and valour in immortal strains, to expose vice and infamous pleasure, and boldly censure tyranny and oppression" (Lonsdale, 178).

This explains the passages (for example, lines 97–134) Gray prefixed to the prophecy itself, a mini-progress of poesy that draws upon his poem of that title to sketch the British bardic line from Spenser and Shakespeare through Milton, all three implicitly deriving from the Tudors' Welsh ancestry imagined in the mythical thirteenth-century Bard. On the basis of that progress—of Milton's prophetic resurrection of Lycidas, who as "Genius of the shore, / . . . shall be good / To all that wander in that perilous flood," coupled with the sun's every-redoubled ray—the Bard is joyously satisfied ("Enough for me") that the fates mete out appropriate justice: to Edward "despair and sceptred care" (a recall of the poem's opening strophe), to the Bard the triumphant knowledge that the ardor of poetic genius will continue its progress unabated "To-morrow to fresh woods, and pastures new."

For all the positive thrust of this explanation, however, my argument is that Gray's Miltonic subtext radically undermines the poem's ostensibly

optimistic, if not fully triumphant, prophetic close. Whatever fresh woods
and pastures new Milton, empowered by the Genius of the shore, may
discover, Gray will discover only an imagined site of distant warblings on
the way to expiration in long (endless) futurity—precisely the depths of
silence into which the Bard's and Gray's voices plunge. The "doom," then,
that the Bard declares the fates have assigned him —that is, to triumph
and die coinstantaneously, presumably in full confidence of the accuracy
of his prophecy—emerges as a kind of bizarre translation of Raphael's
account in *Paradise Lost* of Christ's vanquishing of Satan's rebellious host.
Indeed, Gray subtly emulates in the final six lines of *The Bard* the very
sequence of that account. When Christ advises Michael's armed "bright
array" to stand aside from the battle in favor of his engaging Satan's host
alone, it is because "Vengeance is his [God's], or whose he sole appoints":

> against me is all their rage,
> Because the Father, t' whom in heav'n supreme
> Kingdom and power and glory appertains,
> Hath honored me according to his will.
> Therefore to me their doom he hath assigned.
>   (6. 801, 888, 813–17)

The analogies here are complex but uncannily apt. Where Milton's God
assigns the doom of the rebel angels to Christ, Gray's fates assign a doom
for Edward which is but a pale version of that of the Satanic host ("despair
and sceptred care"); where Christ triumphs and rides through heaven, is
received into glory by the Father, and "now sits at the right hand of bliss"
(6. 888–92), the Bard "triumphs" only to die like Christ's "impious foes"
(831) who "from the verge of heav'n" threw themselves "headlong" into
"the bottomless pit." Moreover, *this* "fate" is a deliberate modification by
Milton of his Book 1 precis of the same battle ("Him the Almighty Power /
Hurled headlong flaming from th' ethereal sky") and, for Gray more tell-
ing, a precise echo of Satan's prophetic fear that, once having passed the
ninefold gates of burning adamant on his way out of hell,

> the void profound
> Of unessential Night receives him next
> Wide gaping, and with utter loss of being
> Threatens him, plunged in that abortive gulf.
>   (2. 434–41)

With no dolphins here to "waft the helpless youth," no "mounting high" to flame "in the forehead of the morning sky," no "undiscording voice" to "rightly answer [Milton's] melodious noise," no renewal of "that song" sung "in endless morn of light," Gray is left to use his own self-descriptive word, "nihillissimo," not only utterly without voice but threatened with utter loss of being. Like West. Not to triumph but to despair and die are *his*. He is irremediably self-sentenced to this "doom" for his Satanic presumption, his attempt to overleap the bounds into Milton's "blooming Eden" and, with the "cherub-choir" and Milton's Godlike "celestial consort," to "live with him," "Singing everlastingly."

There is little doubt that in resurrecting this densely submerged Miltonic subtext into such glaring light I have done some violence to Gray's poem. In fact, I have thrust Gray's dominant text *and* conception into near subtextual status. That *he* would acknowledge, let alone approve, such a reading is at best dubious, since for all their resonating power the three Milton poems I've unearthed from their subtextuality in effect occlude their own visibility. Gray himself, as Lonsdale accurately observes (180), was defiantly aware that his Pindarics (Odikles he sometimes deprecatingly called them) "would perplex many of his readers": they demand, as he wrote to Edward Bedingfield, "a certain measure of learning . . . , & a long acquaintance with the good Writers ancient & modern . . . and without this they [readers] can only catch here & there a florid expression, or a musical rhyme, while the Whole appears to them a wild obscure unedifying jumble" (*CTG*, 478). In fact, it was not until eleven years or so after completing *The Bard* that he acceded to others' demands for notes to *The Bard*, despite his having argued persistently that it only "alluded to a few common facts to be found in any six-penny History of England by way of question & answer for the use of children" (*CTG*, 1002)—a rather wonderful anticipation of Blake's chiding of the obtuse Reverend Dr. Trusler: "You ought to know that What is Grand is necessarily obscure to Weak men. That which can be made Explicit to the Idiot is not worth my care . . . I am happy to find a Great Majority of Fellow Mortals who can Elucidate My Visions & Particularly they have been Elucidated by Children." [5]

However, my own sense about Gray's deployment of Milton, not of history, is that he did not wish his *contemporary* readers to even recognize, much less elucidate, the allusions I have argued for. The subtext, as I have tried to demonstrate, not only does not undercut the power of Gray's historical prophetic conception, but effectively effaces itself paradoxically in the very act of exposing Gray's history of his private self. I would like to think that this self was what he was "really" addressing in his wry comment to Mason in September 1757: "Nobody understands me, & I am perfectly satisfied" (*CTG*, 522). For there were, as W. Powell Jones demonstrated unequivocally sixty years ago, enthusiastic readers of *The Bard* who had both the necessary "certain measure of learning" and at least a decent grasp of literary history ancient and modern.[6]

Even so, along with historical notes Gray did add others to the 1768 edition that glossed "parallel passages . . . out of justice to those writers, from whom I happen'd to take the hint of any line, as far as I can recollect" (*CTG*, 1002). But "those writers" turn out to be Shakespeare (*King John* and *Julius Caesar*), Dryden *(The Indian Queen)*, a painting by Raphael and one by Parmigiano, Milton (but only *Paradise Lost* 1. 537), John Ray *(The Ornithology of Francis Willoughby),* and Spenser *(The Faerie Queene).* That's it—so far as he can recollect. While the paucity of these acknowledged "hints" for a line here and there eloquently bespeaks Gray's fear of being branded a "plagiary," the glosses studiously deflect our notice of *anything* in *The Bard* that might reveal even glimpses of his private agony and despair at having failed miserably to appropriate Milton's power and sublimity—and, above all, Milton's self-conscious trajectory of his illustrious career. Had Gray spoken out the depths of his desire, and had he made poetry of his sense of utter failure even in his most courageously transgressive efforts to attain a voice commensurate with that desire, and had he not resolved, in defeat, to make *his* "pastures new" (non-Milton-inspired), he might well have penned a coda to *The Bard* (or perhaps an epigraph) to match Keats's "On Visiting the Tomb of Burns":

> Burns! with honor due
> I have oft honored thee. Great shadow, hide
> Thy face—I sin against thy native skies.

But the pastures new are, of course, *The Fatal Sisters, The Descent of Odin, The Triumphs of Owen, The Death of Hoel, Caradoc,* and *Conan,* the interstices between these post-*Bard*ic productions being filled with an olio of epitaphs, insouciant lyrics (two at the request of his friend Henrietta Speed), and more or less inconsequential political satires. While I cannot agree with Suvir Kaul (and many of his critical predecessors) regarding the "achievement" of these poems—that in them Gray, by ventriloquizing "the voice[s] of ancient empowerment," nostalgically celebrates "bardic potency," I fully concur with his final judgment that these heroic, bardic, prophetic voices are attained to only "via a formative detour" that itself dramatizes loss.[7] In fact, that detour is in itself a powerful confession of utter failure, for Gray's limited knowledge of the language of the originals led him to rely on Latin translations which, as Thomas Gray, Scholar (not poet), he but retranslated.[8] Thus it is no surprise that the entire Welsh-Norse series dwindles quickly into more and more fragmented, abortive, and in a sense half-baked fits and starts. Other than these we have only a pasture new that is but Gray's old Miltonic territory retrod into trivialization, the *Ode for Music.* Two years after completing that he was dead.

This deep depression, this paradoxically creative self-destruction that is *The Bard* (reminiscent of Coleridge's *Dejection: An Ode* and other Romantic elegies on the death of creative imagination) did not, of course, arise out of a psychic/poetic vacuum. For all the self-consciousness of early-eighteenth-century poets about Milton's unprecedented achievement, even in Gray's relative youth imaginative, creative negotiations of that daunting presence seemed possible. They run a remarkable gamut of poetic forms, genres, and modes, from trivialization to comic defiance to satire, and all involve sometimes shrewd, sometimes awkward, often inept appropriations of Milton's poetry, interspersed with indirect engagements with Milton's sublimity and power (indirect in the sense of deflections or displacements of that power). Without exception, however, in their varying modulations and accommodations they pale before those momentous and moving struggles with Milton's ghost that are dramatically charted by the *Ode on a Distant Prospect of Eton College* (against the groundwork laid several months earlier in *Ode on the Spring*), the *Elegy, The Progress of Poesy,* and *The Bard.*

If, as I have argued in my commentary on *The Bard,* the year 1757 (when Gray finally completed the poem) was a critical turning point in his career in several interlocking ways, fifteen years earlier is the temporal site of the closest he ever came to a genuine annus mirabilis (*pace* the familiar critical claims for the "triumphs" of his Welsh and Norse poems). In 1742, with little or nothing accomplished poetically, Gray took a stab at a tragedy, quickly aborted and largely forgettable now, *Agrippina;* and it was followed by another poetic byway soon abandoned, a translation of one of Propertius's elegies (which he never published but to which I shall return shortly). Early in June, however, he produced *Ode on the Spring,* in August the Eton College Ode, the Sonnet on West's death, and the *Ode to Adversity,* and he possibly began the ultimately unfinished *Hymn to Ignorance.* In between the more or less prolific year of the Norse and Welsh poems,

1761, and the bona fide prolific output of 1742 lie the odd, seemingly incompatible *Ode on the Death of a Favourite Cat, The Alliance of Education and Government* (abandoned six months or so after it was begun), the *Elegy*, and *A Long Story*—the last of which immediately precedes *The Progress of Poesy* (written between 1751 and 1754) and *The Bard* (1755–57).[9]

Before turning to those 1742 poems, however, we need to attend to a few of their predecessors. From about 1725 to 1734 Gray was at Eton, and virtually all of his poetic ventures were Latin school exercises, other Latin verse transcribed in his commonplace book, and a few translations into English of Latin and Italian poetry (notably from Statius's *Thebiad*, Tasso's *Gerusalemme Liberata*, Dante's *Inferno*, and Propertius's elegies). More of the same emerge out of his tenure at Cambridge in 1734–38, except for, in the winter of 1734, the odd, untitled "Lines Spoken by the Ghost of John Dennis at the Devil Tavern" (as it is now known). As Gray's first extant poem in English it ought to be of some general interest, but for my purpose it claims some additional interest as, however peculiar it may seem, his first poetic engagement with Milton. "Engagement," of course, grossly overstates the case, for in the "Lines" Milton jostles with a mélange of other poets and prose writers appropriate to the poem's comic intent: Thomas Brown and Elizabeth Rowe (both working in the Lucian-Fontenelle-Fenelon tradition of comic journeys to the underworld or dialogues with the dead), Dryden, Prior, Pope, Nicholas Rowe, and possibly Nathaniel Lee. Lumped in with them are the beau monde of St. James Park and assorted personages from Alexander to Nicolino Grimaldi and Anne Oldfield, and from Plato to Proserpina to Cleopatra and Queen Elizabeth—and, of course, John Dennis's ghostly self, who not so much speaks as writes ("wrought" is Gray's word in the letter to Walpole that contains the poem) the epistolary lines, replete with a final ten-line P.S. (Toynbee 1: 12–15).

The frame of the "Lines" is, of course, a parodic version of Book 6 of the *Aeneid*, Dennis's ghost rising from the "shady Groves," restful river banks, and "Watersweet meadows" of Virgil's Elysium to revisit the "upper light" and, as Milton put it, to "tell / Of things invisible to mortal sight" (*PL* 3. 54–55). But the fundamental substance of this Lucianic account of the "house of torture and the abyss of woe" derives not from Lucian (nor from imitations of Fontenelle or Fenelon) but from Brown's 1702 *Letters from the Dead to the Living*. Brown's book is hardly an "imitation" of Virgil or Lucian, but he does acknowledge a "relationship" to both in his preface, and he draws on Virgil's point that the dead find in the next world their own irreversible level: "disproportion," Brown writes, "is their punishment," a diminishment, disfiguration, and trivialization of their erstwhile status in the living world. Thus, in the mode of Lucian's *Dialogues of the Dead*, and its mixed-bag progeny, Brown's Semiramis is a barmaid, Cyrus a peddler of snuff, Diogenes a fop, Dido a bedlamite, Hannibal a hawker of Spanish nuts, Hector a hairdresser, Mark Antony an itinerant "with dancing Dogs, a Monkey and a Rope," and Cleopatra sentenced to "feeding Proserpina's Piggs." [10]

Newly popularized in the early eighteenth century, such an antecedent tradition and the poem's tongue-in-cheek epistolary setting militate against our assuming some profound intent or self-revelation. Indeed, the operative occasion for Gray's choice of subject may well have been the publication of Dennis's last work, *A Treatise Concerning the State of Departed Souls*, translated from the Latin of Thomas Burnet. Deadly serious and hardly Lucianic, it would have presented Gray an opportunity for having some youthful poetic fun at the critic's expense and for amusing Walpole in the bargain. Why Dennis, though? The answer may be implicit in my second-chapter account of that critic's writings on Milton, but it is more succinctly evident in Edward Dowden's turn-of-the century reminder that Dennis, deploring "the low estate to which English poetry had fallen at the death of Dryden," "leads the way" in eighteenth-century criticism of Milton.[11] Given that, I hazard here a sharper look at the otherwise forgettable work, particularly the lines following Gray's introductory verse paragraph.

In them he abandons the fiction, barely begun, of an epistle by the dead Dennis (he died in January 1734) to the living Walpole (the Celadon of line 4) in favor of his own authorship (encoded as Orozmades), the names they adopted in the Quadruple Alliance with West (Favonius) and Ashton (Almanzor).[12] In effect Gray thus places himself among the momentarily resurrected dead to recount *his* exploration of the underworld:

> That little, naked, melancholy thing,
> My soul, when first she tried her flight to wing,
> Began with speed new regions to explore.

These phrases oddly, if distantly, may call to mind Milton's Satan "explor-[ing] his solitary flight" "on swift wings . . . toward the gates of hell," as well as Death's ordering him back to hell ("to thy speed add wings") before he can deny he's there "With purpose to explore or to disturb / The secrets of your realm" (*PL* 2. 631–32, 700, 971–72). If the lines indeed do signal Milton's ghostly presence in Satanic disguise (as the four preceding lines of Gray's poem openly are), the passage following the one quoted above seems surely to absent him: flying to explore new regions Gray's soul

> blundered through a narrow postern door.
> First most devoutly having said its prayers,
> It tumbled down a thousand pair of stairs,
> Through entries long, through cellars vast and deep,
> Where ghostly rats their habitations keep.

Is this a wild travesty of Satan, his "cloudy chair" having failed him, blundering into "A vast vacuity" and

> all unawares
> Flutt'ring his pennons vain plumb down he drops
> Ten thousand fadom deep?

Or even of the slippage (near comic in itself) of Milton's line "And swims or sinks, or wades, or creeps, or flies" (*PL* 2. 930–34, 950)? Or perhaps Gray's lines parody Satan's own echoing of Milton's language (in Book 2) in the speech he delivers triumphantly to "the Stygian throng" upon his return: "Long were to tell," Satan begins (cf. Gray's "More to reveal, or many words to use"),

> What I have done, what suffered, with what pain
> Voyaged th' unreal, vast, unbounded deep.
>   (10. 469–71)

And could, then, Gray's "narrow postern door" be "Th' infernal doors" of Hell (2. 881) through which Satan escapes into the realm of Chaos and Old Night?

The allusions or echoes or coincidences I offer here (taken along with Lonsdale's other analogs in *Paradise Lost* 1. 249–50 and 2. 461–62 elsewhere in the poem) suggest less some grand intent in this essentially trivial, even inane exercise than Gray's ready recollection of Miltonic images and phrasings—although his focus on Satanic transgressiveness even as early as age seventeen is worth at least passing note. In any case, the "progress" of Gray's poem itself emulates his soul's blundering down to the underworld by tumbling into a potpourri of fragmentary vignettes modeled on Brown's satirical *Letters*—even as the Milton references may be seen to reflect the fact that, as I argued earlier, if Spenser *was* always in his mind when he composed (as Gray said he was), Gray's ear was far more finely tuned to Milton's "deep-toned shell" and the "genuine ardour" of *his* forays into both "empyrean day" and the "horrors of the deep." But what is surer than all of this is that this comic account of his poetic soul's first flight and descent is both a nascent poetic tactic, used again and again by Gray in his more mature poetry, for displacing Milton's power, and a proleptic (if neither self-conscious nor sober) acknowledgment of the necessity for such tactical displacement. To put that another way, Gray's poetic tomfoolery, for all its jejuneness, should not be allowed to eclipse the implications of his doggerel *reductio* of the sublime to the trivially ridiculous. Given that the Bard's plunge into silence and the struggles of the Eton College Ode, *The Progress of Poesy,* and the *Elegy* are of greater moment in our reading of Gray's submerged and displaced poetic autobiography, there is still that wonderful mastery of trivialization, the *Ode on the Death of a Favourite Cat,* and the strange, allusive Miltonic potpourri that constitutes Gray's farewell to poetry, the *Ode for Music.* To both of these the "Lines" points.

Those poems, of course, are still some years away, however, and here it is significant only to note that Gray's poetic soul, left languishing in the "Lines" among the likes of Nicolini, Anne Oldfield, and Nicholas Rowe's Queen Artemisia at tea, continued its earthbound languor throughout the next six or seven years—a creative (or uncreative) pattern that will be repeated often in Gray's career. And if Milton hovered at all over the sparse and routine verse of these years, he did so only as a benign tutelary deity by example of his early study and writing of Latin and Italian verse. Nevertheless, there are a few glimmers of hope for Gray's poetic career during the years between the Dennis poem and 1741, the eve of his annus mirabilis. Three of them, having to do with Gray's love for West heavily disguised in translations, I have commented on in the previous chapter: the Latin love elegy beginning "Mater rosarum, cui tenerae vigent," the Latin translation of Buondelmonti's "Spesso Amor sotto la forma," and the first fifty-three lines of *De Principiis Cogitandi*—all three in letters to West. Two others, neither of them about West but both sporadically reflecting Gray's continued preoccupation with Milton, are his May 1736 translation of a passage from Statius's *Thebiad* and his abortive attempt at a tragedy, *Agrippina,* begun in late 1741, abandoned in early 1742.

The Statius he sent to West accompanied by a bemused confession of his not doing anything, not reading, and so on, the "employment of [his] hours . . . best explained by Negatives" (*CTG*, 38–41). In this vacant mood, he and Statius "had a game at Quoits together"—that is, the epic discus contest Statius recounts. While, indeed, the translation is but a "playing with Statius," ponderously as it turns out, two rather obvious Miltonic allusions may reflect some modicum of seriousness here, especially as they foreground Milton's Satan. The third candidate for supremacy in the game is "Nesimachus's Son," who "came towring on" just as, on the verge of the great war in heaven,

> Satan, with vast and haughty strides advanced,
> Came tow'ring, armed in adamant and gold.
> (6. 109–10)

With this allusion Gray rather neatly conflates a scene from Book 1, the reaction of the fallen host to Satan's war cry, "War then, war / Open or understood must be resolved":

> out flew
> Millions of flaming swords, drawn from the thighs
> Of mighty Cherubim; the sudden blaze
> Far round illumined Hell. Highly they raged
> Against the Highest, and fierce with grasped arms
> Clashed on their sounding shields the din of war,
> Hurling defiance toward the vault of heav'n.

Here is Gray's radical redaction: the daunting brightness and hugeness of the discus

> With doubled light . . . beam'd against the Day:
> So glittering shews the Thracian Godheads shield,
> With such a gleam affrights Pangaea's field,
> When blazing 'gainst the Sun it shines from far,
> And clash'd rebellows with the Din of war.

However, the scene is but momentary, perhaps predictably in what is clearly an exercise, and there is little else of Milton to detain us here—nor is there in the other letters in the late thirties that have survived. *Agrippina* is far more interesting.

Derived from Tacitus's *Annals* as well as from Racine's *Britannicus* (which is based on Tacitus), Gray's abortive effort at a tragedy was not published until 1775. As Gray left it, there is but an opening scene and a twelve-line fragment of scene 2, the former consisting of 182 lines, of which 149 are spoken by Nero's empress-mother Agrippina, the remainder by her household confidante Aceronia. All three of Agrippina's speeches, occasioned by her son's political machinations which she interprets as efforts to severely reduce her power, are products of a rage that culminates in a vow (in the final line of the first scene) to "sink the traitor in his mother's ruin." The second speech, however, has an interesting Miltonic ring. In it (lines 27–53) she sharply and bitterly contrasts Nero with herself: he is but a "puny boy" who "lived unknown / To fame and fortune" (a line Gray stole for his *Elegy*) and "scarcely dared / On expectation's strongest wing to soar"; but, she says,

> a heart like mine,
> A heart that glows with a pure Julian fire,
> If bright ambition from her craggy seat
> Display the radiant prize, will mount undaunted,
> Gain the rough heights, and grasp the dangerous honour.

This stirring close, replete with a fiery ambition that echoes the "blaze of greatness" a few lines earlier, is clearly intended to undercut Agrippina's seeming acknowledgment just prior to the lines quoted above that Nero's boyhood might have been

> the time
> To shrink from danger; fear might then have worn
> The mask of prudence . . .
>
> (47–49)

This is precisely Belial's counsel against open war in the Pandemonium debate: "To nobler deeds / Timorous and slothful" he says,

> I laugh when those who at the spear are bold
> And ven'trous, if that fail them, shrink and fear
> What yet they know must follow . . .

Thus it is better to "sustain and bear" since "our present lot appears / For happy though but ill, but ill not worst" (*PL* 2. 115–16, 204–6, 209, 223–

24). Satan's response, to Belial, and also to all his lieutenants, is at the heart of Agrippina's ringing assertion in lines 27–53 of her like ambition:

> But I should ill become this throne, O Peers,
> And this imperial sov'ranty, adorned
> With splendor, armed with power, if aught proposed
> And judged of public moment, in the shape
> Of difficulty or danger could deter
> Me from attempting. Wherefore do I assume
> These royalties, and not refuse to reign,
> Refusing to accept as great a share
> Of hazard as of honor, due alike
> To him who reigns, and so much to him due
> Of hazard more, as he above the rest
> High honored sits?[13]
>
> (*PL* 2. 445–56)

In light of West's steady attention to, and achievements in, *his* poetry at this time, Gray, as we have seen in the letters, increasingly regarded his own sporadic efforts as pitifully incommensurate with his ambition, and with what he surely regarded as his substantial creative capacities. That Gray sent Agrippina's long speech to West in March-April 1742 suggests strongly that he meant his friend to read it as a kind of confession of Gray's own static career, something he perennially does in his letters to West. That is to say, Nero as a boy may well be a quasi self-portrait, "haply [eyeing] at distance" some judgeship "of weights and measures; scarcely [daring] / On expectations strongest wing to soar," shrinking from such flights' danger and wearing "The mask of prudence" (39–42, 48–49). On the other hand, Gray's deep-seated desire to be no boyish Nero is thus figured in Agrippina herself who, glowing "with a pure Julian fire" will mount "undaunted, / . . . the rough heights" and "grasp the dangerous honour," the "radiant prize" (50–53). The fact that Gray reused in his *Elegy* Agrippina's characterization of her "puny boy" as "unknown / To fame and fortune," a phrasing repeated yet again in modified form in the Propertius translation he sent West on the very day he abandoned *Agrippina* ("Happy the youth, and not unknown to fame"), adds some measure of additional credibility to my claim for (a possibly unwitting) self-portraiture in the tragedy. What Gray did quite wittingly later on, however, was to refer back to both *Agrippina* and the Propertius translation in the *Elegy*'s epitaph—the epitaph that is at once his own and West's, a matter I shall return to shortly.

Here a few additional observations about the Miltonics of *Agrippina* and about their appearing to be at first blush mere analogies rather than allusions are in order. Retrospectively viewed from the shortly to appear Eton College and Favourite Cat odes, the intersections of *Paradise Lost* and *Agrippina* indeed take on a borrowed power. I have in mind here such passages as, from *Eton College,*

> Some bold adventurers disdain
> The limits of their little reign
> And unknown regions dare descry

and Gray's later reference in the ode to the dire fate awaiting those whom "Ambition . . . shall tempt to rise." And in the Favourite Cat ode, we find in its cautionary moralistic conclusion: since "one false step is ne'er retrieved," one should be "bold" only with "caution";

> Not all that tempts your wandering eyes
> And heedless hearts is *lawful prize* [my italics].

Such retrospectivity on Gray's part, visible here but in rudimentary form, is in fact a crucial characteristic of his subtextual autobiography. Moreover, as I have noted before, his self-referentiality is informed centrally by a swelling chorus of echoes of and allusions to Satan's—and progressively to Milton's own—ambition and transgressiveness. While the better part of wisdom in dealing with this very early stage of Gray's life and barely emergent career dictates that one "be with caution bold" (or must "Be bold but not too bold" as Spenser's Britomart is warned), it seems more than coincidence that, even as *Agrippina*'s progress was stalling, Gray turned from it, and from its Satanic transgressiveness, to his own private, morally transgressive love for West. In fact, discouraged by West's criticism of *Agrippina* in a letter of 4 April 1742 (*CTG*, 189–91), Gray abandoned the play ("she is laid up to sleep, till next Summer: so bid her Good night" (*CTG*, 196) and, in the same letter from which I have just quoted, sent West his translation of Propertius's Elegy 2.1, which Mason carefully excised from his printing of the letter.

It is possible that at least a contributing motive for Gray's writing the translation was a virulent resurgence of West's illness. On 4 April 1742 the latter had written him:

> I have been tormented within this week with a most
> violent cough; for when once it sets up its note, it will go on, cough
> after cough, shaking and tearing me for half an hour together; and
> then it leaves me in a great sweat, as much fatigued as if I had been
> labouring at the plough.   (*CTG*, 190)

Although Walpole and Ashton also knew of West's recurrent illness, there is no evidence that he reported it to them in such graphic detail. Moreover, West's attempt to joke it out of mind by writing a Latin mini-ode to "tussis" could only have intensified Gray's fears for West's life. Eight days later, in a letter of desperately chatty literary criticism (in response to one in kind from Gray) West is compelled to report that his "body continues weak and enervate. And for my animal spirits, they are in perpetual fluctuation: Some whole days I have no relish, no attention for any thing; at other times I revive, and am capable of writing a long letter" (*CTG*, 194–95). In less than a month and a half he would be dead.

In his 23 April letter, Gray responds to West's obvious deterioration by bravely trying to put a hopeful spin on the situation: the length of West's letter, he writes, "is a kind of Symptom of the Recovery of your Health," and he "flatters" himself that West's "bodily Strength returns in proportion." It is in these circumstances, then, that Gray's enclosure of the Propertius takes on greater significance—with respect to his anguished state of mind and heart at what clearly was a critical juncture in his personal life as well as in his poetic career. The Propertius is in many ways an extraordinary poem. It professes more openly than ever before in their correspondence Gray's love for West, only thinly veiled or figured in Propertius's love for his mistress, and movingly reflects, in displaced fashion, his deepening fears about West's health. Even though Propertius's lusty imagining of Cynthia's nakedness beneath her diaphanous "Coan Web" may be a bit much to claim for Gray's imaginings,[14] there is no doubt that the Latin poet's figuring of Cynthia as his "Genius" is deliberately refigured into Richard West as his muse:

> From Cynthia all, that in my Numbers shines;
> She is my Genius, she inspires the Lines,
> No Phoebus else, no other Muse I know:
> She tunes my easy Rhime, & gives the Lay to flow
> . . . .
> In brief whate'er she do, or say, or look
> 'Tis ample Matter for a Lover's Book

> And many a copious Narrative you'll see,
> Big with th' important Nothing's History.
>
> (lines 3–6, 27–30)

What is extraordinary in this last quatrain is Gray's "signature"—the "Nihil" of its final lines he knew West would recognize from the motto of the "medal" he told West he had struck for himself: "O . . . Nihilissimo" (*CTG*, 172). Along with Propertius, this "Nothing" will write no heroic verse but rather elegies that chronicle "A milder Warfare":

> Each in his proper Art should wast the Day:
> Nor thou my gentle Calling disapprove,
> To die is glorious in the Bed of Love.

This is close to, but not quite, Propertius's language, which has as the second line here, "There is credit for dying for love," and for the third, "There is credit again to be privileged with but one love." [15]

Even if we deny West credit for knowing the Propertian original (though it is most likely that he did), my analogical reading is cemented some twenty-five lines later. After cataloging, in language that is a nearly literal rendition of Propertius's, the extraordinary cures "of every Ill, but Love" effected by ancient physicians and magicians, Gray adds these lines that have no precedent in the original Latin:

> For Ills unseen what remedy is found,
> Or who can probe the undiscover'd Wound?
> The Bed avails not, or the Leeche's care,
> Nor changeing Skies can hurt, nor Sultry Air,
> 'Tis hard th' elusive Symptoms to explore,
> Today the Lover walks, tomorrow is no more:
> A Train of mourning Friends attend his Fall,
> And wonder at the sudden Funeral.

This remarkable extrapolation anticipates, of course, the last two stanzas (preceding the epitaph) of the Churchyard Elegy in ways I shall comment upon in due time, but here I want to focus on Gray's equally remarkable putting of himself in West's place by pointedly recalling these closing lines of *Ad Amicos:*

> Yet some there are (ere spent my vital days)
> Within whose breasts my tomb I wish to raise.

Lov'd in my life, lamented in my end,
Their praise would crown me as their precepts mend:
To them may these fond lines my name endear,
Not from the Poet but the Friend sincere.

(CTG, 64)

Gray's coda is:

When then my Fates that breath they gave shall claim,
When the short Marble shall preserve a Name,
A little Verse, my All that shall remain;
Thy passing Courser's slacken'd Speed detain,
(Thou envied Honour of thy Poet's Days,
Of all our Youth th' Ambition & the Praise!)
Then to my quiet Urn awhile draw near.[16]

The moving hyperbole of the parenthesis obviously recalls the shattered
Quadruple Alliance (Propertius's actual phrasing is "our youthful company
of knights"), the lost paradise of Eton days, and the sense of death's immi-
nence; and it thereby reasserts Gray's new-found "identity" as *West's*
("thy") poet, who will sing his honor and his name.

West responds in kind less than two weeks later, the "delay" very possi-
bly due to his efforts to respond *poetically* as well. This letter, of 5 May
1742 (*CTG*, 200–201), opens with an ecstatic reaction to Gray's poem: "I
read [it] over and over with excessive pleasure. . . . I like your Elegy ex-
tremely,"—"so extremely" that he wants to point out certain scholarly/
textual errors, and to discuss them in person with his "Propertius . . . upon
the table between us." But such pedantic and "tiresome" stuff, he then
adds, we should now "banish from our correspondence"—and what we
will write instead are "little Ode[s]" to each other, as West does now.
Ostensibly on the spring, West's little "Ode" is in fact his love-poem re-
sponse to Gray's Propertius. "Dear Gray," the poem opens, "that always
in my heart / Possessest far the better part"—but the thought of his dying
abruptly breaks in:

What mean these sudden blasts that rise
And drive the Zephyrs [West] from the skies?

This pet-name "signature" is repeated in the third stanza, where West
implores "the tardy May" to "Recall the Zephyrs from the west"—the

last word capitalized by West but lowercased by Mason, one of his many "corrections" and "improvements" of the original which Gray happily had copied into his commonplace book. While the entire poem is cast in a *L'Allegro*-like mode—perhaps a kind of deliberate disguise—its verbal allusions to Milton's poem, taken together, suggest that West's string of imperatives ("join," "invocate," "come," "resume," "bring," "rise," "awake," "recall," "restore," "revive," "arise," "come then") are pointedly aimed at Gray. In his almost instantaneous response, after some light-hearted criticism of the ode, Gray says of West's portrait of May that "her bed is so soft and so snug that I long to lie with her." West's invocational implications obviously registered.

Three days later West writes his last extant letter, one mangled and abbreviated by Mason. In it he chides Gray for saying that he (Gray) converses "with none but the dead: They . . . almost make me long to be with them" (*CTG*, 202), and then he exclaims, "What, are there no joys among the living? I could almost cry out with Catullus 'Alphene immemor, atque unanimis false sodalibus!' " Gray did not miss the cue, for he knew Catullus's next line to be "have you no pity now for the one you once called your beloved?" Almost certainly included in this letter were two other translations of Catullus (*CTG*, 203 n), both stunningly disguised in their passionate devotion as well as unusually moving in their reflection of West's sense of imminent death and his seemingly consequent throwing of caution to the winds with respect to his (and perhaps even Gray's) moral reputation:

> Lesbia, let us (while we may)
> Live, and love the Time away,
> And never mind what old Folks say.
> Suns can set, & rise as bright:
> No rise attends our little Light.
> We set in everlasting Night.
>   Count me a thousand kisses o'er,
> Count me a thousand kisses more,
> Count me a thousand still, & then
> We'll count them o'er & o'er again.
> Why should I count? why should I know
> How many kisses you bestow?
> 'Tis better let the Reckoning fall,
> We'll kiss and never count at all,
> And thus we may avoid much Hate;
> Since none can envy at our State;

> When none shall know our total Bliss,
> How often & how much we kiss.[17]

The poem, as Charles Martin has shown brilliantly in his recent translation and introduction thereto, "is an invitation from the poet to his beloved to escape with him from the traditional restraints imposed upon them by Roman society (senile busybodies, gossipmongering elders) and to live entirely for the moment, entirely for the sake of passion." But he also points out that the odd word *conturbare* (which he translates as "cry bankrupt, hiding our assets") may well convey (did it to West? or Gray?) "the disturbing intimation that somewhere down the road, emotional ruin, a bankruptcy of the spirit, is lying in wait for the optimistic lover."[18]

The second Catullus poem has something of the same fear or anxiety, though now it inheres only in the "reckoning of gossips" and "spell-casting tongues of envy" that might retail the number of kisses Lesbia is called upon "to sate" him with, even as "many as the stars in the tacit night / that watch as furtive lovers lie embracing." West softens these lines into:

> Or as many Stars as spy
> From their Watch-Tower in the Sky
> The lawless Thefts of Soft Delight
> That pass beneath the Silent Night.

Gray copied both poems into his commonplace book with the annotation, "Fav: Wrote, May 11, 1742. He died, the first of June following." But apparently West did not die before receiving Gray's final "love letter," a bit of antiquarian history cast in the form of a Latin heroic epistle.[19] The most affecting portion of the poem is Sophonisba's recollection of her first sight of Massinissa, the young Prince of the Massylia. Though it takes up nearly half of the whole, it is worth quoting in full, its present tense, to me, enhancing its tone as intensely personal address:

> A becoming diffidence enhances the beauty of your appearance and longs to steal away from the praise it excites. First manhood has hardly set its mark on your cheeks with its fine bloom and it is only by the deeds of your hand [West's poems?] that we believe you a man. As you walked along, you cast casual glances at every object (whether chance directed your gaze, or Venus), and I felt your eyes linger as they turned on me (or so, at least, it seemed); . . . I felt sure

that your expression softened a little as you gazed and that your feet
went forward more slowly. I looked to see whether there was one of
my companions around me who could have been more worthy of en-
gaging your attention. . . . All night I hardly rested; or, if drowsiness
overcame me and closed my eyes against my will, then sleep held its
own procession and the same image recurred; and once more you . . .
were there.

Memories, dreams of Eton long gone by; and perhaps Gray dreamed a
like dream again on 17 June when he heard for the first time that West
had died. Perhaps he read again, and yet again, the "long verse" by West
that he mentions to Walpole in February 1747 as being in his possession
then, "long Verse . . . *[sic]* on himself, a little before his Death" (*CTG*,
266). Long *painful* verse we can imagine, on love and death and loneliness
and desire. Whatever it was and said, the poem is, sadly, no longer extant.

The Poems (II) and
the Death of West

G ray's penultimate letter to West, which included the Latin *Sophonisba Massinissae*, preceded by three weeks his sending West the *Ode on the Spring*. No letter from West after 11 May has survived, the one of that date a response to an 8 May melancholy letter from Gray confessing he had "none but the dead" to converse with and was "in sad condition." West asks, "But why are you this melancholy?" and then encloses his Catullus translations to "cheer" Gray up. Gray's response to that query, probably written on 27 May (*CTG*, 209), makes the age-old distinction between "black" and "white" melancholy, the latter of which he calls leucocholy. With Milton's twin poems in mind (possibly prompted by West's *L'Allegro*-like "Ode" on the spring, of 5 May), Grays says his allegro-choly "seldom laughs or dances [*L'Allegro*, 32–34], nor ever amounts to what one calls Joy or Pleasure [38–40], yet is a good easy sort of state, and ça ne laisse que de s'amuser." But at the same time it can "give a sort of Ennui, which makes one form certain little wishes that signify nothing." *Little* wishes hardly—for the wish to be with West and the wish to write the poetry of which he knew he was capable had already converged in the Propertius poem he sent West in late April. Thus he goes on to deepen his melancholy into the "loathed" disease of the opening lines of *L'Allegro:* "There is another sort," he writes, "black indeed, which I have now and then felt, that has somewhat in it like Tertullian's rule of faith, Credo quia impossibile est; for it believes, nay, is sure of everything that is unlikely . . . ; and, on the other hand, excludes and shuts its eyes to the most possible hopes, and everything that is pleasurable." [1] The melancholy yet deliciously pleasurable memories evoked in both West's and Gray's mind by the latter's Sophonisba epistle that concludes this letter are the last they were to share.

Read in this context, Gray's *Ode on the Spring,* dated in his commonplace book "the beginning of June, 1742 sent to Fav: not knowing he was then Dead," may be taken as a kind of *Il Penseroso* to West's *L'Allegro.* But, given its rather eerie prescience, the "leucocholy" of Milton's poem darkens quickly into an elegiac lament for the brevity of "the race of man: / . . . they that creep, and they that fly," both "the busy and the gay" who but "flutter through life's little day." Gray's mini-self-portraiture in the phrase "they that creep," as opposed to "they that fly," contrary to his claim of a deficient verbal memory, recalls some Latin verses he wrote at Eton at least eight years earlier: "Man lingers uncertainly on the borders of two worlds, doubtful which one he should draw near to; he knows not whether he should wish to rise up and mingle with the stars or creep over the face of the earth, an inglorious hulk."[2] But the entire stanza proleptically portrays West's "little day" tragically "Brushed by the hand of rough Mischance," with Gray himself left as but "A solitary fly" without the joys of love other "insect youth" find in their "glittering female[s]." Thus, while Gray's opening lines echo the second stanza of West's Spring "Ode"—as well as lines 11–19 of *L'Allegro* itself—they are immediately displaced as "vain deluding Joys" by the Miltonic "Cherub Contemplation" (Gray's "sit, and think") and "shadows brown that Sylvan loves, / Of pine or monumental oak" (Gray's "the oak's thick branches" that "stretch / A broader browner shade").

The poem then does serve as Gray's Miltonic "correction" of West's naive welcoming of a joyous spring, but West's dying at the moment of the Spring Ode's creation prompts some revisioning of the received interpretations of Gray's moralizing. Lonsdale admirably sums up the critical consensus as follows: "The point of the poem for G[ray] lay in the final stanza, in which he moralizes on the moralistic pose he has adopted, undercutting with a characteristic touch of self-derision his own apparent complacency" (48). It is a persuasive reading, and I do not reject it. But if we recall the circumstances of the poem's inception—the progressively hopeless state of West's health, Gray's sense of the futurelessness of his love for West (dying or not), and his increasing conviction of the nihilissimo of his life and career—the fact that Gray originally titled the poem "Noon-Tide, an Ode" suggests a different twist to the conventional patterns of diurnal poems, one that consorts with the tonality and implications of Noon in *Paradise Lost:* the time of the Fall. Spring/May is simply not commensurate with Noon, which is habitually aligned with Summer as Morning is with Spring, Evening with Autumn, and Night with Winter.[3]

Moreover, the "insect youth," usually interpreted broadly to mean all winged insects, Gray presents specifically as bees, which do not merely "flutter through life's little day" but rather, in Milton's words in *Il Penseroso,* are busily "at [their] flow'ry work" while the rest of the world reposes at midday. Or possibly he meant to recall the bees of *Paradise Lost* who

> In springtime, when the sun with Taurus rides,
> Pour forth their populous youth about the hive
> In clusters . . . .
>
> (1. 767–70)

Virgil, Horace, Pindar, and others, of course, traditionally figure the bee as both a busy worker and "an artificer comparable to Daedalus." [4]

Gray, however, neither toils nor spins. His hive is empty; he has no plumage to display. He is alone—not only because he is a "Poor moralist" but because his trite moralizing has come true at the very moment of its utterance. West is dead ("Thy sun is set"), but it is *Gray's* "spring [that] is gone," with nothing, nihil, to show for it. In contrast, West *was* a poet, one who lived and loved and brimmed his hive despite misfortune and "rough Mischance"—and who did *not* merely "frolic, while 'tis May." When he died, part of Gray died too, to be resurrected as a kind of surrogate West, poet, in the burst of creativity that produced the series of odes. If in West's Ode to May "sudden blasts . . . rise" to "drive the Zephyrs from the skies," Gray tries, at least, to undo such a tragic vision:

> While whispering pleasure as they fly,
> Cool zephyrs through the clear blue sky
> Their gathered fragrance fling.

But severely undercutting such (perhaps forced) optimism is Gray's commonplace book notation after his transcription of the Spring Ode ("at Stoke, the beginning of June, 1742, sent to Fav [i.e., Zephyr]: not knowing he was then Dead"), for it reflects, in its stark simplicity, Gray's sense of the belatedness and futility of his poetic effort to dispel the "sudden blasts" that had already driven Zephyr from the skies.

But there is yet more to his tragic context, for Gray's ode also pointedly plays off of West's prophetic *Ad Amicos,* written almost five years earlier, by means of a cluster of allusions that clothe his own ode with the aura of West's depressingly self-elegiac thrust. *Ad Amicos,* we recall, began with an address to the "happy youths [the Quadruple Alliance] on Camus' sedgy side" who "feel each joy that friendship can divide," and with an imagined portrait of Gray "off alone" in "the verdant mazes of the grove" where he used "To catch the zephyr and to court the muse." Gray's Spring Ode opens with the same sequence of images: the zephyrs, the wooded glade, the poet sitting alone with his muse. West next had focused on the injustice of dying before his years "scarcely told their prime," of fate denying him a chance to "stay till age shall blast my withering face"—just as Gray's "rough Mischance" (or the "chill" of old age) annihilates both those who creep and those who fly, leaving them but "in dust to rest." Indeed, part of West's third verse paragraph virtually dictates Gray's language in lines 31–34, which I interlineate here with West's lines:

> To Contemplation's sober eye
> Such is the race of man:
> [How weak is Man to Reason's judging eye!]
> And they that creep, and they that fly,
> Shall end where they began.
> [Born in this moment, in the next we die;
> Part mortal clay, and part ethereal fire,
> Too proud to creep, too humble to aspire.]

"On hasty wings thy youth is flown," Gray concludes in line 48, clearly echoing West's "And fair-fac'd youth is ever on the wing."

This oscillation between the poem's moralistic thrust and linguistic conventionality and its subtextual autobiographical references, coupled with Gray's fear of the imminent fulfillment of *Ad Amicos*'s prophecy of West's early death, suggest strongly that at this critical moment Gray saw himself as the "you" of West's lines:

> From you remote, methinks, alone I stand
> Like some sad exile in a desert land;
> Around no friends their lenient care to join
> In mutual warmth, and mix their heart with mine
> . . . .
> Useless, as yet, through life I've idly run,
> No pleasures tasted, and few duties done.

Looking back to their Eton days together in his penultimate letter to West, Gray had confessed, "I am never a bit the older, nor the bigger, nor the wiser that I was then: No, not for having been beyond the sea." But out of this ignorance came no bliss; yet out of a death and an exile within himself came a poet.

In Fredric Bogel's provocative *Literature and Insubstantiality,* which argues the familiar thesis (albeit with new habiliments) that "the middle of the eighteenth century inaugurates a literary era both more coherent and more decisively distinguishable from the era of Dryden and Pope than it has often seemed to be," he pursues a running analogy "between melancholia and the Literature of Sensibility" that is apropos my probing Gray's state of mind in early June 1742, and in the poems that then flow from his pen in quick succession. Quoting Freud on mourning and melancholia— both of which have to do with "painful dejection, loss of interest in the outside world, loss of capacity to love, and inhibition of activity"—Bogel extrapolates on a distinctive component of the melancholic character as described by Freud: "often prominently and insistently, a severely diminished sense of his own worth that may be expressed in self-reproach, self-reviling, and the delusional expectation of punishment." Moreover, the melancholic withdraws the libido from the object into the ego itself "to establish an *identification . . .* with that object." [5] With this, and the tangled circumstances surrounding Gray's Spring Ode, in mind, Ketton-Cremer's conclusion that Gray's "surge of creative activity" in the late spring and summer of 1742 "happened with extraordinary suddenness" requires some modification. If indeed the creative surge was sudden, its gestation was not. The biographer's conclusion, if only tentatively offered, is certainly more correct: West's "modest talent may have prepared the way for the genius of his friend" (59), a friend, we should add, who like Milton was sorely anguished by knowing his

> hasting days fly on with full career,
> But my late spring no bud or blossom shew'th.
> Perhaps my semblance might deceive the truth,
> That I to manhood am arrived so near,
> And inward ripeness doth much less appear,
> That some more timely-happy spirits endu'th.[6]

One must wonder, indeed, whether Gray's apparent resolve at age twenty-five to push scholarly Latin exercises and other temporizing projects into the background in favor of writing poetry in English owes anything to Milton's comparable resolve (at age twenty-four):

> Yet be it less or more, or soon or slow,
>   It shall be still in strictest measure ev'n
>   To that same lot, however mean or high,
> Toward which Time leads me, and the will of Heav'n;
>   All is, if I have grace to use it so,
>   As ever in my great Task-Master's eye.

If apparently no such religious self-dedication or faith could sustain him, what might have spurred Gray—other than West's death—beyond a mere hope of writing *something* after the Spring Ode was his knowledge that after Milton's two poems on time he produced not only *Comus* but two stunning elegies, *Lycidas* and *Epitaphium Damonis*, one on the premature death of a young poet, the other on the premature death of Milton's most intimate friend.

Whether Milton's burst of creativity registered fully on Gray's consciousness is, of course, finally impossible to determine with certainty, but the seeming confluence of the facts of the early personal and career histories of the two poets could hardly have escaped Gray's notice. Edward King was a schoolmate of Milton's at Christ's College, and though apparently they were not close, Milton poetically describes him as a fellow young poet "dead ere his prime." His elegy, then, wrestles with precisely the questions West raised in *Ad Amicos:* Why should the just man suffer? Why should the good die young? At the time of his writing *Lycidas*, Milton had spent five years in private study preparing himself for an unknown future, and the thought clearly crossed his mind that he too, unaccountably, could be cut off before his life's work was even begun. Indeed, his anguished lament in *Lycidas* might well have been Gray's:

> Alas! what boots it with incessant care
> To tend the homely shepherd's trade,
> And strictly meditate the thankless Muse?

Would there indeed be, as there were for Milton, that bright "To-morrow" and its "fresh woods, and pastures new"?

But the Milton-Diodati Gray-West parallels are even more striking. Both pairs became acquainted in public school, Diodati leaving St. Paul's for Oxford, Milton for Cambridge (the same as Gray and West's divergent university paths). Diodati was training for the profession of medicine (like his father) while West seemed fated for the law (like his father). Neither Milton nor Gray saw his future career at all clearly, the former not before writing *Ad Patrem* at age twenty-four, the latter not until twenty-five and the death of West. With respect to *Ad Patrem* Gray may have remembered that Milton evokes the figure of a bard, "his unshorn hair bound with oak leaves," who "sang of the inspiring deeds of heroes, of chaos and the broad foundations of the world, of creeping gods and divinities . . . , of the thunderbolt not yet sought from the bowels of Etna." Or the fact that Milton thanks his father for not driving him "unto the law and the ill-guarded statutes of our country and thus condemn [his] ears to noisy stupidity." Or, most of all, Milton's vow not to "mingle, unknown, with the dull crowd, and [his] footsteps shall shun the sight of profane eyes." "Be off, wakeful cares," he concludes in *Ad Patrem*, "be off, complaints, and the goatish squint of envy's crooked eye. Spiteful Calumny, do not open your snake-filled jaws, you can do me no harm, loathsome swarm; I am not under your power. With breast safe and secure I shall walk above the reach of your viper stroke."[7] Thus self-dedicated, Milton left England for Italy in 1638, returning after fifteen months; feeling considerably less safe and secure, Gray commenced his tour with Walpole in March 1739, returning to England alone in early September 1741. While Diodati died only a few months after Milton's departure and West lived for slightly less than two years after Gray's return, neither Gray nor Milton was present at the death of his intimate, the latter unable to return and the former rusticating at Stoke. Both poets were devotees (and imitators) of the love poetry of Ovid, Propertius, and Tibullus,[8] and both wrote intensely personal Latin love elegies on the deaths of their friends, Milton's *Epitaphium* and Gray's "continuation" of *De Principiis*. In the sensitive language of Walter Mac-Keller's commentary on the former, these two poems give "spontaneous utterance to deep personal feeling. With inevitable truth [each] expresses the sorrow of one who has suffered irreparable loss. Happy memories of days with his friend, fears for the loneliness of the future, hopes and ambitions which now there is none to share, vain regrets that he was not at [his friend's] bedside to say farewell, all crowd upon him with almost overwhelming force."[9] It was the last but one (*Ad Joannem Rousium*) Latin poem Milton wrote, as the *De Principiis* elegy was the last of Gray's Latin poems, aside from the late addition of the fragmentary "second book" of *De Principiis*, which I shall address below.

What is happening, then, in Gray's anguished, confused state of mind, is that in some odd, complex sense his life had come to replicate Milton's, his own self-dedication literally born out of the ashes of West's death. But if he became a kind of reincarnate West, he is not yet quite Milton redivivus, certainly not the Milton of *Paradise Lost*, though more surely the Milton of *Lycidas* and of the preceding *Comus, At a Solemn Music, L'Allegro* and *Il Penseroso*, the Italian poems, and the six Latin elegies. However, before turning to that maturer Gray-Milton, the poet of the great Pindaric odes, I need to pause a bit longer over Gray's emulation of the *Epitaphium Damonis* in his continuation of the regestating *De Principiis Cogitandi*, the twenty-nine-line beginning of unsubtitled Liber Secundus that is more pointedly "Ad Favonium" than the first book he had sent West in April 1741. In these lines Gray "speaks out" precisely in the way Matthew Arnold lamented he had not, now even more candidly than he had a year earlier in *Ad C. Favonium Zephyrinum*. In fact, he even seems intent on aligning the ostensibly "scholarly" *De Principiis* with that earlier poem—as well as, more distantly, with the *Ad C: Favonium Aristium* of June 1738. The delay in Liber Secundus's composition (it surfaces first in a letter to Walpole of February 1747) was due in large part to his having written the *Sonnet [on the Death of Mr. Richard West]* at Stoke in August 1742;[10] but at the same time the later Latin elegy emerges as a kind of culmination to Gray's mourning, which extends from the Eton College Ode through the West sonnet to *The Progress of Poesy* and the *Elegy*—as well as, to a lesser, different extent, to the *Ode to Adversity* (also written in August 1742). Gray may well have felt empowered yet again, after abandoning Latin verse earlier, to write in Latin of his love for West because, as with Milton, "Latin had been [and still was, after all] the language of intimate feeling," especially for one whom he had loved so passionately and, in his own way, so uncompromisingly.[11]

On the other hand, the delay in composing the Latin elegy may be only apparent after all, for Gray scribbled a marginal note to his commonplace book transcript of it: "Begun at Stoke, June, 1742." While we have no way of knowing how many of the twenty-nine lines constituted that "beginning," or whether the twenty-nine lines *are* the "beginning," the latter is certainly at least possible, in which case the elegy may well antedate the elegiac Sonnet. That possibility verges on certainty in light of the recent discovery (in 1982) of an autograph one-page manuscript of twenty-nine lines "revised, written in red crayon and pencil," which is entitled "Liber Secundus" and is accompanied by Gray's notation, "together with a note on human desires."[12] This manuscript suggests further that Gray's cover letter to Walpole containing the twenty-nine lines may be a deliberate effort at obfuscation: the lines, he writes, make "Part of a large Design, &

is the Beginning of the fourth Book, wch was intended to treat of the Passions" (*CTG*, 267). In any case, and whatever the reasons for Gray's "misleading" of Walpole, neither these twenty-nine lines nor the Sonnet elegy was published in Gray's lifetime, very possibly because of their passionate confessionalism.

Reserving (as it were) certain portions of Milton's *Epitaphium* for his Churchyard Elegy, Gray's Latin is dominated by two of Milton's verse paragraphs, the one beginning at line 112 and the final one. The former reads, in Douglas Bush's prose translation:

> Alas, what restless impulse sent me traveling to unknown shores, over the towering crags of the snowy Alps? Was it worth so much to have seen buried Rome—or even the ancient city that Tityrus [in Virgil's first Eclogue] left his sheep and his lands to see—that I could let myself be cut off from so dear a friend, that I could put between us all the deep seas, and mountains and woods and rocks and roaring rivers? Oh, I might at the end have touched his right hand and closed his eyes at the moment of his quiet death, and have said "Farewell! remember me as you rise to the stars." [13]

Far more anguished than Milton's what-might-have-been is Gray's self-lacerating fiction in the *De Principiis*—that he *had* been present to tend West in the final agonies of his illness: "I myself watched your breast cruelly racked by bitter suffering . . . ; I watched your eyes grow dull and your loving face grow pale." [14] Then a sign of possible, or desperately imagined, abatement of the ravagement:

> and I hoped for the return of Health, with rosy cheeks, and you yourself with it, my dear Favonius! Foolishly trusting, alas, that we might spend the long, sunny days as before. Alas, the hopes, sweet but vain, and the ineffectual prayers! Alas, the sunny days, now spent in mourning, which I am forced to pass without you, in weeping because you are not there, and in vain complaints.   (Lonsdale, 332)

Gray's coda is typical of elegies. As Milton's Damon now dwells "in the pure ether . . . Among the souls of heroes and the immortal gods" draining "ethereal draughts and drink[ing] joys with holy lips," so West is presented as having triumphed over death and rejoicing "in the starry circuit of the heavens and the fire of the pure ether whence you sprang." And as

Milton prays, "now, since you have been granted the rights of heaven, stand by my side and gently favor me," Gray hopes that West will "look down from [his] lofty seat," not merely to stand by and favor him but rather to "look back with pity"

> on the storm of human passion, the fears, the fierce promptings of desire, the joys and sorrows and the tumult of rage so huge in our tiny hearts, the furious surges of the breast; then look back on these tears, also, which, stricken [as I am] with love, I pour out in memory of you; this is all I can do, while my only wish is to mourn at your tomb and address these empty words to your silent ashes. (Lonsdale, 332)

Needless to say, a heart-wrenching guilt emerges from this elegy, coupled with an equally powerful self-lamentation that escapes self-pity (though barely): why, why, "have [you] deserted me in the midst" of this "great . . . task" of writing the *De Principiis?* But the implicit thrust of that charge is West's desertion of Gray at the very moment he had inspired this at-long-last–arrived surge of creativity; as Milton had written, so might have Gray: "But what now is to become of me? . . . Whom shall I confide in? Who will help me to soothe devouring cares? . . . now alone I wander through the fields, alone through the pastures . . . twice wretched is he who loves too late . . . there is no comfort in the present nor any hope for the future."[15]

The guilt is multifaceted, to say the least, but what seems to dominate it is at once Gray's two-and-a-half-year abandonment of West, "ill and unhappy, deeply conscious of his loneliness as he drifted through an unsympathetic world," as Ketton-Cremer puts it (54); his not being present to try to assuage West's final agony but blithely going off to his aunt and uncle's house in Stoke Poges; and his sense that his deep-seated passion had been fully expressed too late, its surging to the surface during West's dying days, moreover, having had but little therapeutic or even consolatory effect on him. Hence, looking down upon him from the empyrean, West will see but "the storm" of Gray's unacted "human passion," "the fears" attendant upon even imagined enactment, "the fierce promptings of desire" suppressed, "the tumult of rage" (at society and its hypocritical moral stance? at himself?), "the furious surges of the breast" beaten back upon themselves out of fear, anxiety, and sexual confusion. All but buried amid this chaos of psychosexual conflict, there is only a fleeting soupçon of "joys." The elegy, in fact, is as much for Gray himself as for West, a kind of death-in-life vision: "this is all I can do."

As notable as Gray's employment of Milton's *Epitaphium* is his echoing at the same time of West's *Ad Amicos*. Writing out of his illness, his "exile" from Gray, and (even in 1737) his fear of an early death, West there had focused on the "real pains, or those which fancy raise" that

> For ever blot the sunshine of my days;
> To sickness still, and still to grief a prey,
> Health turns from me her rosy face away.

Gray's fond thought in the *De Principiis* elegy of the "return of Health, with rosy cheeks" for his "dear Favonius" finds its origin here—though he also knew, of course, that West himself was right: "Health is at best a vain precarious thing, / And fair-fac'd youth is ever on the wing," he wrote in *Ad Amicos*.

> Born in this moment, in the next we die;
> Part mortal clay, and part ethereal fire,
> Too proud to creep, to humble to aspire.
> In vain our plans of happiness we raise,
> Pain is our lot, and patience is our praise.

Ad Amicos, revisited in the moment of Fate's fulfillment of West's prophecy, has now effectively become Gray's autobiography to age twenty-five, neither stooping to creep nor aspiring beyond the quotidian, cruelly stricken with lost love and unable to write even the modest "fond lines" West hoped for at his death. Only "empty words" to "silent ashes." In this moment, the same moment of Horace's conclusion to his Ode 2.6 ("there you may shed the tear you / owe the yet-warm funeral ashes of your / Friend and your poet"),[16] Gray now fully realizes the prescience of West's vision of raising his tomb in Gray's breast: "my only wish is to mourn at your tomb." And it is that mourning which becomes the poetry of Gray's career through *The Bard,* initiated but proleptically in the *Ode on the Spring* and unarguably with the Sonnet elegy on West, probably written at the same time Gray returned to the dormant *De Principiis.*

Ever since Wordsworth's Preface to *Lyrical Ballads* there has been much ado about the overformality and alleged stiltedness of Gray's diction in the sonnet, particularly in its octave, though there are those who argue that the stiffness is a deliberate ironic tactic of Gray's.[17] But if, as Kristeva argues, depressed persons disavow the negation of loss that gives rise to language, such a denial

> would thus be the exercise of an impossible mourning, the setting up of a fundamental sadness and an artificial, unbelievable language, cut out of the painful background that is not accessible to any signifier and that intonation alone, intermittently, succeeds in inflecting. . . . Just the same, they do give the impression that their symbolic armor hasn't been integrated, their defensive shell not introjected. Their speech is a mask—a beautiful facade carved out of a "foreign language."[18]

What Gray cannot do, in her terms, is sublimate his grief and depression "by summoning up primary processes and idealization" in order to "remake nothingness, better than it was and within an unchanging harmony, here and now and forever, for the sake of someone else."[19] Nor can he, in the less psychoanalytical terminology of Suvir Kaul, come "to terms with death and loss" by "ventriloquizing" the diction and poetic vocabulary of the poetic discourse that offers tropes of the regenerative continuities of Nature as hope and consolation."[20]

One of Lonsdale's observations points us more simply in another direction: Gray's diction "is intended to evoke a Miltonic richness which contrasts with the barer language . . . used to describe the poet's barren spiritual condition" (66). But while that contrast is certainly there, Miltonic richness seems to me not to the point; *Paradise Lost* is, and once again West's *Ad Amicos* is. In the former

> Seasons return; but not to me returns
> Day, or the sweet approach of ev'n or morn,
> Or sight of vernal bloom, or summer's rose,
> Or flocks, or herds, or human face divine.
>   (3. 41–44)

For Gray, what does not return are "the cheerful ways of men" and "cheerful fields resum[ing] their green attire." In *his* ever-during physical darkness, Milton can still hear the "wakeful nightingale . . . all night long" singing "her amorous descant" (4. 602–3), but Gray, in his mental and emotional darkness, can only repine for the notes of the more conventional lovelorn nightingale who, again in Milton's words, "Nightly to thee her sad song mourneth well."[21] Thus, the octave becomes, in effect, *his* "amorous descant" to West as if the latter still were there—implicitly echoing Eve's evening speech to Adam:

> With thee conversing I forget all time,
> All seasons and their change, all please alike.
> Sweet is the breath of morn, her rising sweet,
> With charm of earliest birds; pleasant the sun
> When first on this delightful land he spreads
> His orient beams, on herb, tree, fruit, and flow'r,
> Glist'ring with dew; fragrant the fertile earth
> After soft showers; and sweet the coming on
> Of grateful evening mild, then silent night
> With this her solemn bird, and this fair moon
> And these the gems of heav'n, her starry train
> (*PL* 4. 639–49)

But for both Eve and Gray, none of this "without thee is sweet." Without West, Gray's morning is but the mourning of utter, total loss.

I find it difficult to accept Dustin Griffin's suggestion that Gray's final phrase in this octave ("the imperfect joys expire") alludes to Restoration poets' employment of like language to figure "interrupted or imperfect intercourse," and even more difficult to accept Howard Weinbrot's flat statement that the phrase "evokes the impotence of premature ejaculation" and hence "the impotence of love without an object." More to the point of the sonnet as a whole, Peter Manning offers this fine summary of its true thrust (the Restoration crudeness seems to me utterly foreign to Gray's sensibilities, especially on this occasion): "Without West to share his burden of grief, Gray is driven back into a solitary death-in-life; his joys 'expire' in his breast, his mourning is 'fruitless.' Gray's grief feeds on itself and perpetuates its own condition: he weeps the more because he weeps in vain. Gray becomes the tomb of his loss."[22] While it would be absurd to deny the implicit homoeroticism of Gray's poem, his careful degendering of the landscape serves to obviate "the need for the text to specify the principal thing it is prohibited from specifying," the passionate desire, not merely the grief, of one man for another.[23]

Finally, in struggling with his own elegy and with *Ad Amicos* and Milton very much on his mind, Gray obviously recalled West's echoing of the opening of *Paradise Lost*, Book 3, on Milton's blindness: in the "ever-during dark" that surrounds West

> The world will pass as chearful as before,
> Bright as before the day-star will appear,
> The fields as verdant, and the skies as clear.

But the Miltonic recompense of inward irradiation is there neither for West nor for Gray. Spiritually dead, the latter fruitlessly mourns the physically dead; to his own "high requiem" he has become a sod, as Keats fears in his Nightingale Ode. The mild absurdity of Gray's imagining the birds to "complain" in order "To warm *their* little loves" in effect intensifies the inefficacy of his own plaint to imagine even a momentary reincarnation of his greater love—let alone an assuaging of his pain, isolation, unconsolable loss. The sonnet thus turns upon itself, becoming less pointedly an elegy on the death of Mr. Richard West as the title promises (in fact "he" is there only as the anonymous "him" *to* whom Gray mourns) than one on the "death" of Thomas Gray. Accordingly it is suffused with first-person references: "to me," "these ears," "these eyes," "no heart but mine," "my breast," "I . . . mourn," "I weep"—all governed by the thrice-used "in vain." Milton's plaintive line in the *Epitaphium Damonis*, "At mihi quid tandem fiet modo?" should have been the poem's epigraph. West's "tomb" that he wished to "raise" in someone's "breast" *is* this sonnet's "little room." Not exactly Manning's "tomb of [Gray's] loss," Gray's poem is rather the psychic interring of himself into the tomb of his own breast.

It is in this depressed state of mind that Gray began the poem for which he became, and in the eyes of virtually all critics and readers of poetry still is, world famous. *Elegy Written in a Country Churchyard* is the archetypal Gray poem, so go the arguments—with *The Bard* a close second. The still considerable debate about the precise dates of its composition I have no intention of rearguing here, except to observe that, as Lonsdale shows after a splendid summary of the dating controversy, "even if it may appear that most of the poem was written in 1746 and later, it is still possible that G[ray] began drafting it in 1742." Mason originally suggested the same date in the *Memoirs*.[24] Leonard Whibley, on the other hand, concludes his case against 1742 by professing it "hard to believe that within a few weeks Gray, who had only recently begun to write original poems in English, should have written the *Sonnet on the Death of West*, the *Eton Ode*, the *Hymn to Adversity*, and the first draft of the *Elegy*" (*CTG*, 1214); and even Lonsdale himself reminds us that "G[ray]'s method of working on his other poems suggests that he is unlikely to have taken eight years to complete a poem. Usually G[ray] either abandoned a poem without finishing it, or took at most some two or three years, as was the case with his Pindaric *Odes*" (110). Even if we do not insist that 1742 was the year of the poem's inception, the protracted time Gray did take to complete the poem may have had several causes: his struggles with the Sonnet on West, his composing the threnody of *De Principiis*, his drafting of the Eton College Ode and the appropriately entitled *Ode to Adversity*. Clearly none of these he wanted merely to redo or do another version of in the *Elegy*, but all of these poems he might well have thought of assimilating in one all-inclusive elegiac universalization of West's death. On the other hand, the *Elegy* as it actually emerged may have progressively become an attempted act of exorcism. While Milton's ghost does not haunt the *Elegy* as powerfully as it does Gray's other poems, Gray's other assorted demons and ghosts desperately needed laying to rest.

Interpretations of the *Elegy*, of course, are legion, and now even an entire book has been devoted to it, Henry Weinfield's *The Poet without a Name: Gray's "Elegy" and the Problem of History*.[25] Despite its special titular concern it also links itself with other recent efforts to argue West's death as abundantly present, if in submerged fashion, in the poem. Needless to say, I share that view, with less reluctance than Weinfield's argument bespeaks. For example, to Odell Shepard's pioneering argument in 1922–23, countered severely twenty-six years later by H. W. Starr, that Gray's "Epitaph" was "originally written as a separate poem commemorating Gray's friend Richard West," Weinfield responds: "In order to interpret the Youth as a reference to West, who is never, of course, named in the poem, we would have to transfer the locus of meaning from the text itself to the poet's hidden consciousness."[26] Such a transfer is precisely what George E. Haggerty has done in " 'The Voice of Nature' in Gray's *Elegy*." Though I respectfully disagree with a certain excessiveness in his argument as well as with some particulars, I applaud his aligning of the *Elegy* with Gray's *Ode on the Spring* and with his Sonnet on West's death. In fact, my own passing suggestion earlier about the possible impact of the Spring Ode's original title, "Noon-tide: An Ode," is in part supported by Haggerty's claim that lines 101–4 of the *Elegy* are a redaction of the noontide scene in lines 11–27 of *Spring*—though he makes no mention of the ominousness and fatality of Milton's noon in *Paradise Lost*. What I find unacceptable is Haggerty's conviction that Gray "chooses Death as the only expression of a sexuality which terrifies him," as a way, that is, "of redirecting sexual desire and substituting an object—in this case death—for his own threatening melancholy."[27]

Most recently Suvir Kaul provides a new twist to the debate over the *Elegy,* one that diminishes West's presence in the *Elegy* in favor of the idea that, as he writes of the West sonnet, "the absence ... mourned [is] the death of a shared, enabling and validating discourse, poetic tradition, culture." Kaul's explanation is that "After his experience of political marginalisation (his quarrel with Walpole), personal and cultural trauma (the death of West), social loss (the fear that "Epicurean" values had restructured the sphere of culture and discrimination), Gray's depiction of the life of the country as pastoral and communal is defensive, a retreat into a vocabulary that offers both political and poetic retreat." [28] Defensive it may be, but Gray's "retreat" is not solely into a "vocabulary" of "precursory and contemporary discursive practices" [29] in order to console himself over Walpole's political marginalization of him (that marginalization, as I have argued, was there well before the quarrel). Nor is it to console himself for some sort of "social loss," which Gray himself had precipitated by secluding himself at Cambridge, with only vacational and visitational interruptions, from 1734 to 1771. Kaul's word "trauma," however, is exactly right.

For West *is* here, virtually everywhere in the *Elegy,* right from the beginning. The famous opening quatrain with its "massive calm" (Empson's memorable phrase) [30] and Gray's acknowledged allusion to Dante combine richly with the first two stanzas' subtextual recall of Milton's invocation to Book 3 of *Paradise Lost* on the one hand and a reevocation of West's prophecy of sinking "in endless night" in *Ad Amicos.* Building on Lonsdale's note (117 n), Weinfield makes much of the Dante allusion, but neither scholar (nor anyone else I'm aware of) cites the context of the echoed Dantean line ("from afar he hears the chimes which seem to mourn for the dying day"). Dante's whole passage reads, in Mandelbaum's translation,

> It was the hour that turns seafarers' longings
> homeward—the hour that makes their hearts grow tender
> upon the day they bid sweet friends farewell;
>   the hour that pierces the new traveller
> with love when he has heard, far off, the bell
> that seems to mourn the dying of the day. [31]

John Donne was right: that knell is Gray's for Gray as well as for West, the darkness physically West's, psychologically and emotionally Gray's, the latter figured in his appropriation of the "ever-during dark" that "surrounds" Milton in his blindness, "a universal blank" (*PL* 3. 45–47). This allusion seems to me to account for Gray's somewhat odd locution, "Now fades the glimmering landscape on the sight" instead of "on my sight," for it is Gray himself who will "tell" in these lines "Of things invisible to mortal sight," the world of darkness West's death left to him.

West is figured and refigured variously, all but invisible to our sight but movingly seen again and again by Gray's inwardly irradiated eyes. The litany is extensive but needs no comparably extensive comment. I offer, then, but a partial list (with line numbers): "Each in his narrow cell for ever laid" (15); "No more shall [they be] rouse[d] from their lowly bed" (20); "For [him] no more the blazing hearth shall burn" (21); "Can storied urn or animated bust [this elegy?] / Back to its mansion call the fleeting breath? / Can Honour's [Gray's?] voice provoke the silent dust / Or [conventionally epitaphic?] Flattery soothe the dull cold ear of Death?" (41–44); "Some heart once pregnant with celestial fire," some hand that "waked to ecstasy the living lyre" (46–48). More overtly personal, however, are these lines from what is now known as the Eton Manuscript, the earliest extant draft of the *Elegy*, which originally belonging to Mason, who adjudged the lines as "intended to conclude [the poem] before the happy idea of the hoary-headed Swain, &c. suggested itself" (Lonsdale, 130):

> The thoughtless World to Majesty may bow
> Exalt the brave, & idolize Success
> But more to Innocence their Safety owe
> Than Power & Genius e'er conspired to bless
>
> And thou, who mindful of the unhonour'd Dead
> Dost in these Notes their artless Tale relate
> By Night & lonely Contemplation led
> To linger in the gloomy Walks of Fate
>
> Hark how the sacred Calm, that broods around
> Bids ev'ry fierce tumultuous Passion cease
> In still small Accents whisp'ring from the Ground
> A grateful Earnest of eternal Peace
>
> No more with Reason & thyself at strife;
> Give anxious Cares & endless Wishes room
> But thro' the cool sequestered Vale of Life
> Pursue the silent Tenour of thy Doom

Ambiguities of reference abound here, suggesting that Gray initially may have planned to subtly autobiographize the ostensible universality of his themes, an intention that seems inherent in his frequent urgings that his name not be attached to the poem. In fact Lonsdale rather shrewdly suggests that this first conclusion to the *Elegy* may well have failed to satisfy Gray "because it was too explicitly personal for publication" (115). Gray's implicit claim for West's (and perhaps his own) "Innocence" and "Safety" in the first stanza is but one of a number of suggestive personal notes. The "thou" of the second stanza seems clearly Gray himself, mindful of the as yet insufficiently honored West, who had lamented in *Ad Amicos* that "Few will lament my loss whene'er I die" and "Unknown and silent will depart my breath, / Nor Nature e'er Take notice of my death." Gray's "artless Tale," then, the *Elegy* itself with all its artiness or artifice, is in reality the product of his dark night of the soul, by "lonely Contemplation led" lingeringly "in the gloomy Walks of Fate" that West too had trod.

Even more movingly personal, however, is the third stanza of the Eton Manuscript with its brooding calm that now bids Gray's and West's "tumultuous Passion cease" and concludes with the moving fiction of West's "still small accents whisp'ring from the Ground / A grateful Earnest of eternal Peace." This last we need to recognize as a rather remarkable reprise of the final verse paragraph of Gray's continuation of *De Principiis*, where West, released from all cares, will look down from "the starry circuit of the heavens" on Gray's "storm of human passion," "the fierce promptings of desire," "the furious surges of the breast," and his "tears . . . which, stricken with love" he pours out "in memory of" West. When Gray returns to the poem as originally drafted, the first conclusion's explicitness is deliberately fictionalized in the happenstance of "some hoary-headed swain" who may appear, "some fond breast" to elegize someone who has been cast out of "the warm precincts of the cheerful day." But at the same time Gray imports into this fiction his own sense of the ever-during darkness that descended on his life at West's death, out of which he takes, like Adam and Eve, a longing, "ling'ring" last look back to the irrevocably lost paradise of their past together. Milton's "Some natural tears they dropped" becomes Gray's "Some pious drops," and though for Adam and Eve their loss is potentially recompensable in "The world [that] was all before them," bright with the promise of that "paradise within . . . , happier far," Gray's whole world "fades . . . glimmering . . . on the sight."

This shift, however, is governed more broadly at the same time by the coda to West's *Ad Amicos,* where there *is* (not merely a hope that there will be) someone "within whose breast my tomb I wish to raise." Gray's, of course, is that breast, not merely "some kindred spirit['s]," [32] the breast not of "the Poet but the Friend sincere" (*CTG*, 64). No "struggling pangs of conscious truth to hide" here, no "blushes of ingenuous [i.e., honorable] shame" (*Elegy*, 69–70) to repress; rather, with no "denial vain, and coy excuse" here is Gray speaking out in Milton's "lucky words" of him who was "nursed upon the self-same hill, / Fed the same flock, by fountain, shade, and rill." The imagined language of Gray's "hoary-headed swain" is thus transformed via *Lycidas* from mere observation ("oft have we seen him"—West *or* Gray) to Milton's plurally governed recollections, as in

> Together both, ere the high lawns appeared
> Under the opening eyelids of the morn,
> We drove afield, and both together heard
> What time the gray-fly winds her sultry horn,
> Batt'ning our flocks with the fresh dews of night.
> (*Lycidas*, 25–29)

Together both, both together we—"But O the heavy change, now thou art gone, / Now thou art gone, and never must return" (*Lycidas*, 37–38). Thou, thou, I alone, and "what now is to become of me?" as Milton writes in *Epitaphium Damonis*. "But now alone," he continues, "I wander through the fields, alone through the pastures; where branches deepen the shadows in the valleys, there I wait for evening. Over my head rain and the east wind make a moaning sound, and the forest twilight is shaken by the swaying trees."

I cite especially "what now is to become of me?" not only for its appropriateness to Gray's "existential situation" (Weinfield's phrase, page 97) but because Gray himself pointedly alludes to it:

> One morn I missed him on the customed hill,
> Along the heath and near his favorite tree.
> (109–10)

For "customed" Gray originally wrote "accustom'd," evoking not so much "th' accustomed oak" of *Il Penseroso* (whose context does not support the allusion) but "the accustomed elm" under which Thyrsis (Milton) and Diodati (Damon) used to sit together, and to which Milton returns after coming home from Italy only to learn "that his friend was gone." In addition, and more powerfully since it directly addresses West, Gray clearly is recalling in lines 106–14 of the *Elegy* his own translation of Propertius's Elegy 2.1, which he had sent to West a month before his death:

> Today the lover walks, tomorrow is no more;
> A train of mourning friends attend his pall,
> And wonder at the sudden funeral.
>   (96–98)

The "Epitaph," then, is at once Propertius's "short Marble" that but "preserve[s] a Name, / A little Verse, [his] All that shall remain" (100–101), Milton's *Epitaphium,* and the "tomb" West "wish[ed] to raise" in Gray's breast. If it is also Gray's own tomb/epitaph, as so many have claimed, it is so only in the sense I have argued in my commentary on his Sonnet on West's death.[33]

Needless to say, my sharply focused reading of the elegy reflects my inability to subscribe to all of the particulars of the many other interpretations, though often they are not utterly incompatible with mine—and it is admittedly not a full "reading" or explication at all. Yet I do want to offer a broader dissent from those readings that one way or another regard Gray as "disappearing" in the poem, what Pat Rogers, in defining "the characteristic formula of the *Elegy*," calls "the vanishing subject." Poststructuralists tend to argue similarly that the *Elegy* evokes "a twilight which it cannot then move beyond: the text itself (Gray's self) must finally be displaced onto another (the epitaph), which has, it can be claimed, *already* gone through that twilight."[34] On the other hand, if indeed the *Elegy* "dramatizes the Augustan ideal under stress," that stress, which is precisely what Gray exerts upon it so splendidly (if largely unrecognizedly), proves fully capable of extending any and all "Augustan ideals" to accommodate "forms of intense, passionately and extremely private, personal experience," not merely some form of Johnson's "sentiments to which every bosom returns an echo" or "images which find a mirror in every mind."[35] Whether this stress enables the poem to be seen as "closely akin to the 'greater Romantic Lyric,' " as Anne Williams provocatively suggests, I am not prepared to argue here; but I am persuaded by much of her "psychological analysis" of "Gray's lyric speaker," no doubt in part because her broader terms support the particularity of my focus but especially because she demonstrates that Gray, despite his ostensible "reticence about himself and his eventual near-obliteration," achieves "a way of creating a self-portrait after all."[36]

And so, having brought Williams forward with approbation, I conclude with a related passage from Richard Feingold's fine *Moralized Song: The Character of Augustan Lyricism:*

> In the *Elegy* the poem's speaker is both Horace and Virgil: his is both the mastery of a reticent eloquence and the experience of a valued emotional excess.
>
> Gray's gesturing at the presence of what he will not reveal I would define as a sentimental act; it marks the high value the writer places on inward experience, but also his somewhat contradictory suspicion that such experience can have no standing until it is translated into a heard language whose very good manners would give to the inward the grace and status of the social. But then, too, this uncertainty about the standing of the inward is accompanied also by the writer's hostility to the social, the speakable, the authorized. . . . What we are left with finally is the sense that having one's own story is all that counts, but publishing that story can only deface it. Gray's speaker wants, at one and the same time, the privileges of silence and of speech, to walk a stage where passion may brood over itself and still speak to a hearer.[37]

Therein may lie the answer to the inordinately long interval between inception and completion that Lonsdale and others have worried over as so uncharacteristic of Gray. But therein as well, and in my own reading and Williams's, may be the "real" reason that Gray acrimoniously told a friend in 1765 that the *Elegy* "owed its popularity entirely to the subject" (which I take to mean its poetic graveyardism), and "that the public would have received it as well if it had been written in Prose." "Pity," Mason reports his saying to Gray, "that Dr. Young's Night Thoughts have preoccupied it" (that is, the public). "So, indeed, it is" was Gray's reply (Lonsdale, 113). In fact, he rarely mentioned the poem after its publication. The *Elegy* is, then, in its enforced sensibility, modish melancholy, and self-effacingly decorous diction, in my judgment the most uncharacteristic Gray poem we have (along with the valedictory *Ode for Music,* as we shall see). But at the same time the *Elegy* I have argued for is one of the most moving and characteristically personal revelations he has given us—taking therefore a prominent (though not, I think, preeminent) place among the other subtextually rich autobiographical poems I have been presenting, and will continue to present in the following chapters.

The Poems (III)

Into the profoundly personal and intricate elegiac complex I have been developing I must now draw the *Ode on a Distant Prospect of Eton College* (written about a month after West's death), the *Ode to Adversity* (also of August 1742), and the so-called (by Mason) *Hymn to Ignorance: A Fragment*—with a brief aside on the later (1754–55) *Ode on the Pleasure Arising from Vicissitude,* the title of which is also Mason's invention. The first of these has received almost as much critical commentary as the *Elegy,* most of it revolving around some version of Geoffrey Hartman's characterization: Gray's "recessiveness, [his] almost theological self-incrimination, harmonized easily with the neoclassic thesis ... that the age demands something other than genius—in fact, an accommodation of genius to the genius loci"; and while the mute Father Thames *is* that genius loci, his muteness, Hartman says, is eloquent—although he never quite clarifies what that eloquence "speaks." In any case, at the end of the poem Gray "withdraws from envisioning a future that restores a lost happiness," [1] as Hartman claims. Precisely what is lost, however, is more complex than merely Gray's quasi-paradisal childhood and youth, for that ostensibly is freighted with the vanished Edenic days of his youthful, innocent love for West and West's for him. [2]

More recently Marshall Brown has been at some pains to demonstrate what he call the poem's "urbane sublime." That is, Gray learns from his temporal/spatial distant prospect an ability "to contemplate both his childhood and the perils of life with a learned equanimity and ironic detachment," a "disciplined coolness" that "constitutes Gray's answer to the temptations of time-bound worldliness." [3] Although Brown does not apply the word *nostalgia* to this "contemplation," his view seems to me to verge on that pedestrian notion, one that allows S. H. Clark, for example, to argue that the poem's "exquisite nostalgia needs to be adulterated with artifice to enable it to come into being." Therefore the Eton College Ode is "itself ... the 'thought' " that destroys his paradise.[4] Given the poem's rich autobiographical background, my view is that the ode functions in precisely the same elegiac complex as Gray's "versions" of Milton's *Epitaphium Damonis*, West's *Ad Amicos* and *To Mary Magdalene*, and his own Sonnet on West's death, the *De Principiis*, and the translation of Propertius's *Elegy* 2.1. In more general terms, *Eton College*, elegiacally rather than merely nostalgically, remarkably conflates place, time, and love as, in its rapidly receding distance, emblematic of an empty, dark present solaced, if at all, only by memory. Milton's farewell to Diodati ("Farewell! O love me still upon thy starward way")[5] might well have been its epigraph rather than the deceptive cynicism of the Menander line in Greek (translatable as "I am a man; a sufficient excuse for being unhappy") that Gray had jotted next to lines 41–54 in his commonplace book transcription and added as an epigraph only in the 1768 edition of his poems (Lonsdale, 54).

West's *Ode: To Mary Magdalene* (quoted in full in chapter 3) is pertinent both in its specifies and tone to *Eton College*. West, of course, matriculated at Christ Church, not Magdalene, and although he told Walpole (Toynbee, 101–2) it was an imitation of Horace's "divine lyric" beginning "O Fons Blandusiae" (*Odes* 3.13), a translation of which he had sent Walpole earlier (Toynbee, 78–79), his "imitation" has little or no relationship to the Latin poet's ebullient celebratory poem on Fontinalia, the festival of springs. Instead, West's fictionalizing of his academic home as Magdalene transforms its supposed "original" into a tearful elegy for the irrevocably lost (even to dreams) paradise of Eton. His wandering through the "learned awful grove" of the thus allegorized Magdalene evokes the memory "Of sweeter shades and springs" that prompt him to imagine that once again he "tread[s] Etonian ground." But immediately he is startled from that "dear mistake" and, "As [if] disenchanted," wakes:

> Oh! how I long again with those,
> Whom first my boyish heart chose,
> Together through the friendly shade
>   To stray, as once I stray'd!

Here West may be recalling his 14 November 1735 letter in which he and Gray are said to walk at Eton "hand in hand ... Through many a flowery path" (*CTG*, 33), the possible allusion strengthened by the ode's plaintive final stanza with its wish that the Quadruple Alliance were together again so that, "Like paradise," Eton days

> would all appear,
> More sweet around the flowers would blow,
> More soft the waters flow.

For all its somewhat syrupy nostalgia and poetic inexpertness, read in the full context of the letter, the ode bespeaks a profound sense of isolation, the total absence of precisely the sort of consolation West's distant prospect of Eton College ostensibly generates. Indeed, the single word that West adds after the text of the poem to complete his letter is the more eloquent both for this positioning and for its utter simplicity—as well as for its spatial isolation hard against the page's right margin: "Adieu!"

That was in August 1736. There is little doubt that Walpole shared the letter with Gray, as West himself suggested he do: "It is very natural to send [the poem] to you," he writes, "from whom and my other friends it originally came" (Toynbee, 101). Eleven months later West sent Gray the *Ad Amicos* letter, and eight years later (to the month) Gray wrote the Eton College Ode. Whereas, at that temporal distance from West's two elegies, it cannot be considered a bona fide "answer" to them, *like* them, Gray's distant prospect is of Eton but also a "prospect" of West and their youthful love, joy, community, and "bliss"—all now sunk beneath the past's deepening "shade" (a word Gray thrice repeats in the opening eleven lines).[6] It may well be more than mere indecision about the title of his new poem, then, that led Gray initially to absent Eton from the title. "Ode, on a distant Prospect of Windsor, & the adjacent Country" he called it in his commonplace book, almost as if to suggest that Eton was no longer visible, no longer there, although it was actually within sight from his uncle's grounds in Stoke Poges where he was staying at this time. Standing there in a summer-house, gazing back into time, Gray's heart and mind indelibly registered the truth of West's *Ad Amicos* lines:

> From you remote, methinks, alone I stand
> Like some sad exile in a desert land;
> Around no friends their lenient care to join
> In mutual warmth, and mix their heart with mine.

In that recall, with its potent elegiac overtones, coupled with Gray's sense of replicating Milton's life and career immediately prior to and after Diodati's death, Milton's shade (as it were) rises dramatically to share the stage with West, thereby providing Gray's ode an enormously rich, complex subtext pulsing beneath the superstructure of conventional locodescriptive and genius loci patterning. West's "sad exile" has, in effect, become Gray's in an even drier land. Not only is West now dead but Gray's estrangement from Walpole following the European quarrel shows little sign of being mended, and even Ashton has vanished into the preferment for which he had long buttered-up Walpole.[7] If the world in the late summer of 1742 in some sense may have been all before Gray as it was for Adam and Eve, no providence was nigh to be his guide, no Eve with whom to walk hand in hand.

In that psychic desolation, that exile deep inside himself, Gray boldly aligns his distant prospect with Satan's "distant" prospect of heaven (*PL* 3. 501): "Sometimes towards Eden which now in his view / Lay pleasant, his grieved look he fixes sad" (*PL* 4. 27–28). While Lonsdale cites *Comus* (934–35), Pope, and Dyer as possible sources of the ode's opening lines (56 n), none of these rises to Gray's grief-racked, and even guilt-ridden, backward glance with the compelling force of two other Miltonic "prospect" passages, one from *Paradise Lost*, the other from *Paradise Regained*. In Book 3 of the former Milton analogizes Satan's wonder at his first glimpse of "the blissful seat of paradise" to that of a "scout" who, after traveling

> Through dark and desert ways with peril gone
> All night, at last . . .
> Obtains the brow of some high-climbing hill,
> Which to his eye discovers unaware
> The goodly prospect of some foreign land
> First seen, or some renowned metropolis
> With glistering spires and pinnacles adorned.
>   (543–50)

"At sight of all this world beheld so fair" glimpsed from on "high above the circling canopy" (554–56), Satan is seized with "wonder" that quickly darkens into "envy" and ultimately into "despair" (3. 542; 4. 115). In the *Paradise Regained* passage, Satan wings Christ upward to tempt him with the prospect of "fair Jerusalem, / The Holy City," which

> lifted high her towers,
> And higher yet the glorious Temple reared
> Her pile, far off appearing like a mount
> Of alabaster, topped with golden spires.
>   (4. 544–48)

While both passages[8] serve Gray's general association of boyhood days at Eton with prelapsarian innocence, the aligning of his own vantage point, temporally and spatially, with Satan's is startling, not to say jarring.[9] The unsteady mixture of wonder and envy that the *Paradise Lost* allusion imports, as well as Satan's resolute intent to defile Edenic innocence, are deeply ominous in Gray's landscape, especially when taken in conjunction with Satan's fate after his third temptation of Christ in *Paradise Regained:* fourteen lines after the passage quoted above, "smitten with amazement [he] fell." Of course Satan's "Ambition" (which Gray had employed several months earlier in *Agrippina*) had already tempted him to rise while still in heaven (*PL* 4. 49–51), only to be, like Gray's ambitious "wretch,"

> whirl[ed] . . . from high,
> To bitter Scorn a Sacrifice,
> And grinning Infamy
>   (*Eton College*, 71–74)

Reascendant in Book 3, though fallen, Satan's distant prospect of "Eden [College]" (Gray surely suggests the pun) precipitates him "Down right into the world's first region," through

> innumerable stars, that shone
> Stars distant, but nigh hand seemed other worlds:
> Or other worlds they seemed, or happy isles,
> Like those Hesperian Gardens famed of old,
> Fortunate fields, and groves and flow'ry vales,
> Thrice happy isles . . .

—whose inhabitants "dwelt happy there" (3. 562, 565–70) as do Gray's children among the "happy hills" of Windsor.

Indeed, so densely textured with Milton's language are the entire first two stanzas of *Eton College* that it is impossible to unweave that fabric discursively. I offer, therefore, but one more example of Gray's strategic pillaging of *Paradise Lost*. It is from Book 4:

> And of pure now purer air
> Meets his [Satan's] approach, and to the heart inspires
> Vernal delight and joy, able to drive
> All sadness but despair; now gentle gales
> Fanning their odoriferous wings dispense
> Native perfumes . . . .[10]

Gray's second stanza concludes with his soul momentarily soothed by "gales . . . waving fresh their gladsome wing," "redolent of joy and youth," which "*seem*" to enable him "to breathe a second spring." It is the only stanza that employs the first-person pronoun, perhaps thereby recalling West's self-portrait in *Ad Amicos* standing alone, a "sad exile in a desert land" where no gentle gales fan their wings to soothe him (*CTG*, 62). From his friendless perspective (in Oxford), West could only conjure up a mental image of "happy youths" at Cambridge that "feel each joy" of love and friendship while his "weary soul" finds no "second spring" [11] to breathe. The final line of Gray's second stanza glances as well at *L'Allegro* and its coupling of "The frolic wind that breathes the spring, / Zephyr [West], with Aurora playing" (18–19)—both texts, West's and Milton's, amalgamating in Gray's recall of his own final line in the *Ode on the Spring:* "We frolic, while 'tis May." The total effect of this remarkable allusive mélange on our reading of *Eton College* is to untrivialize the "insect youth" of the Spring Ode into the palpable reality of a dead Richard West and a spiritually and emotionally crippled Thomas Gray, neither of whom at Eton were of "The sportive kind" or cleaved the wave or urged the flying ball or otherwise "frolicked." Rather, in retrospect, they snatched only "a fearful joy" because it breathed intimations not of immortality but "of their doom."

It is precisely an awareness of that fact which prompted West's *Ad Amicos* in the first place, the gnawing doubt that he would live much beyond his "prime," and, fully aware of West's state of mind while composing *Ad Amicos*, Gray in effect made the Eton College Ode *his Ad Amicos*, a canny and moving transformation of West's self-elegy on his imagined death into a "real" elegy on its devastating realization. Yet it is also a kind of "elegy" on Gray's utter helplessness (though in 1742 presumably wise beyond his Eton years) to forestall "The ministers of human fate" (West's "Stern Power of Fate") or "black Misfortune's baleful train" (a magnification and multiplication of Gray's "hand of rough Mischance" in his Spring Ode). In fact, *Eton College* echoes *Ad Amicos* repeatedly, those echoes jostling and often merging with the Miltonic echoes; but none is so simply poignant as Gray's implicit nod to West's title and opening line ("Yes, happy youths") in his phrases "Ah, happy hills," "Ah, fields beloved in vain"—just as Gray vainly loved West, *non solum amicus, verum etiam amator.* All in all, Gray's appropriation of West's poem emerges finally as hauntingly ventriloquistic, as if West posthumously were given voice to express the fulfillment of his own prophetic/poetic antecedent and the wisdom gained from that fulfillment. That wisdom, which is of course as much Gray's as the reincarnated West's, powerfully undercuts, even counters the ode's platitudinous moral conclusion, for West's stoic acceptance (at age twenty) of the facts of life, love, youth, and imagined Edens has now been learned by Gray from his experiencing, even if only vicariously, going gentle into that good night.

Gray's actual learning of his friend's death, however, is deliberately veiled from public eye by the poem's seeming "articulation of all that he *needs* to say about himself," as Richard Feingold aptly put it recently.[12] It is a "need" that may be charted by the sequential, ostensibly sharp differences between the speaker's views in the Eton College Ode and West's in *Ad Amicos*. Where the latter rejects the notion that his premature death is punishment for some sin (fratricide, slander, blasphemy, betrayal of "a friend or foe," even a thought not proper for "the world [to] know"), Gray invokes precisely such "fury Passions . . ., / The vultures of the mind" that "tear" *all* mankind—regardless: Anger, Fear, Shame, pining Love, Jealousy, Envy, Despair, Sorrow, Ambition, Falsehood, Unkindness, and so on. And while we are lessoned that "all are men" and therefore "Condemned alike to groan," the only "consolation" the speaker can offer is "To each his sufferings." West, it seems, took the same fatalistic position ("Pain is our lot"), but he evokes patience and quiet fortitude that preclude the need to "repine." "Does life deserve my sigh?" he asks rhetorically. On the other hand, the Eton College speaker angrily and bitterly succumbs to *his* need to melodramatically curse life's "ministers of human fate, / And black Misfortune's baleful train," that "murtherous band" that ruthlessly and savagely seizes "The little victims." West writes, as if answering his own not so rhetorical question quoted above,

> . . . whene'er all-conquering Death shall spread
> His wings around my unrepining head,
> I care not . . .

because

> . . . though this face be seen no more,
> The world will pass as chearful as before,
> Bright as before the day-star will appear,
> The fields as verdant, and the skies as clear.

This remarkable echoing not only of Lycidas's triumph over premature death but of Milton's triumph over the "death" of his eyes bespeaks now in retrospect to the Gray of 1742 the folly of ignorance and the bliss of wisdom his own "Ad Amicos" seems to deny. For it is with Milton's inwardly irradiated eyes that Gray is empowered now to reevoke West's clear seeing in the "ever-during dark[ness]" of his unrelieved, and seemingly unrelievable, despair.

We need to return, therefore, to Milton's presence in the ode, so powerfully entwined with West's as it is. If, in his agony, Gray still could not appropriate West's self-consolation and triumph over despair for his own, it is abundantly clear that Gray was literally inspired by West's courageous life—his creative achievements promising even greater things, his "unrepining" death—to dedicate himself to "continuing" that life, and its poetic career. Henceforth, the feared Satanic transgressiveness of his dangerous love for his friend now seemingly harnessed in poetic creativity, West shall be for Gray "the Genius of the shore" who, in his large recompense, "shall be good / To all that wander in that perilous flood" called the world. And Gray will rise, twitch his mantle blue, and aspire, even in the depths of his melancholy, "To something like [Miltonic] strain." Even so, for all Gray's brave vows, that strain, as he knew even in this moment of "a second spring," could not be fully internalized without risk or fear, as the heart of the Eton ode's opening prospect graphically testifies. Its first two stanzas constitute Gray's bold entrance upon holy ground by way of his imaginative recapitulation of Satan's invasion of Eden, that "room of bliss . . . high advanced" beyond the poorer naive bliss of ignorance.

But this recollective upsurge of Milton's great scenes that I have argued as empowering Gray's burst of creativity in the moment of prospect is complicated as well as underscored by his reemploying them as the contextualizing ground for two subsequent, seemingly disparate scenes in the ode. Both evoke passages in *Paradise Lost* that are at once dissimilar to and interrelated with the *Paradise Lost* and *Paradise Regained* passages already examined. The first of these scenes is:

> Alas, regardless of their doom,
> The little victims play!
> No sense have they of ills to come,
> Nor care beyond today:
> Yet see how all around 'em wait

> The ministers of human fate,
> And black Misfortune's baleful train!
> Ah, show them where in ambush stand
> To seize their prey the murtherous band!
>   (51–59)

Lonsdale cites *The Faerie Queene* and Dryden's *Sigismonda and Guiscardo* to gloss "ambush," the latter nearer to the mark since Dryden's word pointedly recalls (as does Gray's) Milton's commentary on Eve's insistent plea for a "short absence" from Adam:

> O much deceived, much failing, hapless Eve,
> Of thy presumed return! event perverse!
> Thou never from that hour in Paradise
> Found'st either sweet repast or sound repose;
> Such ambush hid among sweet flow'rs and shades
> Waited with hellish rancor imminent
> To intercept thy way, or send thee back
> Despoiled of innocence, of faith, of bliss.
>   (9. 404–11)

Five years later, in his *Ode on the Death of a Favourite Cat*, Gray will again make use of this characterization of Eve on the verge of succumbing to Satan's wily argument about what she can aspire to. But in *Eton College* he moves quickly from Satan's ambush to the dire *immediate* consequences of her, and Adam's, fall: the onset of the "fury Passions," the "vultures of the mind":

> high winds . . . within
> Began to rise, high passions, anger, hate,
> Mistrust, suspicion, discord, and shook sore
> Their inward state of mind.
>   (9. 1122–25)

And, for Gray, "Shame that skulks behind" (*Eton*, 64).[13]

Eton itself emerges from all this as the primal scene of Gray's own self–conscious transgressiveness. If for him, though not "regardless of [his] doom," the "gales" still from Eton/Eden "*seem*" to bestow "A momentary bliss," that moment is of Satan's fleeting, stupefied abstraction "From his own evil" (9. 463–64). Gray's comparable moment is of pathetic, evanescent hope for "a second spring," a hope shattered almost immediately in his refiguring himself as both Satan and the fallen Adam/Eve, whose "gales" are those "high winds worse within." Unredolent of prelapsarian "joy and youth," those gales/winds are tragically unprophetic of the settled quiet of "A paradise within thee, happier far" that Gray fantasizes West as having achieved. The grand philosophizing of the first two lines of the ode's final stanza signals in its very grandness Gray's felt need to deflect or displace his sense of himself as arch-transgressor in Milton's Eden. "Condemned" is Milton's word and it tolls loudly in Gray's sole self: Satan "condemned / For ever now to have [his] lot in pain" along with his "Millions of Spirits for his fault amerced" (1. 607–9); "driv'n out from bliss, condemned / In this abhorred deep to utter woe" (2. 86–87); "condemned / To waste eternal days in woe and pain" (3. 694–95), and so on.

Even though this litany of condemnation and self-condemnation is both powerful and moving, escaping self-pity only through its Miltonic resonances, the converse asserts itself in the palpable absence of self-referentiality in Gray's famous platitudinous conclusion. Adam and Eve's ignorance of good and evil *is* an enforced constituent of their prelapsarian bliss (and an unenforced constituent of the Eton schoolboy's bliss), but Satan's egregious folly in challenging God's omnipotence is another matter. 'Tis *his* folly to be tempted "to rise," and yet again to rerise upon being whirled "from high." [14] What we need to remember here, however, and what Gray did clearly remember, is that Satan aspired not to *be* God but to be literally godlike, just as Gray himself aspired not to *be* Milton but to be Milton like—or, West-Milton-like. "What burden then," Satan asks himself in his extraordinary inner debate (4. 55–57), if "a grateful mind / By owing owes not, but still pays, at once / Indebted and discharged." What burden indeed could Milton's "matchless King[ship]" be in Gray's poetic consciousness? If in the long run fate may be charged with dealing Gray but the genius of inferior angels,[15] it is nevertheless to his enormous credit that he courageously refused to accept that subseraphic status—and thus "stood / not then happy" for at least ten years. In what in fact must have been an excruciatingly painful ten years he finally brought himself, after a kind of last-ditch battle (from late 1751 to December 1754), to admit in *The Progress of Poesy* that *his* "seraph-wings" were capable of carrying him only "Beyond the limits of a vulgar fate" no matter how driven he felt to soar "with no middle flight."

But it is not only Milton's Satan who energized that struggle, for equaling "the most High" is also the core of Satan's casuistical seduction of the "ignorant" Eve to eat the "wisdom-giving Plant" that will empower her to become "A goddess among gods" (9. 679, 724–25, 547). And to *her* aspiring mind it would be "plain then" that what God forbids is "but to know, / Forbids us good, forbids us to be wise" (9. 758–59). Both of these passages, their substance and their language, stand powerfully behind Gray's famous proverbialism in the ode. In most readings, the lines are said to enact an appropriate moral/poetic closure to the hardly revolutionary, if rarely so elegantly articulated, "philosophy" that the ode offers, but in fact they "conclude" the autobiographical undercurrent I have been tracing. That is to say, the foolish ambition that tempts Gray "to rise" (*Eton*, 71) at least seems to him to eventuate in "Falsehood" to his own identity, self-mockery of the kind reflected in his wry self-characterization as "Plagiary," a victim of "keen Remorse," perhaps even of "moody Madness laughing wild / Amid severest woe"—something akin, perhaps, to his *Elegy* self-portrait, "Now drooping, woeful wan, like one forlorn, / Or crazed with care, or crossed in hopeless love" (107–8).

Reperceived from this vantage point, Gray's *Ode on the Spring* but two months earlier takes on an added dimension. If the "sportive kind," about whose fluttering blithely and ignorantly "through life's little day" the speaker has ponderously moralized, in effect rebuke that "poor moralist" in turn for his equally blithe complacency and his fluttering "on hasty wings," *Eton College* rebukes both. With its complex and even daring Miltonic subtext, it emerges as a powerful critique of the poetic mode of the Spring Ode. That mode, of course, was West's as well in his May Ode and it was the mode of the myriad mid- and late-eighteenth-century poets whose own modest creative capacities (or lack of poetic courage) led them to subscribe to *L'Allegro* and *Il Penseroso* as the ground for accommodating Milton's dominating presence rather than aspiring to emulate him. Such poetry, Gray's *Spring* included, is cast in sensibility's comfortable, benign minor key. "Contemplation's sober eye," steadfast and demure, is simply an insufficient imagination to energize the poet to strive toward much less "attain / To something like prophetic strain"; rather it clips his wings to flutter him down to trivial moralizing or to a flat rejection of wisdom in favor of mirth and frolic's carefreeness. For Gray now, in August 1742, his career finally launched and its trajectory taking shape, such fluttering seemed indeed "a vulgar fate" if not anathema.

Gray's resolve in the *Ode on a Distant Prospect of Eton College* to escape such a fate, even to try to soar on the wings of the Theban eagle, Pindar, may seem in one sense to be retarded in this moment of struggle to come to terms with West's death in the Sonnet and the continuation of *De Princi-piis*, but it revives quickly, even remarkably, in his immediate attempt at sublimity in the *Hymn to Ignorance* and the *Ode to Adversity*, both quickly aborted. It is August 1742; the two poems unsurprisingly deal with West's death, the lost Eden of Eton, and Gray's still unalleviated stress of mind. Yet neither (unlike the sonnet on West and the *De Principiis*) is in any sense a "speaking out." Rather they chart a veiled poetic journey into the poet's own lower depths. Perhaps that is why neither was published until years later, *Adversity* in 1753, *Ignorance* only in Mason's 1775 edition (after Gray's death) along with the West Sonnet and *De Principiis*.

The epigraph to the *Ode to Adversity* sums up the poem's professed theme succinctly. It is from Aeschylus's *Agamemnon:* "Zeus, who leadeth mortals in the way of understanding, Zeus, who hath established as a fixed ordinance that wisdom comes by suffering." Lonsdale's suggestion about the inception of the poem, based on Gray's placing of it immediately after the Eton College Ode in his 1768 *Poems,* is that "it appears to have been intended as to some extent a reply to" *Eton College,* "a mature and positive confrontation of the evils of adult life that are described [there] with such unrelieved gloom" (69). Mature and positive perhaps, but such a reading ignores the fact that the entire poem is a plea that Adversity's "relentless power," "Gorgon terrors," and "vengeful band" somehow be transformed. If supplicated properly, perhaps she will appear in her "benign" guise (line 41), becoming thereby (lines 25–29) Milton's Melancholy, who "With a sad leaden downward cast" fixes her eyes "on the earth," that "pensive Nun, devout and pure, / Sober, steadfast, and demure," who is accompanied by "calm Peace and Quiet," "retired Leisure," the "Cherub Contemplation," and who therefore brings "Silence" broken only by that

> Sweet bird, that shunnest the noise of folly,
> Most musical, most melancholy!
> (*Il Penseroso*, 61–62)

However successful such supplication may be, its result seems but a pale dilution of Milton's "something like prophetic strain" into the "philo-sophic train" of a softer, milder adversity. Yet even that watered-down consolation, as yet unwon in fact, is severely undercut by other Miltonic allusions which suggest that *any* consolation is achievable only by some-how negotiating the reascent from hell that Satan and his minions debate.

For it is that hell which Gray summons up in his opening stanza: "Driv'n out from bliss," as Moloch says, Gray too clearly regarded himself as "condemned / In this abhorred deep to utter woe" until "the scourge / Inexorably, and the torturing hour / Calls us to penance" (2. 86–92)—not to peace of mind. Unlike Moloch and Satan, however, Gray is "alone" and "Unrespited, unpitied, unreprieved" (2. 185). The final plea of *Adversity*, then, is not so much an *Il Penseroso*-like thrusting aside of what Gray calls "Self-pleasing Folly's idle brood, / Wild Laughter, Noise, and thoughtless Joy" merely "to be" somehow (facetiously?) "good" or to "know [himself] a man"—for that brood already has vanished with West's love and life and with Eton's paradise; rather, what Gray desperately prays for is the vanishment of the very relentless power Adversity has loosed upon him like an "iron scourge and torturing hour" for some dire sin.

"Teach me to love" in Gray's final quatrain is implicitly (and the more powerfully for its implicitness amid the defeated platitudinizing) "Teach me to love again"; and "Teach me . . . to forgive" is "Teach me to forgive myself." The "ministers of human fate" of the Eton College Ode have become Adversity's vengeful band of Gorgon terrors, the "murtherous band" has seized its prey, and "black Misfortune's baleful train" has done its dirty work. *Adversity* is, then, not only not a poem of "willed self-dedication to that benevolence which [Gray's] age accepted as the root of all virtue" as Lonsdale argues,[16] but rather one of unrelieved despair. Temporally and psychologically contextualized as I have suggested, *Adversity* may well be a repudiation (or at least a serious questioning) of the very idea that either wisdom or virtue resides in mere benevolence. Perhaps that is why Gray receives no answer from that "Daughter of Jove" to his earnest, even desperate beseeching.

Ignorance doesn't answer him either, though in that poem's fragmented state it is only barely possible to even speculate about the question that is asked or what plea is made, or how *this* "Goddess" responds. Possibly, as Mason guesses, the poem *was* to be a "Satire upon false Science and scholastic Pedantry" (Lonsdale, 75), but the uncharacteristic shrillness of the invocatory voice and the implicit and explicit notes of personal anguish punctuating the lines suggest instead that what "satire" may be there is a rather heavy-handed self-protective cloak for confessional utterance akin to *Adversity*'s. The ignorance evoked, for example, consorts with the very "bliss" with which it was equated at the end of *Eton College*, Gray's echoing of that poem pointing toward such an apparently absurd conclusion. While the opening line obviously recalls Satan's "Hail, horrors, hail" in Book 1 of *Paradise Lost* (line 250), the exactness of the quotation carries with it Satan's previous lines, "Farewell, happy fields, / Where joy for ever dwells!"—thus linking them directly with *Eton College*'s

> Ah, happy hills, ah, pleasing shade,
> Ah, fields beloved in vain.

Similarly, *Ignorance*'s "ever-glowing bowers, / . . . gothic fanes and anti-quated towers" by "rushy Camus' slowly-winding flood" recall the "dis-tant spires" and "antique towers" beside "the hoary Thames" that "Wan-ders . . . along / His silver-winding way." Thus when Gray closes his first verse paragraph with "Glad I revisit thy neglected reign; / Oh, take me to thy peaceful shade again," that wished-for return emerges less as Cam-bridge (whose "embrace" he never thought of as "fond" and whose pre-cincts were fled happily, not "weeping[ly] forsook") than as Eton/West/ Eden/Bliss/Ignorance, those "times for ever lost" and "For ever gone— yet still to Fancy new" (*Ignorance*, 31, 33). The "peaceful shade[s]" of Eton College days, and their "soft, salutary power," are now beseeched to generate "dews Lethean" and "steep in slumbers each benighted sense" that plagues the tragic present with its foolish wisdom. Even the "momen-tary bliss" the Eton College Ode speaker fancies as bestowed upon him to soothe his weary soul and foster his breathing a second spring becomes, in the Ignorance Ode, "a momentary day," a product of "wit's *delusive* ray" that, "huddle[d] up in fogs," may quench the "dangerous fire" of full remembrance.

Such an interpretation of this largely neglected poem gains further cre-dence from what Gray appears to recall from his known reading of Edward Young's just-published (5 June 1742) *Night Thoughts*, Night the First ("On Life, Death, and Immortality"). To Gray's lines 14–18 Lonsdale appends (76 n) these of Young:

> *Night*, sable Goddess! from her *Ebon* throne,
> In rayless Majesty, now stretches forth
> Her leaden Sceptre o'er a slumbering world.
>   (1. 18–20)

But as pertinent as these lines are to Gray's focus, the passages that frame them may have effectively suggested to Gray the very exploration of personal grief and loss his own poem articulates. Here is Young's second verse paragraph, for example:

> From short, (as usual) and disturb'd Repose,
> I wake: How happy they who wake no more!
> Yet that were vain, if Dreams infest the Grave.
> I wake, emerging from a sea of Dreams
> Tumultuous; where my wreck'd desponding Thought,
> From wave to wave of *fancy'd* Misery,
> At random drove, her helm of Reason lost;
> Tho now restor'd, 'tis only Change of pain,
> A bitter change; severer for severe:
> The *Day* too short for my Distress! and *Night*
> Even in the *Zenith* of her dark Domain,
> Is Sun-shine, to the colour of my Fate.
>
>   (Young's italics)

And Young's lines immediately following the invocation of "*Night*, sable goddess!" quoted above are:

> Silence, how dead? and Darkness, how profound?
> Nor Eye, nor list'ning Ear, an object finds;
> Creation sleeps. 'Tis, as the general Pulse
> Of life stood still, and Nature made a Pause;
> An aweful pause! prophetic of her End.
> And let her prophecy be soon fulfil'd;
> Fate! drop the Curtain; I can lose no more.
>
>   (1. 21–27)

While the inception of *Night Thoughts* may or may not have lain in Young's having experienced the death of an intimate friend, certainly the poem from the beginning, as Stephen Cornford reminds us, was received "as a distinctively private recitation of the feelings of loss and melancholy" occasioned probably by the death of someone, possibly two or three, whom Young knew.[17]

But even had Gray not seen Young's prefatory statement (published first with Night the Fourth in 1743) confessing that "*the Occasion of this Poem was* Real, *not* Fictitious," Gray would have recognized a kindred soul in distress in Young's opening "Night"—though, of course, his verbal and conceptual borrowings (if indeed that is what they are) pointedly exclude Young's conventional religious consolation and triumph.

Lonsdale cautiously suggests that *Ignorance* "might appear to have been written with a friend such as Richard West in mind as audience," but he adds "there is no reference to it in G.'s letters to West" and therefore the poem may have been abandoned for "lack of an audience" (74). But what if West were not conceived of as the "audience" but as the subject? While we don't know precisely when Gray began to compose it, the temporal coincidence of West's death (June 1) and Young's publication of "Night the First" (June 5) seems no mere coincidence in light of Gray's clear allusion to lines 22–25 of *Night Thoughts* (quoted above) in his Sonnet on West's death: his line, "A different object do these eyes require," derives directly from Young's "Nor Eye, nor list'ning Ear, an object finds." This confluence in June through August of Young's poem, West's death, and Gray's compulsive engagement with that and his own suffering argues the centrality of West in *Ignorance* as well. The poem's composition may well have extended into August, perhaps thereby "explaining" lines 11–12, "Thrice hath Hyperion rolled his annual race, / Since weeping I forsook thy fond embrace"—an arguable reference to West's death itself three months earlier as well as possibly to the final lines of the Sonnet: "And weep the more because I weep in vain." In light of all this, there is little doubt that in November 1742 Gray eagerly read the newly published "Night the Second" of *Night Thoughts*, which even more strikingly confirmed his sense of Young as a "kindred spirit": it is entitled "On Time, Death, Friendship." Here he found himself mirrored in Young's passionate lines 516–21 and 533–37, the former passage punctuated with such language as "Heart meets Heart, reciprocally soft, / Each other's Pillow . . . repose[s on] divine"; but he would also have been warned, as it were, not to continue his own effusions in *Ignorance*, even in their shrilly rhetorical disguise:

> Think'st thou the Theme intoxicates my Song?
> Am I too warm? Too warm I cannot be,
> I lov'd him much; but now I love him more.
> (*Night Thoughts* 2. 594–96)

Wherever Gray may have intended *Ignorance* to go from where he left off is obviously indeterminable, but some years later (1754 or 1755) he produces a related, and equally strange, performance in *Ode on the Pleasure Arising from Vicissitude*. Having written the *Elegy* and *The Progress of Poesy*, and perhaps having begun work on *The Bard*, Gray makes a mighty effort, aborted almost immediately, to gentle "adversity" and "ignorance" into "vicissitude." In an unpublished note he calls the poem a "Contrast between the Winter past & coming spring Joy owing to that vicissitude. Many that feel that delight. Sloth envy Ambition. how much happier the rustic that feels it tho he knows not how" (Lonsdale, 201). A seeming reversion to the mode of his earlier Spring Ode, then, the *Vicissitude Ode* nevertheless purports to undo the wintry trauma and voiced agony of the Sonnet on West's death, the threnody of *De Principiis*, the depression of the Eton College Ode, and the epitaphic *Elegy* by "o'er the cheek of Sorrow throw[ing] / A melancholy grace":

> Behind the steps that Misery treads,
> Approaching Comfort view:
> The hues of bliss more brightly glow,
> Chastised by sabler tints of woe.

In yet another of his repetitive self-portraits Gray then figures himself as "the wretch" who "long has tossed / On the thorny bed of pain" but now "At length repair[s] his vigour lost, / And breathe[s] and walk[s] again." He even ventures so far beyond his losses that

> The meanest flower of the vale,
> The simplest note that swells the gale,
> The common sun, the air and skies,
> To him are opening Paradise.

It is just possible that these lines imply something of the tenor Wordsworth will make of them in his Immortality Ode:

> The clouds that gather round the setting sun
> Do take a sober colouring from an eye
> That hath kept watch o'er man's mortality;
> Another race hath been, and other palms are won.
> Thanks to the human heart by which we live,
> Thanks to its tenderness, its joys, and fears,
> To me the meanest flower that blows can give
> Thoughts that do often lie too deep for tears.

But, taken as a whole, *Vicissitude* emerges as but a virtual reprise of the tenor of his Spring Ode and the opening of *Eton College*. Perhaps that is why, from this point on, the poem rapidly disintegrates into trailing fragments, only the grammatically unconnected and referentially indeterminate "They perish in the boundless deep" standing out starkly. It is impossible, then, to read *this* "bliss," no matter how "brightly" it glows, as other than *Eton College*'s "momentary bliss" that only "seem[s] to soothe" his "weary soul." No wonder *The Bard*'s plunge is not far behind.

Before closing that circle sketched earlier in my analysis of *The Bard*, we need now to attend to the seemingly aberrational *Ode on the Death of a Favourite Cat, Drowned in a Tub of Gold Fishes* (early 1747) and, in a different vein five to seven years later, *The Progress of Poesy. A Pindaric Ode.*

The Poems (IV):
From *Cat* to *Progress*

In one sense it could be argued that the Vicissitude Ode was Gray's self-defeating, last-resort surrender to conventional eighteenth-century sensibility. If not an attempt at self-assuagement, it seemed at least to aspire to a coming to (*some* kind of) terms with his grief over West's death—as well as with the extent to which that event had come to dominate his emotional consciousness and poetic life. Milton's concomitant, contributive codomination was a different matter. As we have seen in the Eton College Ode, *L'Allegro* and *Il Penseroso*-like sensibility was jettisoned by Gray as an insufficient imagination, a kind of poetic capitulation to the obvious, the comfortable, the easy. *Paradise Lost* demanded more, and Gray courageously tackled it head-on despite his fear of replicating Milton's plunge into ever-during night. But "head-on," as perhaps he learned from his juvenile "Lines Spoken by the Ghost of John Dennis at the Devil Tavern," was not the only way to negotiate that poem's dauntingly sublime achievement, nor the only tactic possible to extricate himself from Milton's albatrosslike burden. The "blended form" or "artful strife" of pleasure/grief and misery/comfort mentioned in stanza 5 of *Vicissitude* may have suggested a sort of hybrid serio-comic-satiric stratagem for "gentling" Milton, subduing his power via burlesque diminishment.

Fifty years ago Lord David Cecil suggested three categories of poetry in the Gray canon, the third being a "brief and brilliant category of . . . satirical and humorous verse." Almost thirty years later Paul Sherwin, in order to highlight his contrary view of Collins' career, argued briefly that, like Dryden (in *Absalom and Achitophel* primarily), Pope in *The Dunciad* "comes to terms with Milton in a satiric context." And in 1980 Paul Fry in effect conflated these two positions: *all* of Gray's "odes flirt with parody," their "periphrases" self-defensively screening out "the immediacy and

pain of recollecting high origins."[1] While such a screening-out I find fully
attempted only in the *Ode for Music,* a mingled dish of sauces that I shall
turn to later, the ancestry of that poem's mode lies in Gray's burlesque
potpourri in the juvenile Dennis "Lines" and in the Favourite Cat Ode.
In that underrated poem burlesque, mock-heroic, parody, and even down-
right silliness all jostle as technical companions-in-arms against the para-
bolic, and paradoxical, raising to full poetic consciousness of the impact
on Gray of Miltonic transgression and fall—and (as Wallace Jackson puts
it) "the fate of desire."[2]

Until Sacks's provocative commentary on the poem, which builds on
Fry's five years earlier, virtually no one had regarded the *Favourite Cat* as
worthy of comment beyond steady praise for its "enchanting . . . mixture
of wit and prettiness" that achieved for it "an unexpected immortality."[3]
But most recently Suvir Kaul, in his *Thomas Gray and Literary Authority,*
argues audaciously, if somewhat eccentrically, that the poem is "an allegor-
ical satire on women and a displaced account of the eighteenth-century
British domestication of the imperial ideal," in which woman emerges at
the end as an "excessive, mindless, amoral consumer." The context in
which the *Favourite Cat* "must be read," he goes on, is "the creation of
structural alibis that will validate and affirm overseas expansion."[4] I'm
afraid I do not know how to comment delicately on such a thesis and so I
venture none. On the other hand, the context of Sacks's remarks, revised
and elaborated by Wallace Jackson, is worth pondering here. At the heart
of their position is the conviction that deflection of desire for the unattain-
able object of desire (whether Milton or *some* other) characterizes Gray's
efforts in the *Elegy* and in most of the odes, and that "evasion or incapac-
ity" therefore becomes for Gray "the satisfactory figure of fulfillment."[5] I
find this a persuasive reading in the psychological context Jackson (espe-
cially) develops, but I should like to argue, in the context I have been
developing, that *Favourite Cat* is Gray's first sustained attempt to put Mil-
ton in his place, so to speak.

Such a characterization may seem peculiar or even perverse given the
widely accepted accounts of its verbal (and even conceptual) borrowings:
from Pope's translation of the *Iliad* (Selima is Helen), extensively but un-
persuasively argued mainly by Geoffrey Tillotson; from Dryden's transla-
tion of the *Aeneid* (Selima as Virgil's Camilla in Book 11); from John Gay's
The Toilette (Selima as Lydia); from Ovid's recounting of the Daphne-
Apollo myth; and, to a surprisingly lesser degree, from *Paradise Lost* (Sel-
ima as Eve).[6] Moreover, despite passing reference to one or more of these

"sources" in the criticism we have of the poem, they are always regarded as somehow contributing to a "piece of versified playfulness," a "postured charm" and "gentlemanly archness," or "one of those casual poems, written by grave authors on private occasions"—essentially, that is, Samuel Johnson's contemporary judgment ("doubtless by its author considered as a trifle") though he, of course, adjudged it "not a happy trifle." [7]

The specific terms "playfulness" and "trifle" I shall return to shortly, but first these summary characterizations of the ode, by their very ubiquitousness, deserve some comment. To be generous, they are inattentive to Gray's subtlety (not to say his calculated subterfuge) in repressing, deflecting, or radically displacing the power of Milton's presence. Complicit in this inattention is the commentators' virtual exclusion of Milton from the poem in favor of concerted attention to Pope, the ostensible allusions to whose Helen are at best thin, and to Dryden, whose "real" Camilla is conveniently set aside: for him she is a "Warrior Queen," a "fierce Virago" "pleas'd with Blood," who is bloodily slain on the field of Aeneas's epic battle with Turnus.[8] This critical consensus, then, raises crucial questions about how we can know—or at least try to determine—the difference between a readily recognizable allusion and, at the other end of the spectrum, a mere echo, either accidental or a deliberate appropriation of a felicitous word, phrase, or figure. And, even more important, to what extent, if at all, is the allusion or echo intended to recall for the reader its original contextualization?

My *Blake's Prelude: "Poetical Sketches"* and *Blake and Spenser* essayed some possible answers to these and related questions; and in the course of grappling with the all but ineffable I arrived at a notion of "significant allusion"—that is, one reasonably verifiable by the total thrust of the poem into which it has been imported as evoking its original context, not merely its dictional felicitousness or even its linguistic appropriateness to that poem's general tenor or subject. I shall not rehearse that argument here, but additionally helpful in this regard is John Hollander's excellent taxonomy of degrees of allusion/echo, in *The Figure of Echo*, especially his animadversions on the habitual editorial and critical footnote use of "cf." as an evasion of "the caves of ambience and the chambers of meaning."[9] But what is most important in this regard for the study of Gray is the indubitable fact that he was a meticulous craftsman as well as a shrewd editor of his own final verbal choices—even, as Lonsdale notes (xiii–xiv), of his punctuation and capitalization. And, as I indicated in an earlier chapter, we need also remember that Gray only reluctantly, even irritat-

edly, supplied notes for the 1768 edition of his *Poems,* and then only to
identify allusions which, in the spirit of conventional eighteenth-century
imitation, enhanced or dignified his poetic performance, rather than those
that creatively engaged or interacted with his own poems.

The entire issue is, one must confess, maddeningly complex, but in
light of my last point above about Gray's reluctance to footnote at all, it is
especially provocative that even in the 1768 *Poems* Gray acknowledged no
debt whatsoever to *Paradise Lost,* and, concomitantly, the ode that he him-
self had called (tongue firmly in cheek) "the most noble of my Perfor-
mances latterly" (*CTG*, 277) he adjudged as after all but a "trifle." Gay's
Lydia, then, *may* be another matter, but I leave her in the wings to first
address the pervasive Miltonism of Gray's *Cat. Paradise Lost* is evoked
initially at the end of the first stanza, which depicts Eve's first sight of
herself in the lake, the Narcissistic paradigm auguring well for neither
Selima nor Eve: "There I had fixed / Mine eyes till now, and pined with
vain desire," Eve confesses, until the divine voice warns her away and to
return to the source of her true image, Adam (4. 465 ff). Selima is similarly
mesmerized by her watery image, and "Still had she gazed" except for,
not a divine cautionary voice, but the appearance of an even greater visual
temptation than herself: "Two angel forms" gliding in the lake, "The
genii of the stream." Gray's repetition of "gazed" (6, 13) is a brilliant
stroke, suggesting as it does his awareness that for Milton "gazes" are
invariably suspicious, redolent with desire, ultimately pernicious.[10] It is
Satan who most frequently gazes in *Paradise Lost*—and Eve under Satan's
tutelage—both of them at the Tree, for example, with its "Ruddy and
gold" fruit (5. 57; 9. 578, 735), Satan fixedly at Eve and at Eden (9. 524;
4. 356). And while "Fixed on the fruit she gazed," her "eager appetite" is
raised as the "desire" implicit in gazing "grow[s] to touch or taste" (9. 735,
740–42).[11]

Gray's fish, of course, are not apples nor does Selima, "Forth reaching
to the fruit" (9. 781; cf. Gray's line 22), pluck and eat. On the other hand,
the fish are not fish either, rather "angel forms" arrayed in crimson-purple
armor that "betrays" a "golden gleam" hidden beneath—a rather dazzling
conflation of Satan's fallen "legions, angel forms" (1. 301) and the "wat'ry
gleam" within which Eve sees her own image and pines for it "with vain
desire" (4. 461, 466). But if the fish *are* (as they appear to the *cat's* gazing
eyes) "The genii of the stream," not *Lycidas's* "Genius of the shore," Gray
has already thereby sealed Selima's doom, not only in the pre-Fall context
of gazing and stretching "to reach the prize," but also in her misperception

of the angel forms' fallenness, for they clearly shall *not* "be good / To all that wander in that perilous flood." [12] Hence Gray's line 19 ("The hapless nymph with wonder saw") appropriately replicates not only Eve's "wond'ring" look at her specular image (5. 54) but Milton's address to her as she departs from Adam prior to encountering the serpent: "O much deceived, much failing, hapless Eve" (9. 404). Underscoring this point, the fifth stanza opens with the exclamatory "Presumptuous maid!" which pointedly evokes Adam's calmer, though thereby the more recriminatory, speech after he has branded her fall as defacement and deflowering. Now Eve is, he says, as by now we ought to know Selina is, "to death devote" (9. 900–1). "Bold deed thou hast presumed, advent'rous Eve," Adam continues angrily, "And peril great provoked, who thus hast dared" (921–22). Selima's presumptuousness too inheres precisely in such daring—not merely to "ardent[ly] wish" but, "with looks intent," to stretch and reach: "again she bent / Nor knew the gulf between." The looking and bending effectively recapitulate Eve's gazing "into the clear / Smooth lake" as well as Milton's own unobtrusive echoing of her "As I bent down to look" in the reflected shape's "Bending to look on me." [13] Gray's hyperbolic "gulf between" in the curiously phrased third line of this fifth stanza concatenates God's bending "down *his* eye" to view his universe, including "Hell and the gulf between, and Satan there" (3. 58, 70), with the gulf between Selima's/Eve's transgressive desire and its enactment.

For Gray, that desire is as much a "fall" as his later relegation of self in *The Progress of Poesy* to somewhere in the middle air of the gulf between the Good and Great. It is a stretching to possess the unpossessable, to appropriate the unappropriatable—except, perhaps, in a context that is purportedly a "trifle." If "The slippery verge" is what "beguiles" Selima into her actual fall,[14] the act of falling is made subordinate to Gray's sense of *his* having already fallen by presumptuously committing this outrageous parodization of Milton's sublime—a rather striking prolepsis of Gray's characterizing of Milton's presumption and of Dryden's verge-avoiding "less presumptuous" car in *The Progress of Poesy*. It is no mere coincidence, then, that the "verge" for Milton is that slippery point between "the wild expanse" of the "nethermost abyss" of "Chaos and ancient Night" and the "glimmering dawn" at the "fardest verge" of Nature where Chaos begins "to retire"—a stationing that Gray boldly reverses, or turns upside down, for Selima, unlike Satan, does not "waft on the calmer wave" (*PL* 2. 1014, 969–70, 1034–42). In fact Milton himself alludes to this passage in Book 6 where the apostate angels "headlong themselves . . . threw/

Down from the verge of heav'n" into "the bottomless pit" (864–66). The Lycidean echoes in Gray's next stanza underwrite such parodic as well as autobiographical intent since Gray knows himself to be no Arion, and even if he were, no dolphin is there to waft his hapless self. "Sunk low" like Lycidas/Selima, he is as nonelegiacally untriumphant as Walpole's cat, doomed forever not to mount high like the fallen and resurrected day-star nor to flame again "in the forehead of the morning sky."

What is truly remarkable about the *Favourite Cat*, though, is Gray's extraordinary success in deflecting our attention from his personal poetic agon. Witness the poem's critical history.[15] Before giving further attention to that agonistic matter, however, some comment on the ode's conclusion is in order, for it too contributes in a different, yet collaborative, way to the poem's critical history. This last stanza neatly leaves us satisfied aesthetically that all he has done is to turn a trivial occasion for mock-elegy toward pointing a commonplace, equally trivial moral. Indeed, even the poem's animal-fable ambience becomes subordinated to John Gay's poetic essay on trivialness, *The Toilette*, which outdoes his more "serious" and sprawling *Trivia*. In *The Toilette* Lydia gazes not "on the lake below" but "Reclin'd upon her arm she pensive sate" and in "dumb devotion" stares into "her glass." "Ah hapless nymph," Gay calls her, as Gray calls Selima, for at age thirty-five "conquests" of new lovers or "white glov'd beaux" for Lydia "are no more," and Gray even appropriates for *his* "primal scene" the "prize" given to Lydia by her erstwhile beau Damon, "the tall jar" that "erects his costly pride, / With antic shapes in China's azure dy'd." But here it is the jar that falls, its "shiver'd" shape the emblem of Damon's falseness and his "perjury" in Indian-giving his heart to Chloe.[16]

This wildly disparate circumstance Gray quite wonderfully translates into Selima's plight, his theft signaled by a final allusion to Gay's poem: after "raving" against Damon's perfidy, Lydia's maid rearms her with ribbons, lace, head-dress, and "adjusted" locks to march forth once again into the world of beaux, for "at the playhouse Harry keeps her box." "Harry" was Gray's first choice for one of those (the Tom and Susan of the received text) who fail to hear Selima's mewing in the flood. Uncannily, given the Miltonic context I have suggested, the other was to be "John." Gay called his poem a "Town Eclogue," a subgenre clearly intended as a deliberate trivialization of classical bucolics. It *is* a trifle, which, uninflated by echoes of or references to the direness of Satan's, Eve's, Camilla's, Helen's (or even Agrippina's) desire and transgression, never rises, nor aspires to rise, beyond its essential insignificance. Gray's poem, on the other hand, does rise to soar beyond its surface common-placeness and insistently conventional moralizing—to become at least a minor masterpiece of the trivialized sublime. "Be with caution bold," so goes Gray's moral lesson in his last stanza, and here for once he may have remembered Spenser and Britomart's approach to the House of Busyrane in Book 3 of *The Faerie Queene;* there over the door "thus written she did spye / *Be bold,*" and "*Be bold, be bold,* and every where *Be bold*" (stanzas 50, 54). And while the final doorway legend reads "*Be not too bold*" (stanza 54), very possibly echoed in Gray's line 39, what makes the Cat Ode a significant one in Gray's canon is precisely his ignoring of Spenser's and his own cautionary advice to "ye beauties" in order to poetically emulate Britomart's bold invasion of Busyrane's castle to release Amoret by invading Milton's sanctuary and, at least for the moment, unsaying rather than essaying his sublime. Though *The Progress of Poesy,* and its still not quite "gentled" Milton, are yet to be negotiated, the great achievements of 1742 are now, in the Cat ode, five years behind Gray; and, almost as if delaying any renegotiation of his enduring "problem" of Milton, what soon follows *Cat* is the untypicality of the *Elegy* and of his abortive foray into Welsh and Norse antiquarianism.

And so I have come nearly full circle. The career trajectory that Gray pursues now seems predictable: the resolute rejection of Milton as model in *The Progress of Poesy* (even to the omission of his name), the "deep depression," as I called it, heralded by *The Bard* and reflected in its progeny, and finally the desperate (if in its own way daring) misappropriation or garbling of Milton that at once undergirds and subverts the dutiful pompousness of Gray's farewell to the muse, the *Ode for Music.* That final "performance" (the word Gray tellingly used to describe the Cat Ode), I suggest, derives in large measure from the complex mixture of serious self-scrutiny and trivialization that constitutes the achievement of *Ode on the Death of a Favourite Cat,* for the Music Ode emerges as a kind of exorcistic elegy that enables Gray to disengage himself from Milton's palpable presence and ultimately to lay his ghost to rest to a deliberately less than solemn music. Mock-heroic, then, may *really* be the right descriptive term for the Favourite Cat Ode after all, not in its "bathetic disproportion of diction to occasion" as Rodney Edgecombe recently put it, echoing virtually all his predecessors,[17] but rather in its exquisite Miltonic diction courageously and fully proportionate to the occasion of Gray's creative agon— still very much at the center of his poetry in 1751–54 in the struggle with *The Progress of Poesy.*

I do not intend here yet another "reading" of *The Progress of Poesy*, nor to rehearse the various interpretations and commentaries it has received and attempt to adjudicate among them. What I do intend is to situate the Gray of the early 1750s in the context of his perception of *his* progress, fraught as it continued to be with wafflings, and in the context of the extent to which his career is informed, even dominated, by his struggle with a Milton who was, unobligingly, neither mute nor inglorious. Something like that "situating" has been done most recently, and brilliantly in my judgment, by William Fitzgerald in his study *The Pindaric Mode in Pindar, Horace, Hölderlin, and the English Ode* especially in the chapter "Progress and Fall," centering on "Horace's treatment of his relation to his great forebear Pindar."[18] While that relationship inheres largely in the political contexts of those two poets' careers, Fitzgerald's analysis suggests an important basic point about Gray: no matter how magnificent his attempt, he fails to emulate Horace's successful rereading of the past and its myths in order to situate himself "in the earlier context . . . according to the demands of the present" (103). In somewhat the same fashion that Suvir Kaul argues Gray's relationship to earlier and contemporary poetic modes and discourses, Fitzgerald regards Horace's use of Pindaric forms as his way of linking "the individual poet with his tradition, poetic or historical," and working "out his own relation to the past, as lesser and yet better than its towering figures" (86). That, of course, is precisely what *The Progress of Poesy*'s final lines seem to declare with respect to Gray's history of poetry's migrations. But of course *his* past, his "tradition," in the poem turns out to be a notably unhistorical (or ahistorical) "search for sublime images . . . necessarily closed off from the history of which Gray should be part" (90)—an ersatz Other not figured *in* Milton but nevertheless, subtextually in the *Progress*, fully constituted *by* Milton.[19]

Accordingly, despite its obvious evocation of Pindar's Aeolian music (as well as Cowley's Anglicizing of his forebear's "trembling strings": "Awake, awake, my lyre"),[20] the opening stanza of *The Progress* subliminally introduces not Pindar, nor Horace's "version" of Pindar, but a solidly Miltonic subtext. Although the specifics of the allusions themselves ring some changes on those I've focused on in earlier poems, the story is the same. *This* subtext too oscillates between Satanic power and transgression on the one hand, Eden inviolate on the other—beginning with Gray's imaging of the ode's narrative thread (the "progress" proper) in his stream-of-music trope. An ancient figuration, its locus classicus is Horace's *ode* 4.2:

> Any poet seeking to rival Pindar,
> Iullus, puts on Daedalus' wings of wax to
> Rise in soaring flight, and a sea shall keep his
>   Name and his body.
>
> Like a river headlong from mountains pouring
> Forth to drown its banks with the glut of rainfalls,
> Pindar's language, seething with boundless power,
>   Bursts like a torrent.[21]

While Gray obviously knew both the Pindaric and Horatian passages, and leans no doubt on both, his version associates itself as well, if far less openly, with Eden's river in *Paradise Lost*. Passing underneath the mount of Paradise, its "rapid current" is

>   through veins
> Of porous earth with kindly thirst up drawn
> [As] a fresh fountain, and with many a rill
> Watered the garden; thence united fell
> Down the steep glade, and met the nether flood.

Divided there into "four main streams" that run "diverse, wand'ring many a famous realm," these "crisped brooks,"

> Rolling on orient pearl and sands of gold
> With mazy error under pendent shades
> Ran nectar, visiting each plant, and fed
> Flow'rs worthy of Paradise.
>   (4. 227–31, 238–41)

Gray's use of "mazy" (line 4) is of course hardly innovative in the eighteenth century, especially given Spenser's and Milton's precedents, but given this poem's immersion in *Paradise Lost*, Gray's alteration of "mazy error" to "mazy progress" arguably sounds a muted uncertainty of direction for this "rich stream of music" despite the firmness of the word "progress." In fact, Gray's employment of the entire trope ceases abruptly with the dispersion of that stream in Greece, figured in the proverbial objective correlative for mazy error, "Maeander's amber waves" (its renowned muddiness) that "In lingering lab'rinths creep" (69–70).

Though such hints and indirections may make but a shaky case in themselves for Milton's imposition here, when we turn back from them to the ode's intensely personal opening exhortations, we find that case already solidified. For his first line Gray initially wrote (in his commonplace book) "Awake, *my* Lyre, *my* Glory" (my emphasis), an obvious theft from Psalm 57: "Awake up, my glory; awake, psaltery and harp. . ." (verse 8). But if for David God is the "muse," for Gray Milton's "Heavenly Muse" is even nearer to hand, for thence Milton

> Invoke[s his] aid to [his] advent'rous song,
> That with no middle flight intends to soar
> Above th' Aonian mount . . .
>   (*PL* 1. 6, 12–15)

No mere distant way this, no modest mounting beyond a vulgar fate, no middle flight above the good but far below the great. But Gray's early version of his first line is even more richly proleptic than this dual allusion suggests: "my Lyre" rather than the substituted indeterminate "Aeolian lyre," and "my Glory" rather than the anonymity of the exhorting self signaled by the absence of David's phrasing in the revisions. Into this studious second-thought and self-effacement, as well as into the context of Milton's invocation of the heavenly muse that inspired Moses on Horeb and Sinai, Satan's resounding cry to his fallen cohort inserts its dissonant note: "Awake, arise, or be for ever fall'n!" (1. 330). The arguable impertinence of that suggestion is mitigated by Gray's later shift (already alluded to) from the "stream of music"/Edenic river trope to metaphors of poetic soaring, of Miltonic/Satanic transgression—and, of course, of being "blasted with excess of light" (and flight) into the same endless night to which the Bard will shortly commit himself. As Fitzgerald demonstrates with respect to the opening of Pindar's *Olympian* 3, when "the poet is a receiver of divinity [cf. Gray's later labeling of his lyre as "divine," line 112], a mediator between God and human, . . . there will be a danger of presumption in the poet's too active appropriation of divinity," a presumption that risks a tragic fate.[22]

Finally, then, it is Dryden's hands alone that grasp and "explore" "the lyre" in his "less presumptuous" middle flight—as distinct from Shakespeare's hand on his "pencil,"[23] from the absence of any such instrument in Milton's ride sublime, and from Gray's grasping of nothing. Perhaps this is why Dryden, as Paul Fry reminds us, is accorded more lineage in the poem than any of Gray's illustrious predecessors; and he is, of course, the

only one *named*. Fry may well be right to suggest therefore that Dryden
here "is Gray's self portrait." [24] To me, however, Gray's sense of his own
identity takes on a darker hue from this penultimate passage in *The Prog-
ress:*

> Oh! lyre divine, what daring spirit
> Wakes thee now? Though he inherit
> Nor the pride nor ample pinion,
> That the Theban eagle bear
> Sailing with supreme dominion
> Through the azure deep of air:
> Yet oft before his infant eyes would run
> Such forms as glitter in the Muses's ray
> With orient hues, unborrowed of the sun.
>   (112–20)

Many have noted the deflationary thrust of this passage, from "daring
spirit" to "infant eyes," which (possibly) passively view some unspecified
"forms" that glitter only as reflections of the Muse's ray—what Fitzgerald
accurately calls "the collapse of narrative into image." [25] Nor is it entirely
new to cite the reiterated deflection here of Gray's self (the original my
lyre, my glory) to the anonymity of the third person. But should we not
ask as well why *"infant* eyes"? So fine a classical scholar as Gray could not
have written that phrase without knowing that *infans* is (one) unable to
speak, and the association is especially likely in view of his revising his
original choice here, "visionary eyes." Nowhere in the final twelve lines
of the poem do the infant's hands *do* anything, nowhere is music heard,
nowhere does *this* child dauntlessly stretch forth his little arms and smile
(as the "immortal boy" Shakespeare does in lines 87–91),[26] nowhere are
there Drydenian "words that burn." Instead this "daring spirit" merely
mounts some "way" and "keeps" it in silence, precariously poised, or wan-
dering, somewhere between the good and great. Wherever that some-
where is, "Some mute inglorious Milton here may rest," his infant ear still
vainly, despairingly attuned, perhaps, to David's psalm: "My heart is fixed,
O God, my heart is fixed: I will sing.... I will sing unto thee among the
nations" (57:7, 9).

To Gray's famous final couplet Lonsdale suggests two Horatian paral-
lels, *Ode* 3.2, lines 21–24, and *Ode* 4.9, lines 3–4, in Pope's translation, but
neither in their contexts seems to speak to Gray's point.[27] Fitzgerald's
model of Horace's use of "Pindaric forms . . . to work out his own relation

to the past" and thus to be "lesser and yet better than its towering figures" does so speak—though I would demur to his paradoxical interpretation of Gray's concluding lines: "Gray, too, will fly, but his flight will accuse Milton and Pindar, outbidding them by being weaker." "Weaker" I understand; "outbidding" seems to me not to Gray's point, for in fact he hardly "bids" at all, not daring (being unable?) to "fly." Rather than, as Fitzgerald argues, "exorcis[ing] his sense of failure at being unable to assume a position in the great tradition" and thereby going "beyond Horace's ambivalent relation to the heroic past, which allows him to feel superior in being less great,"[28] Gray exorcises nothing. Rather, he stakes a claim to a place in "the great tradition" that befits a poet who has come, agonizingly, to know himself—something like what prelapsarian Adam learns from Raphael: "Consider first," Raphael says, "that great"

> Or bright infers not excellence: the earth
> Though in comparison of heav'n so small,
> Nor glistering, may of solid good contain
> More plenty than the sun that barren shines.
>   (8. 90–94)

Or God's words about his Son:

> By merit more than birthright Son of God,
> Found worthiest to be so by being good,
> Far more than great or high. . . .
>   (3. 309–11)

In any case, if self-knowledge is what Fitzgerald calls Gray's "independence" from a poetic tradition whose progress he "seems to have repudiated"[29] in favor of imagistic forms that "glitter in the Muse's ray," that "independence" turns out to be but an abortive abandonment of the tradition entirely and a momentary fraternization with Norse-Welsh bards that falls apart virtually at the moment he pledges himself to it.

My big guns having now all been fired, it remains but to mop up with a brief survey of the other evocations of *Paradise Lost* that consort with the ones already cited in *The Progress*. Virtually all dramatize the final throes of Gray's Miltonic agon: his sense that the transgressiveness and punishment articulated in lines 95–102 reflect but Milton's *inadvertent* identification with Satan, and hence his own greater presumption, under no Uranian auspices, to risk a direr fate by soaring into Milton's sublime heaven of heavens. He obviously knew that it was not Milton who "rode sublime / Upon the seraph-wings of Ecstasy" but Christ, He who "on the wings of Cherub rode sublime," not to spy into the secrets of the abyss but to do battle with Satan's legions (6. 771 ff); and it is Satan's address to Chaos, Old Night, and their entourage whose language Gray appropriates:

> Ye Powers
> And Spirits of this nethermost abyss,
> Chaos and ancient Night, I come no spy
> With purpose to explore or to disturb
> The secrets of your realm.
>
> (2. 968–72)

Even more ominously Satan boasts to Gabriel,

> I therefore, I alone first undertook
> To wing the desolate abyss, and spy,

not the abyss but God's "new-created world, whereof in hell / Fame is not silent" (4. 935–38). So forcefully did these conflicting resonances echo in Gray's ear that in his 1768 notes he deliberately attempts to deflect his readers' notice of them by linking Milton's transgressive overstepping "the flaming bounds of place and time" solely to a Lucretian passage on the "lively power" of the imagination coupled with the more obvious source of Milton's "seeing" the "living throne, the sapphire-blaze" in Ezekiel.[30]

This entire history of the poems of 1742 through 1754, then, represents the peak of Milton's haunting of Gray. Unlike Collins, for whom (in Paul Sherwin's words) "the way to freedom, from both his cultural anxiety and the anxiety of Milton's influence, is the venture of undoing Milton's poetics of purification, or sublimation" in *L'Allegro* and *Il Penseroso*, Gray more courageously (or with supreme foolhardiness) seemed fatally compelled to somehow accommodate within his own poetic enterprise "the mind [that] hears, and sees, and knows itself divine"[31]—the mind, that is, to which his own aspires. I find in this agon little sense of what Fry calls "writing [as] Gray's fortunate fall," for there is in his work nothing of Milton's revaluation of "fallen humanity as a hopeful purgatorial venture, vouchsafing a teleology to time and a sustaining future to the Christian wayfarer-warfarer." [32] Instead Gray presents the alternative teleologies of the conclusion to *The Progress of Poesy* (which tonally and substantively echoes that of the Eton College ode) and the Bard's self-defeating plunge into endless night, both of which impinge upon the tenor of the *Elegy* composed between them.

Finishing

Chapter 5 discussed in some detail Gray's deep depression as that is reflected in *The Bard:* Richard West was dead; Gray's love for him, first frustrated and anxiety-ridden, was now unpursuable; Eden-Eton was hopelessly lost but to memory; and his own poetic career had plunged into an endless night of enveloping silence. After the joint publication of *The Bard* and *The Progress of Poesy* in August 1757, headed by the motto in Greek taken from Pindar's second Olympian Ode ("vocal to the intelligent alone," his "private message to the elect, and his signal of defiance to the ignorant and unworthy"),[1] Gray was understandably crushed that even the intelligent condemned the odes for their impenetrable obscurity. Though he wrote to Mason in September, "Nobody understands me, & I am perfectly satisfied," this was an obvious defensive posture, maintained for only a line or two before he confesses resignedly, "I know my day is over" (*CTG*, 522–23). There were exceptions to the public's negative responses, of course—David Garrick and Richard Hurd, for example. The latter wrote a letter almost immediately after the odes' publication: "Everybody here [Cambridge], that knows anything of such things, applauds the Odes. And the readers of Pindar dote upon them" (*CTG*, 521).[2] But the overwhelming consensus was that they were "nothing to the *Churchyard*," and some even said that had Gray written the odes in prose to say what he really meant, they might have bought them "& put [him] in their pocket (*CTG*, 532).

Despite the few positive responses that appeared during Gray's post-publication flurries of anxiety over their reception, he almost immediately ceased to even mention the odes again. Ketton-Cremer inexplicably states flatly that "he did not grow bitter or resentful," even though Gray's letters immediately after publication, all of them reeking with anger and woundedness, consistently pillory the obtuse intelligentsia, as well as those of

166

less learning. "The next thing I print," he wrote wryly to Mason, "shall be in Welch [*sic*]" (*CTG*, 524). But by the end of 1757 printing (or even writing) *anything* seemed far from Gray's mind, as the conclusions of the Eton College Ode and *The Bard* presaged. To Thomas Wharton in February 1758, he writes that he holds his "employment cheap enough . . . the drift of my present studies is to know, wherever I am, what lies within reach, that may be worth seeing. Whether it be Building, ruin, park, garden, prospect, picture, or monument" (*CTG*, 564). That is to say, from 1757 on, "apart from [writing] a few occasional pieces," Gray "withdrew more resolutely even than before into private study and the private life."[3] The fact that he was by 1757–58 the foremost poet in Britain—Collins insane, the Warton's having turned to criticism and scholarship, Johnson not writing verse, Churchill's satires as yet unpublished—was even less consolation than the occasional favorable reviews, since that fame rested firmly on the *Elegy Written in a Country Churchyard*, the wide popularity of which prompted greater and greater misgivings about its true quality.

In these circumstances, however, and despite what he wrote to Wharton, Gray did not simply withdraw into private contemplation of "what lies within reach" but rather turned to the solace of scholarship, a kind of emulation of the Wartons' career turn, interrupted only by vacational visits to his few close friends. Off and on since 1746 he had been occupied with an elaborate research project on ancient Greek civilization, classical literature, and travel books—and later on Romance, Germanic, and Celtic poetics and philosophy, and medieval English poetry (Lonsdale, 211); and by 1758–59 he plunged into the study of English history and antiquities, stimulated and abetted by the opening of the British Museum in 1759: "My only employment & amusement in Town," he writes to Mason, "has been the Musaeum" but "I have been rather historically than poetically given." But then, after saying "I can write you no news from hence," he adds mysteriously that he *has* "lately heard *ill-news*, wch I shall not write" (*CTG*, 646).

That "*ill-news*" (the italics are Gray's), I suggest, is the suicide of Gray's longtime friend from Peterhouse days (the early 1740s), Henry Tuthill, who in February 1757 had been adjudged by the Master of Pembroke (to which Tuthill had migrated in 1747), on the basis of "common fame," as "having been guilty of great enormities"; and since, for reasons no one knows, Tuthill did not appear to clear himself, the college Register concludes "there is good reason to believe he never will" (*CTG*, 1208). While the precise nature of these "enormities" has never been uncovered, there is plenty of circumstantial evidence to indicate that they had to do with Tuthill's homosexuality and the public knowledge of it.[4] This seemingly tangential or irrelevant circumstance does have a bearing, however, on Gray's state of mind at this crucial point in his life and career. As Norton Nicholls writes in his 1805 *Reminiscences,* whenever West was mentioned in their frequent conversations Gray "looked serious, & seemed to feel the affliction of a *recent* loss" (*CTG,* 1300; my italics), and given the power-ful impingement of West's *Ad Amicos* on *The Bard* and *The Pleasure Arising from Vicissitude* in 1754–57, Gray's "affair" with West (though hardly an "enormity") and his fear of public exposure would have been even at this late date a vivid presence in his consciousness—particularly now with the exposure of Tuthill's affair, which Gray might have feared would lead, at least in some quarters, to recollections of his own close friendship with Tuthill, even if that was almost twenty years ago.

In fact Gray in some way may have seen himself in Tuthill's situation but for the grace of God, and it is no mere coincidence to find that Mason obliterated or excised from the letters Gray exchanged with Thomas Wharton about the Tuthill affair all reference to Tuthill, even those indi-cated merely by the initial "T." (*CTG,* 232 n). Wharton was, and Mason knew he was, a driving force in attempts to secure a fellowship for Tuthill at Pembroke, and Gray himself also wrote Mason about the matter, pre-sumably because the latter not only knew Tuthill at Pembroke but was elected a Fellow there at the same time Tuthill was (March 1749). None of those letters has ever been discovered either (*CTG,* 1208–9). The Rev. John Mitford, into whose hands Mason consigned this correspondence (though probably not all of it), restored without comment Tuthill's name in his edition of *The Works of Thomas Gray* (1816), and rather bitterly re-called even as late as 1843 the "mutilated state of the manuscript" of the letters Mason lent to him (*CTG,* 232 n). While Gray no doubt *was* "deeply moved" by Tuthill's plight since he "had been his intimate friend," it is virtually impossible that his own private fears, presumably by this time no longer pressing, did not resurface rudely in the guise of his friend's igno-miny rather than his merely worrying "lest the scandal should do serious harm to the college," as Leonard Whibley suggests.[5] Perhaps such private fears are what Gray alludes to in his mysterious first *extant* letter to Whar-ton (there were obviously others prior to this one) after Tuthill's "sen-tence": "a part of what I imagined, has already happened here, tho' not in the way I expected" (Tuthill's not showing up to defend himself?). Then he goes on, "in a way indeed, that confutes itself," that is, presumably, Tuthill's absence confesses his guilt; "but I will not answer for the truth of this ... I can not interpose at present, lest I make the matter worse" (*CTG*, 495).

While my guess about the "ill-news" he says he will not give Mason in the 6 October 1759 letter cited above is supportable only on the slim grounds of Mitford's statement in 31 January 1828 that "the name of Gray's friend, who drowned himself was *Tuthill*" (*CTG*, 1210 n), Whibley conjectures similarly that the "suicide may have taken place soon after his disgrace" (*CTG*, 1210); and Mitford, even as late as 1847, is still worrying about the entire catastrophe, especially the "considerable gloom" it spread "over Gray's mind, and perhaps permanently affected his spirits"—though he adds, paradoxically, that "it is quite useless to draw [the "circumstances"] from the obscurity in which they have been placed" (*CTG*, 1210 n). My point in drawing them forth here may by now be clear, to try to capture as much as we can of Gray's state of mind after the publication of *The Bard* and *The Progress* and during his subsequent precipitate plunge into the antiquarian scholarship that produced *The Fatal Sisters* and *The Descent of Odin* in 1761, *The Triumphs of Owen* and *The Death of Hoel* in 1760–61, and the last-gasp fragments of "Caradoc" and "Conan" sometime in the early 1760s. All of these *Bard*ic progeny, as I indicated earlier, lean heavily on Latin translations of the originals by various hands. As a result, the poetic voice we hear is even more deliberately impersonal and non-self-revelatory than the famous prevailingly manneristic sensibility and studied decorum of the *Elegy*'s surface. Both are disguises, the Norse and Welsh translations differing from the earlier poem only in their absolute impenetrableness into Thomas Gray's breathing, passionate self.[6]

Somewhat more penetrable are the two curious, usually ignored lyrics supposedly written to gratify Gray's sometime friend Henrietta Speed's desire to "possess something from his pen on the subject of love."[7] Though that story may well be apocryphal and neither poem was published in Gray's lifetime (one appearing only in 1791, the other in 1797), both are of interest here because of their contemporaneity with the Norse and Welsh translations and their pertinence to my claim for the persistence in Gray's memory at this time of his affair with West. " 'Midst beauty and pleasure's gay triumphs," one song begins (referring presumably to his three summer weeks with Miss Speed and Lady Cobham et al. at Stoke in 1761),

> to languish
> And droop without knowing the source of my anguish;
> To start from short slumbers and look for the morning—
> Yet close my dull eyes when I see it returning;
>
> Sighs sudden and frequent, looks ever dejected,
> Sounds that steal from my tongue, by no meaning connected!

For all its insipidity, the poem's final-line address to "Delia," and the ear-marks of Gray's attempt to escape in rhyme "the company and cards at home, parties by land and water. . . , and (what they call) *doing something*," reflect at once "the sulkiness of [his] disposition" and a desire to "be alone with pleasure" (*CTG*, 693) that hints at a real, persistent "anguish" (the word "droop" in one version is "weep") as well as a revival of his perennial sense of his own "nothingness" and psychic emptiness. So too with the other song, an address to Thyrsis (only coincidentally Milton's pastoral name for himself in *Epitaphium Damonis?*) to return before the spring, and a lament that spring was already advanced in "untimely green." Is this, then, a recollection of Gray's sense of guilt, one that matched Milton's, at Diodati's death, at not attending West on his deathbed at the end of May 1742, indeed at not even knowing he had died? Though one need not insist on this connection (the advanced season, however, is "right"), these lines nevertheless do reflect a perpetuation into the sixties of what Gray himself calls, in August 1763, "the nothingness of his history"—and, as he more than once confessed throughout his career, his inability to write *anything*, least of all something openly "ingenti perculsus amore" ("under the spell of a mighty love") as Virgil had.[8]

Gray's ultimate escape, not merely from the Speed-Cobham ménage's "racketting about from morning to night" (*CTG*, 693) but from his self, was twofold. On the one hand we have from his pen a quick burst of political satire, notably *The Candidate* in 1764 (on Gray's detestation of the Duke of Newcastle's Chancellorship at Cambridge and its rancorous aftermath) and in 1768 "On L——d H——s Seat near M——e, K——t," which reflects Gray's interest, stimulated largely by Walpole, in the unscrupulous self-interest and scheming of Henry Fox.[9] Gray saved nothing of the first among his papers, and the second, which appeared in the *New Foundling Hospital of Wit* of 1769, was published without his permission (Ketton-Cremer, 204; Lonsdale, 260–61). In fact, he is said (by Walpole) "to have condemned all his satirical works,"[10] however much they might have been, in Byron's terminology, the lava of the imagination that prevents the earthquake. The other mode of "escape" was more typically Grayesque, Latin verses on and interleaved annotations to his copy of Linnaeus's three-volume *Systema Natura* (10th edition, 1758–59), a project to which Gray assiduously applied himself throughout the rest of his life.

Yet even these enterprises failed to stem Gray's melancholy, nor, more accurately, did they relieve his despair at the failure of his career. The litany of epistolary confessions of creative sterility throughout the sixties is heart-wrenching, and though it may have been exacerbated by repeated attacks of gout (about which he and Walpole, a fellow gout sufferer, exchanged detailed letters), he made no poetry of that affliction as West had of his cough. In March 1766 Gray is "in a gentle stupefaction of mind" (*CTG*, 919); in August he is "in no spirits, and perplex'd besides with many little cares" (*CTG*, 935); in January 1767 "many *desagremens* . . . surround [him]: they have not dignity enough to be called *misfortunes:* but they feel heavy on my mind" (*CTG*, 948); and, at the heart of the "litany," in February 1768 he replies to Walpole's urging him to "write more" with: "What has one to do, when *turned of fifty*, but really to think of finishing. . . . If I do not write much, it is because I cannot" (*CTG*, 1018)—because, he adds, of "a want of alacrity in indulging any distant hopes" (*CTG*, 1027; a faint recall of the "distant way" of *The Progress of Poesy?*). The "finish" is just around the corner. The two separate editions of the collected poems, Dodsley's in London and the Foulis brothers' elegant edition in Glasgow, both appeared in 1768 (both, of course, incomplete since the *Ode for Music* is a year away); Gray accepted the Regius Professorship in Modern History at Cambridge in July 1768 (hardly a crown of poetic laurel); and the idiosyncratic, self-confessedly inept *Ode for Music* was performed at the Duke of Grafton's installation as Chancellor of Cambridge University on 1 July 1769. This last would be *the* finish to a career, if not to a still passionate inner life that would terminate in a devastatingly destructive replay, with Charles-Victor de Bonstetten, of his love affair with West.

Of the Regius Professorship a detailed account is unnecessary. While I see less evidence than Ketton-Cremer does of its being a "long-standing ambition" of Gray's,[11] he did seem nearly overwhelmed by the honor, recounting the details to his aunt Mary Antrobus and to Wharton, Mason, Nicholls, and Beattie in quick succession. (Oddly no such account was sent by Gray to Walpole for over a year, even though they had been corresponding regularly up to March 1768.) Still Ketton-Cremer is correct about Gray's regarding "the professorship as [nothing] but a sinecure"—though

of course privately he may have regarded it as a proper, well-earned re-
ward for his scholarly enterprises.[12] Even Nicholls chastised him in May
1771 for claiming that his "duties" prevented him from accompanying
Nicholls to Paris to see Bonstetten: "For God's sake how can you neglect
a duty which never existed but in your own imagination, what catches
every alarm too quickly? it never yet was performed, nor I believe ex-
pected" (*CTG*, 1190). But Whibley does show conclusively that Gray actu-
ally had ambitious scholarly plans for his students: the study of geography,
languages, moneys, antiquities, law and government, manners and educa-
tion, public papers, treaties, letters of princes and ministers, memoirs,
chronicles, and monkish historians. No literature, no poetry. Although
Whibley claims that "he had an enthusiasm in imparting his knowledge
to individual pupils," Gray apparently had no pupils nor did he deliver
any lectures, and more than once his declining health, continuing funk,
and troubled conscience about his inactivity led him to contemplate even
resigning the professorship (*CTG*, 1257–59).

In short, this "escape" from his self proved largely as futile as his ex-
tended tour of the lake country in September-October 1769, even though
he wrote a detailed multiletter account of it to Wharton that extended
into 1770. Despite these efforts to do *something*, when Gray wrote an af-
fecting letter of consolation to Richard Stonehewer whose father had
just died, the last part of it reflects his own unabated guilt at being absent
when West died: "I feel for the sorrow you have felt, and yet I cannot
wish to lessen it: that would be to rob you of the best part of your nature,
to efface from your mind the tender memory of a Father's love, and de-
prive the Dead of that just and grateful tribute wch his goodness de-
manded from you" (*CTG*, 1081). The obvious contrast here between
Stonehewer's deeply felt loss and Gray's troubled relationship with, even
fear of, his own father and his consequent lack of grief at his death in 1741
surely informs this graceful tribute—but so did his own state of mind at
his mother's death in 1753, which we find him still lamenting as late as
1766.[13] Yet, at the same time, in the paragraph that follows the quotation
above he is thinking about West: "I must . . . remind you, how happy it
was for him, that you were there with him to the last; that he was sensible
perhaps of your care, when every other sense was vanishing"—a patent
reprise of the first verse paragraph of book 2 of the *De Principiis* elegy.

The dual publication of his collected poems, however, did please Gray,
especially the elegant Glasgow edition, although even amid his elation
and pride he could not forget the paucity of his "works." To James Beattie,

for example, in a not very long letter, he begs his pardon "for taking so long about it [that is, saying why he is writing]: a little more and my letter would be as big as all *my works*" (*CTG*, 983); and to Beattie again he virtually apologizes for *The Fatal Sisters, The Descent of Odin,* and *The Triumphs of Owen,* which were included, he says, because they "make up (in bulk) for the omission of that *long story*" (*CTG*, 1002–3), a reference to his poem *A Long Story,* that he repeatedly said "was never meant for the publick." He makes the same point later to Walpole: without these three poems "*my works* [would] be mistaken for the works of a flea; or a pismire," and even with them "I shall be but a shrimp of an author" (*CTG*, 1017–18). It is here that the passage on "finishing" quoted at the beginning of this chapter is written: "If I do not write much, it is because I cannot."

He did write more, if hardly much: the satires and two lyrics commented upon above, a few dutiful elegies, and finally the obligatory *Ode for Music.* If West manifestly had not been forgotten, Milton seems to have all but disappeared from Gray's mind after *The Bard.* The Norse and Welsh poems, distantly reminiscent of his Latin poetic exercises at Eton, emerge only as ersatz self-empowerment, second-handedly and ventriloquistically evoking other voices—perhaps in an effort to drown out whatever might have remained of Milton's sublimity in his creative consciousness. Part of that remainder seems fittingly relegated to his tour journal written to Wharton in 1769–70, which is punctuated by easy, comfortable, unanxious quotations from *Paradise Lost, Comus,* and even from *Samson Agonistes.* That these occur not only sparsely but after his writing of the *Ode for Music* suggests that their effortless, nonsubtextual comfortableness stems in some measure from the extraordinary exorcism of Milton's ghost that Gray performs in that ode. To that farewell to the muse, that finishing, then, I now turn.

Following the precedent of the Duke of Newcastle's installation as Chancellor of Cambridge and of Mason's ode on that occasion, a similar celebration of the Duke of Grafton's installation was held on 1 July 1769, and, given his appointment by the Duke to the Regius Professorship, Gray "thought [himself] bound in gratitude to his Grace unasked to take upon [himself] the task of writing" the installation ode, even though such verses, as he later told Beattie, would be "by nature doom'd to live but a single day." Or, if they were to live longer, it would be only in "newspaper parodies, and witless criticism" (*CTG*, 1070). The task was, he said, "the worst employment" he had ever had and he predicted wryly to Nicholls that when it was over his Parnassus would be but Skiddaw, which was inaccessible to other "mere mortals" only when it rains (*CTG*, 1057, 1061, 1066).

In light of Gray's self-deprecative chorus of and his repetitive references to the ode's dutifulness, my suggestion that it is exorcistic may well appear excessive. It has been almost eleven years since the Bard, West, and Gray himself, accompanied in some sense by Milton, all plunged into endless night, an eleven-year stretch since Thomas Gray ceased trying to be the poet he always thought he could be. And if West patently was still there gnawing at his innards and Milton's ghost really had faded mutely into oblivion, it seems but a folly to argue that the latter miraculously rematerializes in lines not in duet with Dennis in the Devil's Tavern but rather soaringly intoned in the more sublimely hallowed precincts of the senate house of Cambridge University, set to a solemn music by Charles Burney, and performed by an orchestra, chorus, and distinguished soloists under the direction of the professor of music at Cambridge "with saintly shout and solemn jubilee" and "undiscording voice." Perhaps this epiphany was prompted by Gray's assumption that the august occasion itself demanded neither Mr. Gray of *Elegy* renown nor the wild-eyed persona of his Bard but rather *something* akin to the organ tones of Milton's *At a Solemn Music*, from which I have taken the above-quoted phrases. However outrageously, but certainly audaciously, Gray thus assumes Milton's posture in the prelude to the "Hymn" proper of *On the Morning of Christ's Nativity:*

> Say, Heav'nly Muse, shall not thy sacred vein
> Afford a present to the infant God?
> Hast thou no verse, no hymn, or solemn strain,
> To welcome him to this his new abode . . .
>   (15–18)

Such an extraordinary poetic maneuver, not merely to hymn like Milton but to *be* Milton, eventuates in Gray's one shining moment in the poem, the superb eight-line "Air" in the precise measure of the Nativity Ode (lines 27–34).[14]

I set aside for the moment the fact that for all their tonal and substantive felicity those lines also reflect Gray's "gentling" of Milton's central event into a typical mid-eighteenth-century penserosoism (they constitute a virtual pastiche of portions of that poem) in order to add a subsidiary suggestion as to why Milton irresistibly self-resurrects after all those years. I advert here to my earlier contention, supported by the analyses of Gray's prior poetry, that Milton's music and words, rather than Spenser's, were always at the tip of his imagination when he took poetic pen in hand. For example, squarely in the midst of the senate house on installation day "There sit[s] . . . the bard divine," not Gray's Bard but rather he

> whom genius gave to shine
> Through every unborn age and undiscovered clime.
> Rapt in celestial transport [he],
> Yet hither oft a glance from high
> [He sends] of tender sympathy
> To bless the place, where on [his] opening soul
> First the genuine ardour stole.[15]

Oft a glance indeed, for Milton here is everywhere—though, as I shall argue in a moment, not so much as a "Divinely warbled voice" never sounded before to "[answer] the stringèd noise" of the Nativity Ode (95–97) but as a Scarronic, ventriloquized brutalizing of Milton's "deep-toned shell" and "choral warblings." Moreover, my invoking *At a Solemn Music* at the outset only reflects the fact that the nakedness of Gray's allusion to it near the end of the *Ode for Music* (lines 87–88) is but the climactic element, the *terminus ad quem*, of a series of deliberate (perhaps desperate?) Miltonic misappropriations that are subliminally insistent enough to constitute a covert, subversive subtext. Thus Gray's lines prefatory to that allusion present Granta as submitting "the fasces" of "her sway" of consular power to Grafton's "gentle hand" with the same "modest pride" (83–85) Eve evinces in yielding "with coy submission" to Adam's "Subjection" ("required" by him but "with gentle sway"—*PL* 4. 308–10). Should we ask with studied ungenerosity whether Eve's "sweet . . . amorous delay" and the Miltonic pair's unconcealed "mysterious parts" (311–12) are somehow present as well at the installation, with Satan high atop the Tree of Life ogling voyeuristically?

The ode's opening lines, of course, loudly say no: "Hence, avaunt, ('tis holy ground) / Comus and his midnight-crew"—and Gray avaunts as well Ignorance, Sloth, Sedition, Servitude, Flattery, Envy, Gain, seemingly a mixed bag of *Comus*'s "brutish" transformations of the "Th' express resemblance of the gods," the "human count'nance," now become assorted foul disfigurements that somehow threaten to profane Gray's sacred occasion. Yet, as if to remind us of his initial establishment by fiat of that "holy ground" (a phrase repeated in the first twelve lines), Gray's concluding

two lines of the poem's final recitative are not only a redaction of the
conclusion to *At a Solemn Music* but an echo, signaled by his phrase "loud
symphonious lay," of Milton's own echo of his Seraphim's blowing in the
poem's first sixteen lines "loud up-lifted Angel trumpets" and of "those
just spirits that wear victorious palms" "Singing everlastingly" (*Solemn
Music*, 11, 14, 16). Now that Grafton holds sway, not only do "men below"
stand once more "In first obedience and their state of good" (24) but
Satan's "horrors of the deep" are gilded into serene submission by the
House of Brunswick's smiling-star-empowered fiat.[16] Holy ground re-
stored, Paradise regained.

Whereas it is at least arguable that Gray regarded the occasion as de-
manding hyperbolic hallowing, his own contemptuous designation of his
poem as an "Odikle" (with that term's odd Byronic resonance)[17] may give
us some pause. The grounds for pause may seem tenuous at first blush,
but confirmation proves not long in coming, for the road to Cantabrigian
Eden redivivus is paved with a curious gold. The ode's opening allusion
to *Comus* is, in fact, a remarkable corruption of Milton's anti-masque, for
it transforms Comus's banishment of Rigor, "scrupulous" Advice, "Strict
Age," and sour "Severity" into a banishment of Gray's version of the seven
deadly sins, personal, social, political, and economic (*Ode for Music*, 3–9),
perhaps to hide Gray's own "serpent-train" of "painted Flattery" "in
flowers"—or in the "grave saws" of "Strict Age" and "scrupulous head[s]",
and appropriate "Rigor"? For Gray immediately swoops us, via the Atten-
dant Spirit's preludic lines in *Comus*, to the "realms of empyrean day"
where sit "The few whom genius gave to shine" (notably, of course, Mil-
ton) to bless Milton's own undergraduate home, now the locus of the in-
stallation (*Ode for Music*, 13–23). The Spirit's speech needs to be before us
here to appreciate what Gray is working from:

> Before the starry threshold of Jove's court
> My mansion is, where those immortal shapes
> Of bright aerial Spirits live insphered
> In regions mild of calm and serene air,
> Above the smoke and stir of this dim spot
> Which men call Earth, and with low-thoughted care,
> Confined and pestered in this pinfold here,
> Strive to keep up a frail and feverish being,
> Unmindful of the crown that Virtue gives,
> After this mortal change, to her true servants
> Amongst the enthroned gods on sainted seats.

> Yet some there be that by due steps aspire
> To lay their just hands on that golden key
> That opes the palace of Eternity.
>
> (*Comus*, 1–14)

It is well nigh impossible, given the graphic waning of Gray's career, to read this passage without seeing in it an allegory of his own aspirations and his awareness of their failure. The former are figured here as one of "those immortal shapes / Of bright aerial Spirits" enthroned on the "sainted seats" of Parnassus (or at the very least hovering at its threshold)[18] and crowned with laurel—the reward won only by those who "by due steps" and with "just hands" grasp the brass ring of immortality. The failure is confessed in the same breath: "Confined and pestered in this pinfold" earth, Gray succeeds only in keeping "up a frail and feverish being" in vain pursuit of "the crown that" poetic "virtue" proffers tantalizingly, the one Milton wears so effortlessly.

Accordingly, at the end of his first recitative Gray uncharacteristically (recall the absence of Milton's name in *The Progress*) has Milton by name sing the second air of the ode (27–34)—not *Comus*-like now nor in its Attendant Spirit's accents but, as Mason and Beattie among others noted, in the deeper tones of the Nativity Ode.[19] What is disturbing here, as I suggested earlier, is the jarring inappropriateness of *that* solemn music as a vehicle for Gray's redaction of *Il Penseroso* (what I called a "gentling"): Milton's introductory avaunting of Folly's "vain deluding Joys" and his "studious cloister's pale" whose windows cast "a dim religious light" become Gray's "cloisters dim, far from the haunts of Folly," lit by Cynthia's silver-white gleam; the "archèd walks of twilight groves, / And shadows brown that Sylvan loves" become Gray's "brown o'er-arching groves, / That Contemplation loves." And he then concludes this idyll (the air of lines 27–34) by elevating quiet, "soft-eyed melancholy" to the status of muse, one which evokes Milton's "Goddess sage and holy" whose "rapt soul" sits in her eyes—in effect thereby penserosoistically disempowering Urania, the "Heav'nly Muse" petitioned by Milton in the Nativity Ode. Melancholy, however, remains on Gray's stage no longer than a line. After an intervening recitative (35–56) on the founders of Cambridge's colleges who, though dead, now "hail their Fitzroy's festal morning come" (a Scarronic "translation" of the Nativity Ode's "happy morn" when "the son of heav'n's eternal King" delivers from above "Our great redemption"), Gray essays a second disempowerment, this time of his Melancholy Muse in

favor of the "Goddess fair and free" of *L'Allegro*, "heart-easing Mirth," thus
reversing the implicit "progress of poetry" that Milton's paired/sequential
poems suggest. Instead of *Il Penseroso*'s thrust toward pealing organ music
and full-voiced choirs "In service high and anthems clear" till "old experi-
ence do attain / To something like prophetic strain," Gray offers a radically
reductive precis of the "soft Lydian airs," notes of "linked sweetness,"
and "melting voice[s]" of *L'Allegro* (lines 133–44): "Sweet is," Gray writes,

> Sweet music's melting fall, but sweeter yet
> The still small voice of gratitude.[20]

Even such syrupy flattery Gray does not allow to remain quietly gratula-
tory, however, for that gratitude is "crie[d] aloud," in the recitative that
immediately follows, by Margaret "from her golden cloud" (line 65 ff).
The mother of Henry VII and foundress of St. John's and Christ's Col-
leges, she appears here in the bizarre guise of Milton's God who "From
midst a Golden Cloud" expresses his gratitude to Abdiel for having well
"fought / The better fight" to maintain

> Against revolted multitudes the cause
> Of truth, in word mightier than they in arms.
> (*PL* 6. 29–32)

The hyperbolic close of the *Ode for Music* now seems prepared for. Yet not
quite. Not content to liken Grafton to Milton's "servant of God," Gray in
his final recitative grotesquely transforms Cambridge itself into a personi-
fied likeness of just-created Eve as Adam describes her to Raphael:
"though divinely brought" she is

> Yet innocence and virgin modesty,
> Her virtue and the conscience of her worth,
> That would be wooed, and not unsought be won,
> Not obvious, not obtrusive, but retired,
> The more desirable . . .[21]

Also "Not obvious, not obtrusive," according to Margaret, Granta (with
Eve-like "modest pride") offers "No vulgar praise, no venal incense
flings" to welcome Grafton, but rather graces his brow with "The laureate
wreath, that Cecil wore," and like Eve submits herself to Grafton's Adamic

"Absolute rule" (*PL* 4. 301). But, as I noted initially, mixed into this strange olio of allusions is, even more oddly, Satan's first vision of Eve, who, as Milton describes her, "wore" her "unadornèd golden tresses" down to her waist, which "implied / Subjection, but required with gentle sway,"

> And by her yielded, by him best received,
> Yielded with coy submission, modest pride,
> And sweet reluctant amorous delay.
> Nor those mysterious parts were then concealed.
>   (*PL* 4. 304–12)

Grafton as Adam to Cambridge's Eve, "the loveliest pair / That ever since in love's embraces met," the assembled dignitaries (Gray's "men below") voyeuristically joining "with glad voice the loud symphonious lay"? One at least must wonder how even so sharp-eyed a critic as Coleridge could see "something very majestic in Gray's Installation Ode" as distinct from *The Bard* and the rest of his lyrics," which he thought "frigid and artificial" (quoted from *Table Talk* by Lonsdale, 267).

I have gone on here in such detail because, as Gray's final performance (so far as we know) and as surely one of his most Milton-haunted poems, the *Ode for Music* tells us more about the final state of Gray's mind with respect to Milton's vestigial presence there than it does about Grafton and the politics of Cambridge's chancellorship. More shrewdly than he knew, George Montagu, in a letter to Walpole, called the poem "Grey's [*sic*] copy of himself" (Lonsdale, 267), for in it Gray's distaste at the entire enterprise from inception to aftermath arguably underlies an apparent effort to satirize not so much the occasion or Grafton (to whom he was genuinely grateful) but rather his own hyperbolic, self-consciously inept performance. And it was, after all, an *actual,* even bravura performance, not certainly "a genuine rekindling of the fires of noble poetry," as Ketton-Cremer would have it (236). Were it indeed intentionally satiric (and Gray's respectable talent for satire at least allows that possibility), it is wonderfully appropriate that "the proceedings began in confusion, with the waiting crowds rushing the building with no regard for those with tickets, ladies losing their shoes and even their jewels, and the proctors vainly endeavouring to restore order." [22]

But if some satiric intent was in the back of Gray's mind, there is little doubt, given the wild inappropriateness of much of its allusional texture (and contexture), that Gray seized the occasion (which prompted a last, reluctant poetic effort) to radically domesticate, if not finally to exorcise, Milton's still importunate ghostly presence. "Domesticate" is no doubt imprecise, but no better term occurs to me to justify the studied subversive mélange of Miltonic allusions. Trivialization, in the *Favourite Cat* mode, is surely here as well—as is utter frustration, even anger, at himself and at Milton. And along the way also subverted is the very solemnity, dignity, and ritualistic panoply of the installation ceremony, Gray maneuvering his political flattery of Grafton (a requisite of the occasion) so as to turn it against itself. The means to this is the same garbling of Milton's grandeur, the same wildly shifting and shuffling of the Miltonic contexts from which Gray wrenches the allusions. Moreover, the confused, often conflicting analogizing of his ode's main characters with Milton's disparate cast creates an undercurrent of satanic comment not only on the event the poem celebrates but on Gray's own grudgingly performed poetic celebration.

Such celebration becomes precisely the "painted Flattery" ostensibly banished from the scene in the poem's opening air—a kind of diabolical enterprise shrewdly disguised in the lineaments of unfallen angelic brightness, or in the "flowers" of Milton's awesome sublimity, genuine passion, and consummate grace. By "flowers" I mean to recall Satan's "ambush hid among sweet flow'rs and shades" in the "consecrated bowers" (as Gray initially calls Cambridge) of Eden: "Now hid, now seen / Among thick-woven arborets and flow'rs," Satan with "his tortuous train / Curled many a wanton wreath in sight of Eve" (*PL* 9. 408, 436–37, 516–17), guilefully leading her "into fraud" with "his persuasive words, impregned / With reason, to her seeming, and with truth." [23] Indeed, Eve's initial reaction to Satan's seductive vision of her imminent deification might well have served as an epigraph to *Gray*'s guileful performance: "thy overpraising leaves in doubt / The virtue of that fruit" (615–16). No such imagining is necessary, however, to appreciate Gray's veiled assumption of Satan's role in an ostensibly Urania-empowered ode as a confident and assured (if almost manic) strategy for coming to terms with, if not once and for all laying to rest the ghost of, Milton's intimidating, and in its own way subversive, influence over Thomas Gray, poet. His legendary statement, recorded over thirty-four years after this death by the sixty-seven-year-old Norton Nicholls, "I felt myself the bard," is not, finally, the same as "I am the bard."

West's "ghost" was another matter. Whereas Milton could be laid rather rudely to rest in *Ode for Music,* to the publication of which Gray even refused to attach his name (hardly an "affectation" as Toynbee and Whibley say—*CTG,* 1068n), when Bonstetten appeared on the scene a little over a year later (December 1769), all of the conflicting, largely repressed feelings involved in Gray's intense relationship with West—not to mention his continuing guilt at not tending him at his deathbed—surged to the surface. Unpent at last, they were overwhelming and obsessive. Bonstetten was twenty-four at this time; West was twenty-six when he died. Gray's activities since *The Bard* and his short-lived career "revival" in the Norse and Welsh fiascos were almost entirely scholarly, intellectual, touristy, and gossipy. While these nonpoetic enterprises possibly were, as Jean Hagstrum suggests, "socially and personally accepted substitutes for the more dangerous passions, which may not be fully understood and are neither mastered nor suppressed" [24] (the sort of "escapes" I discussed earlier), with Bonstetten's appearance on the scene those escape hatches suddenly seemed to close. What opened were those "dark passages" Keats acutely saw Wordsworth exploring after *Tintern Abbey,* and vowed to explore himself,[25] though for Gray such darknesses were neither Wordsworthian nor Keatsian. Ketton-Cremer could not be more wrong in his overdelicate claim that Bonstetten occasioned the arousal of "emotions such as [Gray] had never experienced before" and which "filled [him] with disgust" because they "could not for one moment be contemplated by one who had been, all his life long, a strict observer of the laws of God and the laws of man" (*Thomas Gray,* 251). These emotions unquestionably *were* contemplated, compellingly, even though to what extent, or indeed whether, they were acted upon clandestinely during Bonstetten's three-month stay with Gray at Cambridge will never be known—at least not until more of the letters exchanged by the two somehow miraculously surface. The total correspondence extant consists of three letters from Gray, all written after Bonstetten returned to France, and none from Bonstetten, although Gray himself in 1770–71 mentions "many letters, which he had received from Bonstetten after he left England," and we know of several written to Gray before that departure (*CTG,* 1114 n, 1113).

Bonstetten himself was predictably circumspect in discussing his sojourn in England in his letters to his mother and in his *Souvenirs* of 1831, but in the latter he does say of Gray that "I dine every day with him, I go to his quarters at all hours, he reads with me whatever I wish, I study in his rooms." On the other hand, he tells his mother that while he informs Gray "all about [his] life," the latter "never talked to me about himself.

With Gray that was an insuperable abyss between the present and the past. When I wished to touch on it, dark clouds appeared to cover the subject." He then adds, logically and with a kind of uncanny percipience, "I believe that Gray had never been in love, which was for him an enigmatic word; the result was a sadness of heart, which contrasted with his forceful and profound imagination that, instead of being a source of happiness, proved only a torment." [26] Did they, then, or did Bonstetten, at least talk some of love, however awkwardly or tentatively, and whatever talk they had is what prompted Bonstetten to conclude that even the word, for Gray, was "enigmatic"? Possibly. But if nothing more than mere conversation eventuated, Gray did express with striking openness a good deal about the relationship to his intimate, Norton Nicholls, who was instrumental in their meeting in the first place.

Except for a short postscript that Gray added to a letter Bonstetten wrote to Nicholls on 6 January 1770 about his studies at Cambridge, Gray's first letter to Nicholls about his "affair" is on 20 March 1770. It is the only one extant that was written before his French friend returned to France. Angry with Bonstetten's "cursed F[athe]r" (who may have reminded Gray of his own) for ordering his son home by autumn of that year, Gray writes that the young man "gives me too much pleasure, and at least *an equal share* of inquietude. You do not understand him so well as I do, but I leave my meaning imperfect, till we meet" (*CTG*, 1114). Whether he did make his meaning perfect, even to Nicholls, we do not know, but if so he clearly had trouble doing it as he confesses to Nicholls less than a month later: "I thought my mysteries were but too easy to explain, however you must have a little patience, for I can hazard only word of mouth" (*CTG*, 1121). As usual, he relies on the sort of encrypting we have seen before, for example a passing quotation from Virgil's ninth eclogue in his 20 March letter to Nicholls, "sed non ego credulus illis" (but I trust them not). While the epistolary context within which the quotation occurs is not entirely clear—"I have seen (I own) with pleasure the efforts you have made to recommend me to him, *sed non ego credulus illis*, nor I fear, he neither"—what Gray seems to be saying is that Nicholls flatters Gray by deeming him the right person for Bonstetten to study with—because, as Gray oversubtly implies (at least in my judgment), like Lycidas in Virgil's dialogue, he "too, the Pierian maids have made a poet." Lycidas continues, "I, too, have songs; me also the shepherds call a bard, but I trust them not. For as yet, me thinks, I sing nothing worthy of a Varius or a Cinna, but cackle as a goose among melodious swans." Virgil's

Moeris then responds in the same vein: "Oft as a boy I recall that with song I would lay long summer days to rest. Now I have forgotten all my songs. Even voice itself now fails Moeris." [27] Would Nicholls have got the message? Maybe. In any event, if, as Moeris says just prior to this passage, "Time robs us of all, even of memory," time robbed Gray of no memory of West, nor of Milton, nor of his own failed career. Bonstetten unwittingly fueled those memories, indeed intensified them, perhaps especially because he quickly learned Milton sufficiently well during his stay to be able to quote him effortlessly in at least the few letters to Gray that we know about.

Bonstetten sailed for France on 24 March 1770, acceding to his father's demands that he "pass thru France to improve his talents and morals" before returning home, as Gray put it in his 20 March 1770 letter to Nicholls (*CTG*, 1114). At this defection Gray hurriedly and woundedly wrote to Nicholls, "*Was never such a gracious Creature born!* and yet—but no matter! burn my letter that I wrote you [of 20 March], for I am very much out of humour with myself and will not believe a word of it. you will think, I have caught madness from him (for he is certainly mad) and perhaps you will be right . . . I am destitute of all things. This place never appear'd so horrible to me, as it does now" (*CTG*, 1115–16). To Bonstetten himself, however, now safely distant from his tutor's unrestrained (and no doubt in some way expressed) desire, Gray writes on 12 April 1770: "Never did I feel, my dear Bonstetten, to what a tedious length the few short moments of our life may be extended by impatience and expectation, till you left me . . . I did not conceive till now (I own) what it was to lose you" (*CTG*, 1117–18). It might well have been written to West's ghost. But then after lessoning Bonstetten in avuncular or tutorial fashion on the character of a genius truly inclined to philosophy, essentially paraphrasing Plato's *Republic*, Gray agonistes almost compulsively silences Thomas Gray, scholar: "Show me your heart simply and without the shadow of disguise, and leave me to weep over it (as I do now) no matter whether from joy or sorrow" (*CTG*, 1119). The thought, and indeed the very language, of this plea repeats astonishingly a passage from West's letter to Gray thirty-four years earlier: "In one of these hours I hope, dear sir, you will sometimes think of me, write to me, and know me yours"—followed by West's quotation in Greek from the *Iliad*, "speak it forth, hide it not in thy mind, that we both may know it" (*CTG*, 58). The memory lingers on, as a Tin-pan Alley song put it long ago.

On 19 April 1770 we have the second (presumably unexpurgated, since

Mason had no access to it) of Gray's three extant letters to Bonstetten,[28] which includes another striking reminiscence of West, this time as he "appeared" in one of Gray's earlier letters to him. Writing from Turin in 1739, Gray says, "If I do not mistake, I saw you too every now and then at a distance among the trees; il me semble, que j'ai vu ce chien de visage la quelque part. You seemed to call to me from the other side of the precipice" (*CTG*, 128). To Bonstetten this becomes: "My life now is but a perpetual conversation with your shadow.—The known sound of your voice still rings in my ears.—There, on the corner of the fender you are standing, or tinkling on the Pianoforte, or stretch'd at length on the sofa . . . I cannot bear this place,. . . since you left me" (*CTG*, 1127). And, again echoing a West letter of long ago, Gray's final extant letter to Bonstetten includes: "It is impossible with me to dissemble with you. Such as I am, I expose my heart to your view, nor wish to conceal a single thought from your penetrating eyes" (*CTG*, 1132).

A year later, even to Nicholls (who was in Paris visiting Bonstetten) Gray ceases all mention of Bonstetten, their abortive "affair" (almost certainly one-sided) apparently too traumatic for mere words, though nonetheless indelibly inscribed in his memory. Despite Nicholls' repeated urgings, cajolings, and even semiangry responses to Gray's endless excuses for not going to France with him, Gray could not bring himself to go. Possibly his adamance was fueled by Bonstetten's having become something other than the West redivivus Gray had first imagined him to be. When Bonstetten sent his portrait, Gray petulantly regarded it as "no more like than I to Hercules: you would think, it was intended for his Father, so grave and composed: doubtless he meant to look, like an Englishman or an owl" (letter to Nicholls, *CTG*, 1157). And on 3 May 1771 he tells Nicholls of a "strange" letter from Bonstetten in which he seems "either disorder'd in his intellect . . . or has done some strange thing, that has exasperated his whole family and friends at home . . . I am quite at a loss about it" (*CTG*, 1184). As far as we know, Gray didn't write back, and he cautions Nicholls "not [to] speak of it [Bonstetten's letter] to anybody."

This strange letter is probably the one James Brown comments on to Nicholls in September 1771 after Gray's death: "I thought it might be some satisfaction to you to know that I had disposed of the Letter you mention according to your desire" (*CTG*, 1280). Why? To protect Bonstetten, safely in France, seems inconceivable. To protect Gray's reputation, as Mason assiduously had always done, is far more likely, and perhaps that concern is why Brown (in the same letter) mentions seven or eight other letters presumably from Bonstetten to Gray, possibly from Gray to Bonstetten: "Be assured they are sacred," Brown concludes. Nothing further is known of these letters, whether destroyed by Brown himself (who with Mason was joint executor of Gray's will) or sent to Nicholls for disposition. Just three days before Brown's letter Gray was buried beside his mother in the churchyard of Stoke Poges on 3 September 1771. Nothing was left; nihilissimo had triumphed at last, as the "blind Fury with th' abhorred shears, / . . . slits the thin-spun life. 'But not the praise,' / Phoebus replied and touched [the] trembling ears" of posterity (*Lycidas*, 75–76).

Such a death, of course, carried with it nothing of the Bard's defiance, although one might fantasize Gray recalling on his deathbed his first version of the Bard's final words: "Lo! to be free, to die, are mine" (Lonsdale, 200 n)—free of Miltonic oppression, of guilt about West and Bonstetten, of a failed poetic career, of a living nihil. However, before dying Gray, like his Bard, "spoke" his life and his life's work—indeed, spoke out in ways Arnold may not have fully understood had he heard; and even now few hear or understand because of those words' obscurantive cloak of sensibility. Marshall Brown recently has argued that Gray's poetic mode was the "urbane sublime," whose "chief virtue . . . is its discretion," speaking "in generalities and with indirection," never descending to particulars.[29] Needless to say, I cannot subscribe to that view as *the* view of Gray, however much it may be applicable, as Brown shows, to Thomson's *Seasons*, Collins' odes, or Young's *Night Thoughts*. For Gray, "human passions" are not "irrational demons that can be contained by preserving the native English purity and simplicity of manners"[30] but rather something like what Wordsworth calls powers (a word that for him also includes great poets) that erupt unbidden to be only partially contained by the veneer of English purity and simplicity of manners, or by a special decorum (disguise), or even by "the turnings intricate of verse."[31]

If this speaking out seems in itself insufficient to elevate Gray's place in literary history to some species of bardic, sublime, or heroic triumph, there is nevertheless a quieter heroism in his poetic efforts not merely to find his "place" in literary history but to make his own history out of a tortured, struggling self, one seemingly seduced by what Brown calls those "great enemies of genius,. . . stasis, the inertia of conventionality and popular wisdom,"[32] but valiantly resisting that seduction even as his poetic surfaces ostensibly succumb to them. For Gray's was a "dauntless breast" that withstood no "little tyrant of his fields," rather the more fearsome one of Milton's paradigm of innocence, transgression, fall, and re-

demption, all stunningly replayed in the depths of Gray's own poetic psy-
che—and in the allusive depths of his texts. This replay or, as David
Simpson recently called it with respect to Wordsworth's poetry of dis-
placement, this "recapitulation and recuperation" of the drama of *Paradise
Lost*,[33] in fact emblematizes Gray's own perception of his poetic progress.
Transcribing a subject in dire conflict, and energized alternately by tactical
efforts to displace the regnant source of poetic power and voice, and by
brave thrusts toward possession of that power which possessed him, Gray's
poetry subversively and evasively furnishes both the polarities and inter-
stices of his imagination. It is, in fact, as we have seen, a kind of speaking
in tongues whose constituent accents are those of Milton's entire cast.
More precisely, with a kind of Keatsian negative capability Gray's "little,
naked, melancholy thing," his poetic soul, in some sense becomes, indeed
is (not merely ventriloquizes through or tries out the vocalities of) God,
Messiah, Satan, Raphael, Abdiel, Michael, Adam, Eve—alternately, sever-
ally, oscillating betwixt and between but ever pushing his soul forward
through the history of cosmic *and* human fall.

That push, or thrust, however, is not so much toward redemption as
toward expulsion and the lesser sublime of unspectacular heroism figured
in Adam and Eve's descent "To the subjected plain" (*PL* 12. 64 ff).
There, we recall, the ministering Archangel "disappeared." There too
Milton fades into a kind of notation on the limits of Gray's hard-won sense
of the true power and poetic efficacy of his own brand of sensibility. At
the end of *Paradise Lost* Adam and Eve looked back and "all th' eastern
side beheld / Of Paradise," but neither "side" was ever for Gray *his* happy
seat" except in the special Miltonic terms of the Eton College Ode. Nei-
ther was "The world all before" Gray except with respect to his seeming
to "choose" his "Place of rest" in both the *Elegy* and *The Bard*.

My own word "dauntless" above I intend to resonate, as it does (per-
haps oddly) for me, with Byron's affecting "On This Day I Complete My
Thirty-Sixth Year." Though rarely noted, Byron's *Hours of Idleness* reflects
a youthful admiration for Gray that suffuses such poems of loss as the
following with a Grayesque melancholy: "On a Distant View of the Village
and School of Harrow on the Hill" (obviously modeled on the Eton Col-
lege Ode), "Childish Recollections" (replete with Quadruple-Alliance-
like pet names for school friends), "Lines Written beneath an Elm in the
Churchyard of Harrow," "The Adieu," "On Revisiting Harrow," among
others—as well as translations of Catullus, Tibullus, and his late Thyrza

poems to the young chorister Edward Edleston. From "On This Day" are these lines:

> Yet, though I cannot be beloved,
>   Still let me love!
>
> My days are in the yellow leaf;
>   The flowers and fruits of love are gone;
> The worm, the canker, and the grief
>   Are mine alone!
>
> The fire that on my bosom preys
>   Is lone as some volcanic isle;
> No torch is kindled at its blaze—
>   A funeral pile.
>   . . . .
> If thou regret'st thy youth, *why live?*
>   The land of honourable death
> Is here . . .
>   . . . .
> Then look around, and choose thy ground,
>   And take thy rest.

The heroic tonality of "choose thy ground" should not be lost on any sensitive reader of Gray's poetry.

Yet Gray's psychic recuperation of Milton's drama enables him to *choose* as well that other "subjected plain" with which he had earlier figured the stream of music's, and the Muses', descent from Parnassus, "the Latian plains" in *The Progress of Poesy*. Thereon, "with wand'ring steps and slow," and hand in hand with Adam and Eve, bloody but remarkably unbowed, Gray took his "solitary way" *out* of *Paradise Lost*. As Adam says, after Michael's historical dissertation is over,

> Greatly instructed I shall hence depart,
> Greatly in peace of thought, and have my fill
> Of . . . what this vessel can contain;
> Beyond which was my folly to aspire.
>   (*PL* 12. 557–60)

Finally, he was himself, his own subjectivity—mayhap "by small / Accomplishing great things" (*PL* 12. 566–67).

I see Gray finally, then, as of his age yet not of his age, often (and increasingly) as retrospective and recollective as Wordsworth but without his great successor's triggering moments of tranquillity; his "subjected plain" to which Adam and Eve were led at the end of *Paradise Lost,* was the human heart that Keats recognized as Wordsworth's central concern; and his past prefigured the past-haunted Byron of *Hours of Idleness.* If Gray did not play out in his poetry the history of his age as Byron did, he did play out, like Byron, his inner conflictual personal life—its love and death and guilt and fear and despair and, above all, its joy "whose hand is ever at his lips bidding adieu." Although Hartman may be correct in assessing Gray's "boldest poems" as finally evincing "a reluctance to rouse the English lyre from its torpor," I must dissent from his judgment that "Gray refuses to engage in a reversal of the destiny of poetry in the Enlightenment." [34] Failing in a "reversal" of a *destiny* seems an oversevere charge to levy against any poet. Even that archiconoclast William Blake "reversed" little in his nevertheless extraordinary debut in *Poetical Sketches* twelve years after Gray's death. Somewhere behind Hartman's, and most Gray critics', sense of Gray's failure to revolutionize Augustan poetry is the inordinate fame of the *Elegy,* whose proverbial lapidary form gives to sentiments, in Johnson's phrase, what every reader "persuades himself that he has always felt." But, more broadly, Gray has been charged with depersonalizing his reminiscences and reflections, which "occur mainly in general propositions" that are "sometimes expressed as *sententiae*" but more often than not, "in the standard artifice of the contemporary ode, are converted into the tableau-and-allegory form that Coleridge derogated as . . . 'translations of prose thoughts into poetic language.' " [35] Or, it is argued, whenever emotional strength is apparent in his poems, it is so combined and expressed with " 'classical' and un-Wordsworthian detachment" that the subject, scene, or emotion is said to become an unmergeable "other." [36] But if one attends to the double, intersecting personal agons I have traced throughout this study, albeit carefully shrouded in the above-charged accoutrements, what emerges in the poetry, as well as in Gray's life, is far more powerful and moving than the pleasing melancholy of the eighteenth-century sensibility tradition—certainly something akin to and prefigurative of what M. H. Abrams describes as the greater Romantic ode's often "profound sadness, sometimes bordering on the anguish of terror and despair, at the sense of loss, dereliction, isolation, or inner death . . . inherent in the speaker's existence." [37] Of few, if any, of Gray's compeers can this be said except perhaps for a poem here and there.

To return, then, to Hartman's judgment, I venture to claim that Gray's poetry *is* the destiny not of Enlightenment but rather of post-Enlightenment, post-Miltonic poetry on its "distant way" toward the revisionist Miltonic poetry of Wordsworth and Keats (and to some extent Shelley) and their exploration of the dark passages of the psyche and the soul. In that sense Gray is *the* poet of *his* mid- to late-century age, in Bertrand Bronson's words an age "discontented, restless, uncommitted, unwilling to stay [Augustan], yet undetermined to go," an age whose opposing tensions give it a "waywardness, an unpredictability, that are continually engaging one's surprised attention." [38] While I would quarrel here with "undetermined to go" (Gray's determination *was* to go but he knew not quite where), there have been far less attractive denominating adjectives applied to this age, which with some trepidation I offer as the Age of Gray, fully worthy of rubbing shoulders with the less forward-looking but more famous, and critically more acceptable, Age of Johnson or Age of Sensibility.

Notes

Chapter 1　Introduction

1. Wallace Jackson, "Thomas Gray: Drowning in Human Voices," *Criticism* 28 (1986): 361–77; "Thomas Gray and the Dedicatory Muse," *ELH* 54 (1987): 277–98; with Paul Yoder, "Wordsworth Reimagines Thomas Gray: Notations on Begetting a Kindred Spirit," *Criticism* 31 (1989): 287–300. Three even more ambitious reopenings postdate these essays: Henry Weinfield's *The Poet without a Name: Gray's "Elegy" and the Problem of History* (Carbondale: Southern Illinois University Press, 1991), Suvir Kaul's *Thomas Gray and Literary Authority: A Study of Ideology and Poetics* (Stanford: Stanford University Press, 1992), and *Thomas Gray: Contemporary Essays*, ed. W. B. Hutchings and William Ruddick (Liverpool: Liverpool University Press, 1993). While I shall refer especially to the first two of these in the following pages, here it is useful to mention that Kaul chastises Jackson for what is called his refusal "to consider any but an 'utterly and completely personal' account of Gray's impasse," thus returning us "once more to a critical model of the man who suffers (desire) and the poetic imagination that closes in upon itself" (247). I have a similar quarrel with Jackson's approach, but my own shares something of his perspective even as it also shares something of Kaul's claim that the "formal and thematic elements" of Gray's poetry exist "in a (largely agonistic) counterpoint with precursory and contemporary discursive practices" (4). My view of that agon, however, is at once narrower (Milton as the dominant precursor rather than, or perhaps in addition to, these "practices") and based on deeper excavation into Gray's career and life. Quotations from Kaul's book will hereafter be noted parenthetically.

2. Northrop Frye, "Towards Defining an Age of Sensibility," *ELH* 23 (1956): 144–52.

3. John Sitter, *Literary Loneliness in Mid-Eighteenth-Century England* (Ithaca: Cornell University Press, 1982), 77; Marshall Brown, *Preromanticism* (Stanford: Stanford University Press, 1991). The Cassirer quotation I have also taken from Sitter, whose view of Gray and history is sharply countered by Weinfield's book cited in note 1 above, although "history" there is massively marshaled mainly to elucidate every jot and tittle of the *Elegy*.

4. Northrop Frye, Plenary Address at 1989 meeting of ASECS in New Orleans, published in *Eighteenth-Century Studies* 24 (1990–91): 173–95.

5. Jackson, "Dedicatory Muse," 277. Kaul refuses the word *failure* in favor of

disappointments (247). For a different argument as to the reasons for that failure (which yet fails finally to "explain" it), see Linda Zionkowski, "Bridging the Gulf Between: The Poet and the Audience in the Work of Gray," *ELH* 58 (1991): 331–50.

6. Lord David Cecil, "The Poetry of Thomas Gray," *Proceedings of the British Academy* 31 (1945): 43–60; F. Doherty, "The Two Voices of Gray," *Essays in Criticism* 13 (1963): 222–30; Patricia Spacks, "Statement and Artifice in Thomas Gray," *SEL* 5 (1965): 519–32; Roger Lonsdale, "The Poetry of Thomas Gray: Versions of the Self," *Proceedings of the British Academy* 59 (1973): 105–23; Leon Guilhamet, *The Sincere Ideal: Studies in Sincerity in Eighteenth-Century English Literature* (Montreal: McGill-Queen's University Press, 1974); Paul Fry, *The Poet's Calling in the English Ode* (New Haven: Yale University Press, 1980).

7. See note 1 to this chapter.

8. Jackson, "Dedicatory Muse," 284, 285.

9. Paul S. Sherwin, *Precious Bane: Collins and the Miltonic Legacy* (Austin: University of Texas Press, 1977).

10. My emphasis. The incidence in the *Elegy* of the word *some* is in itself reflective of Gray's sense of his own poetic achievement's inadequacy, even in the *Elegy* itself, when measured against his hopes or ambitions. For more on this, see my discussion of that poem later on. In addition to the "some" phrases quoted, there are also "some heart" (line 46), "some village-Hampden" (57), the pivotal "Some mute inglorious Milton" (59), "Some Cromwell" (60), "Some frail memorial" (78), "Some pious drops" (90). On the presence of *Lycidas* in the *Elegy* see John Guillory's superb recent analysis, which in my judgment goes far beyond any prior effort at contextualizing the entire poem. *Cultural Capital: The Problem of Literary Canon Formation* (Chicago: University of Chicago Press, 1993).

11. The Spenser comment is cited in Roger Lonsdale, ed., *The Poems of Thomas Gray, William Collins, Oliver Goldsmith* (New York: Longman, 1969), xvii; hereafter cited parenthetically in my text as Lonsdale. Gray's comment on Milton's ear is in his *Common-Place Book*, 2: 757–59.

12. But see Guillory's *Cultural Capital*, 87 ff, for the substantial role Gray's commonplace book had as the "matrix of compositional practice," particularly with respect to the *Elegy*.

13. Bruce Redford, in *The Converse of the Pen: Acts of Intimacy in the Eighteenth-Century Familiar Letter* (Chicago: University of Chicago Press, 1986), calls this felicitously "the distorting resonance of an echo chamber" (98). While his point is about Gray's letters, it is equally applicable to the poetry, where the reader is presented with something more formidable than an "embarrassment of choice"; there one finds a studied obliquity and imaginative verbal contortionism.

14. The most notable exception to this critical consensus is Kaul's *Thomas Gray and Literary Authority*, though his emphasis is less on diction and phrasings than on precursory discursive practices as well as "socio-cultural formations"—in short on generic poetic representations and canonical methods that Gray's poet-figures "ventriloquize" as "contestatory responses to changing literary practices" (247, 74–75). See also Guillory, *Cultural Capital*, passim.

15. *The Correspondence of Thomas Gray*, ed. Paget Toynbee and Leonard Whibley,

with additions and corrections by H. W. Starr, 3 vols. (Oxford: Clarendon Press, 1971), 1:251. Subsequent references, in my text and notes, will be to *CTG* plus the page number (the three volumes are paginated consecutively).

16. Lonsdale notes most but not all of these, and adds many other echoes, analogs, and parallels, the great bulk of which are commonplace locutions deriving ultimately from Horace, Anacreon, Ovid, Lucretius, Virgil, Propertius et al. and employed widely from Dryden through a host of early-eighteenth-century poets.

17. Whalley, "Thomas Gray: A Quiet Hellenist," in *Fearful Joy*, ed. James Downey and Ben Jones (Montreal: McGill-Queen's University Press, 1974), 164; Eric Rothstein, *Restoration and Eighteenth-Century Poetry 1660–1780* (Boston: Routledge & Kegan Paul, 1981), 98. On this point see also note 23 below, and Kaul's entire argument in *Thomas Gray and Literary Authority*, which takes severe issue with such "helpless" conclusions and dutiful apologia.

18. Actually the death penalty for homosexuality in England goes back to 1533, though executions were rare before the late seventeenth and early eighteenth centuries, when according to Louis Crompton, "the law appears to have been seriously enforced." *Byron and Greek Love* (Berkeley: University of California Press, 1985), 15. George S. Rousseau goes even further in saying that the 1740s were particularly "crucial in England for the perception that sodomy was spreading rapidly." "The Pursuit of Homosexuality in the Eighteenth Century: 'Utterly Confused Category' and/or Rich Repository," in *"Tis Nature's Fault": Unauthorized Sexuality during the Enlightenment*, ed. Robert P. Maccubbin (Cambridge: Cambridge University Press, 1985), 151. See also in that volume Randolph Trumbach's "Sodomitical Subcultures, Sodomitical Roles, and the Gender Revolution of the Eighteenth Century." These facts about Gray's sociolegal milieu and his commonly acknowledged aspiration to Miltonic poetic achievement seem to me to call into question Kaul's argument that to focus on the individuality of Gray's psyche or inner life "is to misunderstand the construction of the (speaking) figures in Gray's poems" (67).

19. Sherwin, *Precious Bane*, 101. Sherwin's argument that Collins refused, or was unable, to "venture beyond pastoral innocence, the domain of Evening," and that therefore Milton became for him only a "benign presence from which he is able to draw inspiration" (123, 102), would place Collins in even sharper contrast to Gray than I would suggest. Though he was substantially different from the Gray I shall paint, I would not portray Collins as, at his best, "remarkably unassertive, not eager for a punctual revelation, content to announce a presence whose meaning does not need to be interpreted" (Sherwin, 113). Sherwin's point is oddly reminiscent of Arnold's famous judgment of Gray as one who "had almost spoken out, had almost opened his soul and delivered himself to things too deep for tears," but less oddly reminiscent of Geoffrey Hartman's view of Gray's "early style" as avoiding "the prophetic, the speaking out." Only the Norse poems, for Hartman, do that. The Arnold reference is quoted from Ian Jack, "Gray in His Letters," in Downey and Jones, *Fearful Joy*, 39; the Hartman quote is from his "Blake and the Progress of Poesy," in *Beyond Formalism* (New Haven: Yale University Press, 1970), 313—his comments on Collins constituting, in my judgment, the seeds of Sherwin's entire thesis.

20. Richard Wendorf, *William Collins and Eighteenth-Century English Poetry* (Minneapolis: University of Minnesota Press, 1981), 183–84.

21. I adopt Sherwin's phrase despite Wendorf's proper questioning of precisely what Sherwin means by it, because I do mean by "personal" personal—not Gray's "character apart from his work," not certainly his "literary character" or "broadly conceived intellectual portrait." Rather I essay precisely what Wendorf (whose phrases I employ here) says is not possible for Collins: "a more convincing portrait" of the whole-man-poet Gray, one that if not exactly "reconcil[ing] the man of flesh and blood with the character of his work" will allow us to see that whole-man-poet *in* the poems *and* in the letters in ways that we have had but glimpses of before.

22. See, e.g., Brian Fothergill, *Beckford of Fonthill* (London: Faber & Faber, 1979), and Haggerty's "Literature and Homosexuality in the Late Eighteenth Century: Walpole, Beckford, and Lewis," *Studies in the Novel* 18 (1986): 341–52. The Haggerty quotations in my text are from an unpublished paper. By far the best essay on this aspect of Gray is Jean Hagstrum's "Gray's Sensibility," in Downey and Jones, *Fearful Joy*, 6–19. It is worth noting that even as recently as twenty-five years ago Peter Watson-Smyth's "On Gray's Elegy" (*The Spectator*, 31 July 1971) stirred up a hornet's nest of outraged responses throughout the rest of the year because he dared to say, "As Gray was, like Walpole, particularly devoted to his mother, it will surprise no psychiatrist that such a background produced a homosexual whose first and greatest love, I believe, was Horace Walpole" (166). Later on I shall challenge Watson-Smyth's claim about the Gray-Walpole relationship, and "first and greatest" is surely in error. In fact, Eve Kosofsky Sedgwick, in her highly acclaimed *Between Men: English Literature and Male Homosocial Desire* (New York: Columbia University Press, 1985), describes Walpole as only "iffily . . . in some significant sense" a homosexual, though she regards Beckford as one for sure, Monk Lewis probably. She doesn't mention Gray.

23. The spur to this fissuring may well have been Jean Hagstrum's "Gray's Sensibility" (Downey and Jones, *Fearful Joy*), but I add as well Paul Fry's *The Poet's Calling in the English Ode* and Joshua Scodel's *The English Poetic Epitaph: Commemoration and Conflict from Jonson to Wordsworth* (Ithaca: Cornell University Press, 1991). In *Thomas Gray and Literary Authority*, Kaul in effect makes a critical/poetic virtue out of Gray's "artifice," which nevertheless, along with his "special decorum," persists as a critical term in otherwise shrewd readings of the poetry. Pat Rogers, for example, writes (in an acute brief commentary), "Gray was seldom able to find the right public occasion to express his deep private emotions. It is as though he had to satisfy the confessional urges of a Rousseau within the bland social register of a Prior." *The Augustan Vision* (London: Weidenfeld & Nicolson, 1974), 140. See also Richard Feingold's argument that the *Elegy* demonstrates how "inward experience . . . can have no standing until it is translated into a heard language whose very good manners would give to the inward the grace and the status of the social." *Moralized Song: The Character of Augustan Lyricism* (New Brunswick: Rutgers University Press, 1989), 10–11.

24. The closest we have come to answering such questions seems to me Hagstrum's conjecture that "Gray's intellectual interests are socially and personally ac-

cepted substitutes for the more dangerous passions, which may not be fully understood and are neither mastered nor suppressed" ("Gray's Sensibility," 8). In fact Hagstrum may be echoing here Edmund Gosse's early aperçu about Gray's "habit of drowning consciousness in perpetual study. . . , an excess of reading" that suggests his "treating the acquisition of knowledge as a narcotic." Edmund Gosse, *Gray* (London, 1882), 67. On the other hand, one should consult as well the more conventional, eminently sensible argument for such abundant allusions and echoes advanced by Eric Rothstein in chapter 3 of his *Restoration and Eighteenth-Century Poetry, 1660–1780*, as well as Kaul's argument in *Thomas Gray and Literary Authority* for Gray's deliberate ventriloquizing of precursor discourses in order to contest them.

25. Cf. Rothstein's distinction between "real" allusions in Gray, however we determine them (only via Gray's acknowledgments perhaps?), and those that are merely "a welcome presence with a faint charge of *déjà-vu*" (*Restoration and Eighteenth-Century Poetry*, 108). Redford more sharply characterizes the opposition as forcing the reader (and especially the allusion hunter) to run the risk of "the embarrassment of choice and . . . distorting resonances" (*The Converse of the Pen*, 98).

26. Louis Crompton, *Byron and Greek Love*, passim. The quotation that follows is from p. 66. See also Bruce R. Smith's *Homosexual Desire in Shakespeare's England* (Chicago: University of Chicago Press, 1991), in which he explores the "imaginative vocabulary" that sixteenth- and seventeenth-century writers employed "for talking about homosexual desire" (19).

27. See note 18 above.

28. Ibid., 138–42.

29. T. A. J. Burnett, *The Rise and Fall of a Regency Dandy: The Life and Times of Scrope Berdmore Davies* (London: John Murray, 1981), 13–14.

30. *CTG*, 1 n. The quotation is from Mason's *Memoirs*, p. 16 n. I shall have more to say about Mason's editing later on. Toynbee and Whibley print the only Eton letter, which first appeared in 1915 in Toynbee's two-volume *The Correspondence of Gray, Walpole, West, and Ashton*. It is one of thirty-eight extant letters from Gray to Walpole written between 1734 and 1739, of which Mason printed but one and fragments of five others (*CTG*, 1 n). Mason indeed promises his "reader that he shall, in the following pages [of the *Memoirs*], seldom behold Mr. Gray in any light than that of a Scholar and Poet" (*CTG*, xiv).

31. Royston Lambert, *The Hothouse Society: An Exploration of Boarding-school Life through the Boys' and Girls' Own Writings* (London: Weidenfeld & Nicolson, 1968), 339. A more modern version of this, eerily relatable to Gray's "affair" with West, appears in Simon Gray's autobiographical *An Unnatural Pursuit:* "While in the History Sixth [at Westminster] I had a passionate friendship, which never became quite an affair, with a more clever and daring boy who was frequently and romantically ill (he died at Oxford in his early twenties) and I dramatically renounced all games and corps, in order to devote myself fully to an intellectual life that was all the more shapely in form and epigrammatic in expression for being barren of content." Quoted from John Clum, "'Being Took Queer': Homosexuality in Simon Gray's Plays," in *Simon Gray: A Casebook*, ed. Katherine H. Burkman (New York: Garland, 1992).

32. Raymond Flower, *Oundle and the English Public School* (London: Stacey International, 1989), 230.

33. Rousseau, "The Pursuit of Homosexuality," 156; Sedgwick, *Between Men*, 92–93.

34. Arthur C. Benson, *Fasti Etonensis* (London: Simpkin Marshall, 1899), 147. Benson is quoting Judge Hardinge.

35. Anna de Koven, *Horace Walpole and Madame du Deffand* (New York: Appleton, 1929), 126; Martin Kallich, *Horace Walpole* (New York: Twayne, 1971), 27–28.

36. On the relationship between homosexuality and homophobia and gothic romance see, especially, Sedgwick's *Between Men* and George Haggerty's "Literature and Homosexuality in the Late Eighteenth Century: Walpole, Beckford, and Lewis" (see note 22 above).

37. Rousseau, "The Pursuit of Homosexuality," 136; Hagstrum, "Gray's Sensibility," 13, 11 respectively.

38. George Haggerty, unpublished essay, " 'The Voice of Nature' in Gray's *Elegy*," 2 (my italics).

39. Rousseau, "The Pursuit of Homosexuality," 144. While I have not included Norton Nicholls among the main characters in Gray's agon, Gray's later-life intimacy with Nicholls (they met when the latter was about eighteen, Gray about forty-three) is at least worth noting briefly, especially since it was Nicholls who introduced Bonstetten to Gray in December 1769. But we also know that Nicholls' father deserted his wife soon after their marriage, that (in T. J. Mathias's words) Nicholls had a "reverential attachment to his mother . . . singularly affectionate, unremitting and unvaried," and that "with the single exception of . . . Richard West, Mr. Gray was more affectionately attached to [Nicholls] than to any other person." Thomas J. Mathias, *The Works of Gray*, 2 vols. (London: Shakespeare Press, 1814), 1:524, 518). On the other hand, I find no evidence at all in their substantial correspondence of anything beyond friendship or what Rousseau neologizes as homoplatonism.

40. Alan Bray, *Homosexuality in Renaissance England* (London: Gay Men's Press, 1982), 98.

41. William Epstein, "Assumed Identities: Gray's Correspondence and the 'Intelligence Communities' of Eighteenth-Century Studies," *The Eighteenth Century: Theory and Interpretation* 32 (1991): 279.

42. Ibid., 279, 276, 286 n. More recently Linda Zionkowski argues that the Quadruple Alliance was primarily a "nurturing literary community" in which "literary and affective relationships [were] fostered and cemented by their circulation of texts," which she regards as evidence of a kind of literary effeminacy at a time when "the commercial market in texts . . . led to a redefinition of the poet's status in English culture, a status expressed in terms of a new concept of masculine conduct." "Gray, the Marketplace, and the Masculine Poet," *Criticism* 35 (1993): 596, 590.

43. Robert Wyndham Ketton-Cremer, *Thomas Gray: A Biography* (Cambridge: Cambridge University Press, 1955), 5–6. Further references to this standard biography will be given parenthetically in the text. The Quadruple Alliance coined other names for other friends (e.g., Tydus, Plato, Prato, Puffendorf), and Walpole, espe-

cially, had a number of friends outside the "secret" Alliance—even though he confessed (as did his close friends) that he "was never quite a schoolboy" in the conventional Etonian sense (Ketton-Cremer, 6–7). On the basis of a single anonymous pamphlet of 1767 Linda Zionkowski (see note 42 above) extravagantly claims that Gray "was ridiculed [in England] as a 'butterfly' who was too feminine to accept the rigors of life at Cambridge" (590).

44. Ketton-Cremer, *Thomas Gray,* 12.

45. The quoted phrase is from Robert Lance Snyder's "The Epistolary Melancholy of Thomas Gray," *Biography* 2 (1979): 125.

46. Roger Martin, *Essai sur Thomas Gray* (London: Oxford University Press, 1935), 8–19.

47. Ketton-Cremer, 3, 7. Cf. Walter Ong's judgment that "male bonding groups are associations of lovers" in which "each assures himself that everybody is a friend though at the same time is on his own and keeping everybody else at arm's length—an admiring arm's length, in a kind of diffuse communal narcissism." *Fighting for Life: Contest, Sexuality, and Consciousness* (Ithaca: Cornell University Press, 1981), 81.

48. Snyder, "Epistolary Melancholy," 125–26, 132.

49. Ibid., 126; Hagstrum, "Gray's Sensibility," in Downey and Jones, eds., *Fearful Joy.*

50. James Olney, *Metaphors of Self: The Meaning of Autobiography* (Princeton: Princeton University Press, 1972), 43.

51. Brown, *Preromanticism.*

52. Paul de Man, "Autobiography as De-Facement," in *The Rhetoric of Romanticism* (New York: Columbia University Press, 1984), 69. References in the rest of my paragraph to this essay (originally published in *Modern Language Notes* in 1979) will be by page number in *The Rhetoric.*

53. De Man's point about prosopopeia is that it is *the* "trope of autobiography, by which one's name . . . is made as intelligible and memorable as a face" (76).

54. Smith, *Homosexual Desire in Shakespeare's England,* 16–17, 104. On Latin as code-language, Smith cites especially Virgil (most notably the second eclogue) and Horace, both of whose poems, as we shall see, are an integral part of the encodings buried in the Gray-West correspondence. Gagnon and Simon's terms are developed in their "Sexual Scripts," *Society* 22 (1984): 53–60.

Chapter 2   The Miltonic Background

1. My last phrase echoes one by Cowper in a late-century letter that I have been unable to track down again. It reads, in part, "The consciousness that there is much to do, and nothing done, is a burthen, I am not able to bear. Milton especially is my grievance; and I might almost as well be haunted by his ghost, as goaded with continual reproaches for neglecting him." Presumably the letter (to Hayley?) has to do with their collaborative four-volume *Milton's Life and Poetical Works* ("with Notes by William Cowper"), ed. Hayley (Chichester, 1810).

2. I center my point on these two figures rather than the larger company of critics who brewed what has come to be called "the Milton controversy," since the

sniping by poets at Milton reflected their sense of his uselessness to their kind of poetry or the poetry they wished to write rather than as ex cathedra pronouncements about literary-historical hierarchies. Some of these latter, of course, emanated from Middleton Murry, Herbert Read, F. R. Leavis (perhaps preeminently), and later A. J. A. Waldock, all of whom aimed at lowering Milton's two-century reign on the English Parnassus. For a brief account of the controversy and its critical bases (and biases) see Bernard Bergonzi, "Criticism and the Milton Controversy," in *The Living Milton*, ed. Frank Kermode (London: Routledge & Kegan Paul, 1960), 162–80.

3. While I have learned from him, I also have some differences with Harold Bloom's *Anxiety of Influence* (Oxford: Oxford University Press, 1973). Both will, I trust, be apparent. Here I take issue only with his pronouncement that Wordsworth was the first great post-Miltonic "revisionist" (33)—though Bloom's own word "great" here does its own historical fudging. Hartman's almost identical position is that, after the mid-eighteenth-century "tension between the high Miltonic mode and the vernacular," Wordsworth's "simple produce of the common day" (in which "the spirit is sufficed, the need for fictions dispelled, the burden of the mystery lifted") constitutes a "Wordsworthian Enlightenment," and "unghostly poetry . . . born" in "true vernacular, 'words that speak of nothing more than what we are.' " "Blake and the Progress of Poetry," in *Beyond Formalism* (New Haven: Yale University Press, 1970), 319, 329. The general point is unexceptionable, but I'm afraid I don't read Wordsworth Hartman's way; his poetry is suffused with Miltonic debts and revisionary, even contentious, allusions. Nor can I fit Gray neatly into this critical-historical paradigm, a fitting that would implicitly argue that Gray was some sort of precursor of Wordsworth (or the Romantics generally). Lucy Newlyn, a Bloom disciple, has recently claimed, for example, that somewhat like Gray, the Romantics were "excited by the extent to which Milton . . . seems prepared to transgress moral boundaries." *Paradise Lost and the Romantic Reader* (Oxford: Clarendon Press, 1993), 84–85.

4. Much of "Miltonic" eighteenth-century poetry offers itself as *prima facie* evidence supporting such a generalization, but Raymond D. Havens' monumental survey of *The Influence of Milton on English Poetry* (Cambridge: Harvard University Press, 1922), goes further to define that influence as one of "style, diction, prosody, and subject-matter" (68). "Subject-matter," however, he construed narrowly and vaguely as "epic," "philosophical," or "religious," thus reinforcing his conviction that style, diction, and prosody constitute virtually the whole case for "influence." Havens' list of "The Characteristics of *Paradise Lost* and Their Relation to Eighteenth-Century Blank Verse" particularizes these as "Dignity, Reserve, and Stateliness," the "Organ Tone," "Inversion of the Natural Order of Words and Phrases," the "Omission of Words not Necessary to the Sense," "Parentheses and Apposition," the "Use of one Part of Speech for Another," "Vocabulary," a "Considerable Number of Proper Names" in comparative short passages, and "Unusual Compound Epithets" (80–85). Cf. Walter Raleigh's earlier argument that eighteenth-century poetic diction is in large measure due to "the plastering of a Miltonic manner over themes with which it had no proper correspondence"—precisely the opposite, oddly enough, of Dryden's enterprise in *The State of Innocence*. The lan-

guage here is Edward Dowden's redaction of Raleigh's in "Milton in the Eighteenth Century (1701–1750)," *Proceedings of the British Academy* (London: 1907–1908), 3:281.

5. Thomas Greene, *The Descent from Heaven: A Study in Epic Continuity* (New Haven: Yale University Press, 1963), 3.

6. Edward N. Hooker, ed., *The Critical Works of John Dennis* (Baltimore: Johns Hopkins University Press, 1939), 512. The phrases quoted are Hooker's cullings from a variety of Dennis's works. In 1734 Jonathan Richardson raised the encomia ante even further: *Paradise Lost* should be treated "like the revealed Word of God." From *Explanatory Notes and Remarks on Milton's "Paradise Lost,"* quoted in Leslie E. Moore, *Beautiful Sublime: The Making of "Paradise Lost," 1701–1734* (Stanford: Stanford University Press, 1990), 158.

7. Havens, *The Influence of Milton*, 93.

8. Only Dryden exceeds Milton in frequency of reference and numbers of his lines quoted, the vast majority of these being from his translations of Virgil.

9. John Shawcross, *Milton 1732–1801: The Critical Heritage* (London: Routledge & Kegan Paul, 1972), 2.

10 Ibid., 30. The quotation is from Cibber's *The Lives of the Poets* (London, 1753), 2:108.

11. Arthur Johnston, "Poetry and Criticism after 1740," in *Dryden to Johnson*, ed. Roger Lonsdale (London: Sphere Books, 1971), 368.

12. Roger Lonsdale, "Gray and 'Allusion': The Poet as Debtor," in *Studies in the Eighteenth Century IV*, ed. R. F. Brissenden and J. C. Eade (Canberra: Australian National University Press, 1979), 32.

13. Andrew Marvell, *The Rehearsal Transpos'd: The Second Part* (London, 1674), excerpted by Shawcross in *Milton: The Critical Heritage* (New York: Barnes & Noble, 1970), 80. A useful recent summary of this view, which frequently included the idea that Milton's blindness was God's punishment for his political transgressions, is in Moore's *Beautiful Sublime: The Making of "Paradise Lost,"* 168 ff.

14. Davies' poem appeared in *A Collection of Original Poems and Translations* (London, 1745), 182–86. Its final phrase is tantalizingly anticipative of Gray's "blasted with excess of light" in *The Progress of Poesy*, and it is at least possible that Gray knew Davies personally. They are almost exact contemporaries (Davies' dates are 1709–69); Davies was on the foundation at Eton and afterwards was a scholar and fellow at Cambridge (King's College); and he probably knew Walpole since his publisher was John Whaley, also of King's and a sometime tutor of Walpole. Moreover, Davies was widely known to be homosexual, as George Hardinge's account of him not always delicately shows—in John Nichols' *Illustrations of the Literary History of the Eighteenth Century* (London, 1817), vol. 1. See especially pp. 510–11, 672–75, though the entire "biographical memoir" occupies pp. 481–709.

15. These passages are in Shawcross, *Milton, 1732–1801*, 97, 241.

16. This is a particularly striking anticipation of Hazlitt's analysis of Satan in *Lectures on the English Poets*, which reads in part: "His ambition was the greatest, and his punishment was the greatest; but not so his despair, for his fortitude was as great as his sufferings.. . . . The vastness of his designs did not surpass the firm,

inflexible determination with which he submitted to his irreversible doom" (121–22). The Webb quotation is from Shawcross, *Milton*, 256.

17. Shawcross, *Milton*, 307–60.

18. William Hayley, "An Essay on Epic Poetry" (1782), ibid., 314.

19. I am quoting Leslie E. Moore's redaction of Richardson's position, in *Beautiful Sublime: The Making of Paradise, 1701–1734*, 159. She goes on to argue that Richardson's biography of Milton "clearly displays the biographer's fear that a 'sublime Milton,' brilliant and isolated, may be aligned with the Satan of the 'Tow'r' simile" in 1.590–91 (172; see also 177). In *The Prophetic Milton* (Charlottesville: University of Virginia Press, 1974) William Kerrigan makes the same point this way: "The epic is offered as another Testament. Writing with the divine inspiration higher than 'those Hebrews of old,' Milton assumes divine authority for every word, every event in *Paradise Lost* that does not appear in Scripture" (264). See also Lucy Newlyn's *"Paradise Lost" and the Romantic Reader*, 224–30, in which she cites Gray (along with Collins) only briefly, concluding conventionally that Gray's "need is to define an Augustan tradition to which he can comfortably and modestly belong."

20. William B. Hunter argues that this reference to Christ at Siloa as "healer of maimed and impaired human nature" constitutes a "veiling [of] Milton's personal prayer for amelioration of his own blindness." *The Descent of Urania* (Lewisburg: Bucknell University Press, 1989), 33.

21. As fine a scholar as Gray was, he may also have been aware, as Walter Schindler argues Milton was, "of the long tradition that held that invocations themselves were 'evidence of arrogance and presumption'—a view held by Castelvetro" among others. *Voice and Crisis: Invocations in Milton's Poetry* (Hamden, Conn.: Archon Books, 1984), 47. In this regard see also Jonathan Culler's broader discussion of apostrophe in *The Pursuit of Signs* (Ithaca: Cornell University Press, 1981), 146 ff.

22. Hunter, among others, reminds us also of Matthew 3:16: "And Jesus, when he was baptized, went up straightway out of the water: and lo, the heavens were opened unto him, and he saw the Spirit of God descending like a dove and lighting upon him" (*The Descent of Urania*, 32).

23. "Utter" calls to mind the "utter darkness" of the fallen angels' "prison" (*PL* 1.71–72) as well as the "utter darkness, deep engulfed" into which the disobedient will be "Cast out from God and *blessed vision*" (5.611–15; my italics).

24. Satan himself, of course, "reads" it this way in his parodic hymn to the sun in 4.32 ff.

25. Bloom, *The Anxiety of Influence*, 19–20.

26. Riggs' is the most sustained argument for Milton's success in overcoming his sense of presumptive transgressiveness, as his title implies: *The Christian Poet in "Paradise Lost"* (Berkeley: University of California Press, 1972). The quotation is from p. 25. For the opposite view, to my mind diametrically opposed to Gray's, see Denis Saurat, *Milton, Man and Thinker* (New York: Dial Press, 1925); and for a kind of middle ground (at least in her language and tone) see Regina Schwartz, *Remembering and Repeating: Biblical Creation in "Paradise Lost"* (Cambridge: Cam-

bridge University Press, 1988): "Milton expresses the apprehension that his own inquiries may be forbidden, that his own revelations may be only quaint conjectures, and that his own aspirations may be, after all, presumptions" (59).

27. Hunter, *The Descent of Urania*, 32.

28. Cf. Milton's rising "to the highth of this great argument" in 1.24, as well as the more uncertain, problematic lines following Satan's epic face-to-face confrontation with Michael in Book 6. Though the language is put into Raphael's mouth, it is Milton we hear as well:

> . . . for who, though with the tongue
> Of angels, can relate, or to what things
> Liken on earth conspicuous, that may lift
> Human imagination to such highth
> Of Godlike power?
>
> (6.297–301)

29. Hunter, *The Descent of Urania*, 33.

30. Dawson W. Turner, ed. and trans., *The Odes of Pindar* (London: Henry G. Bohn, 1852). Turner's translations are in prose, to which were added just before publication metrical versions by Abraham Moore. The passage quoted appears on pp. 428–29, accompanied by a footnote in which Moore cites Milton's imitation of the passage.

31. Cf. *Comus*, lines 37–39: "the perplexed paths of this drear wood, / The nodding horror of whose shady brows / Threats the forlorn and wand'ring passenger."

32. J. B. Broadbent, *Some Graver Subject* (London: Chatto & Windus, 1960), 235.

33. Hunter, *The Descent of Urania*, 43, 37.

34. I must agree with Sherwin that in general Collins accommodated himself to Milton, not to his "sublimity" but rather to his "pastoral innocence, the domain of Evening," where "Milton ceases to be a withering force. . . , becoming instead a benign presence from which he is able to draw [presumably 'human'] inspiration." *Precious Bane* (Austin: University of Texas Press, 1977), 12, 123, 102.

35. Edward Young, *Conjectures on Original Composition* (London: Miller & Dodsley, 1759), 20–21.

36. Ibid., 31. Such imitation, however, even for Young risked Satan-like presumption: "What glory to come near, what glory to reach, what glory (presumptuous thought!) to surpass our Predecessors" (23). Cf. also my comment in note 3 above on Geoffrey Hartman's generalization about mid-century poems in his fine essay "Blake and the Progress of Poesy," in *Beyond Formalism*, 319.

37. Young, *Conjectures*, 17. A kind of inadvertent "translation" of the positive side of Young's argument is Bloom's conception of "the triumph of having so stationed the precursor, in one's own work, that particular passages in *his* work seem to be not presages of one's own advent, but rather to be indebted to one's own achievement, and even (necessarily) to be lessened by one's greater splendor" (*Anxiety*, 141). That "stationing" is what I believe Gray tried heroically, but finally vainly, to achieve.

Chapter 3   Gray, West, and Epistolary Encoding

1. Ronald Sharp, *Friendship and Literature: Spirit and Form* (Durham: Duke University Press, 1986), 77–78.

2. Jean Hagstrum, "Gray's Sensibility," in *Fearful Joy*, ed. James Downey and Ben Jones (Montreal: McGill-Queen's University Press, 1974).

3. Cecil S. Emden, *Poets in Their Letters* (London: Oxford University Press, 1959), 43; Geoffrey Tillotson, "On Gray's Letters," in his *Essays on Criticism and Research* (1942; Hamden, Conn.: Archon Books, 1967), 118; Ian Jack, "Gray in His Letters," in Downey and Jones, *Fearful Joy*, 31.

4. All quotations and other references to Gray's, West's, Walpole's, and Ashton's letters will be to the three-volume *Correspondence of Thomas Gray*, ed. Paget Toynbee and Leonard Whibley (Oxford: Clarendon Press, 1971), the 1935 original ed. corrected and supplemented by H. W. Starr (cited in my text as *CTG* and page numbers). On some occasions it will be necessary to cite Toynbee's earlier two-volume edition of *The Correspondence of Gray, Walpole, West, and Ashton* (Oxford: Clarendon Press, 1915), indicated in my text as Toynbee plus volume and page numbers.

The most recent comment on these early letters is disappointingly old-hat in an otherwise provocative book, Suvir Kaul's *Thomas Gray and Literary Authority* (Stanford: Stanford University Press, 1992), 57. They are, he says, "self-consciously clever in the displays of their developing sensibilities, disingenuous in their ironic, yet ostentatious, assumption of the trappings of scholarship and learning, celebratory of their having established a community of like-minded souls." Among the shrewdest of brief commentaries on the general characteristics of Gray's letters is still, to my mind, a passage in Hazlitt's essay on "Letters of Horace Walpole"—in Ronald Blythe, ed., *William Hazlitt: Selected Writings* (London: Penguin Books, 1970), 421.

5. *CTG*, 33. The sixteenth-century ballad to which West is referring contains no such lines as West "quotes," as he himself acknowledges (they are from his "pen"). It is worth noting, however, that the children of the ballad are sister and brother— she "framed in beauty's mold," he "a fine and pretty boy"—and that "These pretty babes, with hand in hand" did wander "up and down" in the wood, their parents dead, and deserted even by the one who "rescues" them from the murderer hired by their uncle/guardian in his scheming to get their inheritances.

6. *CTG*, 34–35. In a later chapter, I shall address the vexed issue of the kind of editorial "suppression" evident even in these early "innocent" letters. This Gray letter, for example, is available only in Mason's transcript in his 1775 *The Poems of Mr. Gray. To which are prefixed Memoirs of his Life and Writings* (London: Dodsley), a transcript that actually combined parts of two letters by Gray to West (the other written about five months later). The whole is dated by Mason as 8 May 1736. In Toynbee's 1915 edition he argued that the first eight lines or so of the Gray letter I have just commented on was a concoction of Mason's. In *CTG* Whibley reevaluated whatever evidence there was for Toynbee's conjecture and decided to include the lines as Gray's since, he himself says somewhat unclearly, "the substance

of the passage is probably Gray's" (*CTG*, 34, n.2). No salutation or closing is present in either Toynbee or *CTG*, reflecting both Walpole's and Mason's assiduousness in cutting away or otherwise obliterating over-affectionate phrasings and the pet names the "Quadruple Alliance" had adopted at Eton. More on this below.

7. Recently Joshua Scodel hazarded the guess that this was Tibullus's love elegy 1.3, addressed to Messalla (to whom this first book was dedicated) on his departure. The poem begins "Messalla, will you go without me through the Aegean? / Do not forget me there, my guard, my other self!" The translation is Constance Carrier's in *The Poems of Tibullus* (Bloomington: Indiana University Press, 1968), 40. Scodel may be right, but there are certainly other appropriate Tibullus candidates, his elegies being, as Carrier says, major vehicles "for Latin amorous expression" (8). Scodel's guess is in his *The English Poetic Epitaph: Commemoration and Conflict from Jonson to Wordsworth* (Ithaca: Cornell University Press, 1991), 324, where he also correctly reports that "Gray and West frequently sent one another translations from the classics, and their versions of Roman poems are simultaneously literary exercises and displaced but still deeply felt explorations of their personal relationship."

8. All the translations of Horace I have taken from Charles E. Passage, *The Complete Works of Horace* (New York: Frederick Ungar, 1983). Epistle 1.2 is on pp. 262–64.

9. Ten lines prior to this passage Horace evokes Ulysses's homeward journey and addresses Lollius thus: "Songs of the Sirens you know of, you know of the potions of Circe: / How, had he greedily drunk them in folly, as did his companions, / He would have languished, a slave to a slut, in brutish existence, / Foul as a dog and rejoicing in filth like a pig in a quagmire." Perhaps West meant Gray to think of these lines as applicable to the fleshpots of Europe, but their very excessiveness in detail and language suggests West's anxiety about Gray's possibly succumbing to Walpole's widely known attraction for other men.

10. Toynbee 1:318 n. Toynbee took the word "badinage" from Duncan Tovey's note to West's letter to Gray of 5 June 1740: "A letter of Ashton's, partly badinage, partly flattery, and neither in good taste . . . was directed" to West at Mrs. Sherard's in Prince's Court near Story's Gate, Westminster." *Gray and His Friends* (Cambridge: Cambridge University Press), 139.

11. "The Pursuit of Homosexuality in the Eighteenth Century: 'Utterly Confused Category' and/or Rich Repository," in *'Tis Nature's Fault': Unauthorized Sexuality during the Enlightenment*, ed. Robert P. Maccubbin (Cambridge: Cambridge University Press, 1985), 133, 142. Rousseau goes on to claim, on reasonable if not compelling evidence, that the 1740s was "a decade . . . crucial in England for the perception that sodomy was spreading rapidly" (151). In his *Byron and Greek Love* (Berkeley: University of California Press, 1985), Louis Compton provides a mini-history of British statutes branding homosexuality a capital offense, parliament having established it so in 1533. Blackstone supported this position as derived directly from biblical authority, and "both learned and popular opinion in England" overwhelmingly sided with both. Moreover, the English clergy "repeatedly whipped up animosity against the nation's gay minority in essays, sermons, and

scriptural commentaries," and "it was seemingly impossible for a newspaper or magazine to report an arrest or trial for sodomy without laying down a barrage of scurrilous epithets" (15–53 passim).

12. Since we know Ashton wrote his first letter to West at Oxford in October (Toynbee 1:44–46), it clearly must have crossed West's to Walpole in the mail. No earlier letter from Ashton to West is extant, hence West's obvious irritation here.

13. Robert Wyndham Ketton-Cremer, *Thomas Gray: A Biography* (Cambridge: Cambridge University Press, 1955), 15. All further references to this standard biography will be made parenthetically in the text.

14. *CTG*, 38 n. A little later in May Gray sent West a translation of a further passage from the Statius poem, a "letter" that Mason "created" by adding the translation to a piece of Gray's 20 December 1735 letter to West. When properly separated, we are left with *only* the translation, no salutation, no closing, no addresses to or from.

15. Carrier, *The Poems of Tibullus*, 14, 16.

16. Georg Luck, *The Latin Love Elegy* (London: Methuen, 1959), 71.

17. Ibid., 71, 64, 32, 73 respectively.

18. Carrier, *The Poems of Tibullus*, 43–44.

19. Ibid., 56.

20. *Horace Walpole's Correspondence with Thomas Gray, Richard West, and Thomas Ashton*, ed. W. S. Lewis, G. L. Lam, C. H. Bennett (New Haven: Yale University Press, 1948), Yale ed. of Horace Walpole's Correspondence, 13:127.

21. Ibid., 130–32.

22. The odd singular here, "heart," speaks eloquently to West's *only* concern, Gray.

23. These lines, as well as lines 4–8 of the second verse paragraph, *may* have something to do with the "mystery" Ashton wrote West about. In that connection it is worth noting as well that in September 1737 approximately (Toynbee 1:156–57) Ashton referred to two letters from West (neither of which has survived) which gave Ashton serious "Concern."

24. *The Correspondence of Alexander Pope*, ed. George Sherburn (Oxford: Clarendon Press, 1956), 148. All subsequent quotations from the letter are from this page. It was first printed in *The Guardian*, no. 132 (August 1713).

25. Passage, *The Complete Works of Horace*, 187–88.

Chapter 4   Gray, West, Walpole, and the Letters

1. Several lines later West adds, citing Ecclesiasticus, if "Friendship be the physic of the mind," Gray should "prescribe to him" and he "shall be a most obedient servant." But then he adds, adapting Horace, "Non ego / Fidis irascar medicis, offendar amicis," presumably to assure Gray that *he* does not "annoy" him or "try his patience" (*CTG*, 70). Would West have counted on Gray's recalling other lines from the same source, Horace's epistle 1.8: "I plan many splendid / Projects but live neither wisely nor happily"; and "Things proven harmful I do, and avoid doing those that might help me" (Passage, *Horace*, 275)?

2. *The Greek Anthology*, Loeb Classical Library (London: William Heinemann, 1917), 2:97.

3. Passage, *Horace*, 187–88. "Aristius" was the friend to whom Horace addressed his ode 1.22, the first line of which Gray also may be recalling for West's pleasure and consolation; "One whose life is clean and by crimes umblemished" (ibid., 160). Cf. Horace's epistle 1.10 where Aristius is addressed as a "lover of city life" in contrast to Horace's cherishing country life—but in all other respects "we are almost like twins"; and Horace closes with: "Happy in every respect of my life save that you are not with me" (ibid., 277–78).

4. J. A. Hendrickson's translation in *The Complete Poems of Thomas Gray*, ed. H. W. Starr and Hendrickson (Oxford: Clarendon Press, 1966), 141.

5. Actually his first thank-you is in a brief letter before his leaving for Epsom—with no mention of his health and certainly in good spirits (*CTG*, 88–89). The Epsom poem is in *CTG*, 91–92.

6. *CTG*, 91–92, 121, 190. I am indebted to my classics colleague Professor Peter Burian for the translations of West's Latin poems.

7. On West's health generally at this time Ketton-Cremer refers to his "depression . . . darker and more constant" than Gray's, and to his being "tormented by a persistent cough and violent nervous headaches" (23), but he says nothing specifically about West's health precisely at the time he moved to his mother's house at Epsom. More than likely it was no better, possibly even worse.

8. It is of some pertinence here that in his first letter to West from the Continent, a long sprightly travelogue and diary of socializing and theater-going, Gray does not ask about West's health. On the other hand, without salutation and closing, that letter (available only in Mason's *Memoirs*) is almost certainly incomplete.

9. For example, two letters by Gray to West in French Mason admits to excluding (in their place inserting one of Gray's letters to his mother!), two letters in Italian from Gray to West Mason labels as "lost," and two others (or more) are incomplete or Mason-engineered pastiches of more than one letter—or even partly written by Mason himself.

10. *CTG*, 119. That West wrote far more often is further suggested by Gray's writing in April 1739 to thank Ashton for the "heap of letters" he had just received from Ashton and West. The earliest *known* letter West wrote to Gray was in June of that year.

11. *Horace Walpole's Correspondence*, ed. W. S. Lewis et al. (New Haven: Yale University Press, 1955), 28:151.

12. The translations are by a "Mr. Gantillon" in *The Elegies of Propertius*, ed. Walter K. Kelly (London: H. G. Bohn, 1854). Constance Carrier's more recent translation, in *The Poems of Propertius* (Bloomington: Indiana University Press, 1963), 145–46, is less "flowery" and more intense; it concludes with "O Bacchus,. . . grant me release: / free me from her, great god! O give me peace!" Gray owned J. G. Graevius's edition of *Catullus, Tibullus, et Propertius* (Utrecht, 1680).

13. I quote from the text printed by Duncan Tovey in *Gray and His Friends* (Cambridge: Cambridge University Press, 1890), 127–28. *CTG* does not print the letter but refers to Tovey's text, which is identical to that in Paget Toynbee's 1915

edition of the *Correspondence*, where it is assigned erroneously to West's letter to Walpole of 21 June 1739 (1:229).

14. The translations are Charles Martin's in *The Poems of Catullus* (Baltimore: Johns Hopkins University Press, 1990), 46.

15. While Mason may have blue-penciled part of this letter as well, we owe the text of Gray's poem to his transcription of it in his commonplace book. He also sent a handwritten copy of it to Walpole (*CTG*, 158–59 and nn.).

16. The translation is Hendrickson's in *Complete Poems of Thomas Gray*, 145. For all its seeming modesty and gracefulness of compliment, Gray also betrays his gnawing sense of creative inactivity by confessing himself but "a novice of the lyre" struggling "with limping numbers."

17. *CTG*, 151–52 n. How much of the full story West confided to Gray is unknown, but Gray's language in the rest of his comments to Nicholls seems to bespeak something far direr than merely news of an affair: for example, the "treachery of a supposed friend" who "intrigued" with Mrs. West, and the "viciousness of a mother he tenderly loved." It may indeed be possible, then, that "West's death was hastened by mental anguish, there having been good reason to suspect that his mother poisoned his father," a story recounted by Edmund Gosse, *The Works of Thomas Gray in Prose and Verse* (London, 1884), 2:113.

18. Hendrickson's translation of Gray's Latin, in *Complete Poems of Thomas Gray*, 150; the translation of the Italian, by James D. Powell, is on p. 263.

19. Hendrickson's translation, *Complete Poems of Thomas Gray*, 162–67.

20. Hagstrum goes further than I by arguing that the "pattern" of Gray's life (excessive love of his mother, fear and loathing of his father, et al.) is reflected in *De Principiis*, beginning with Gray's focus on the sense of touch instead of sight as primary (see the Latin original on p. 158 and Hendrickson's translation on p. 164 of *Complete Poems of Thomas Gray*). Hagstrum's remarks are on pp. 13–14 of his "Gray's Sensibility," in *Fearful Joy*, ed. James Downey and Ben Jones (Montreal: McGill-Queen's University Press, 1974).

Chapter 5   The Poems (I)

1. Lonsdale notes the Young source. Milton's only use of "blooming" in *Paradise Lost* is, however, in the context of Satan's first view of Eden, though the word is attached specifically to the Tree of Life (*PL* 4.218–19).

2. Fredric Bogel makes a similar, though less sweeping, point in his *Literature and Insubstantiality in Later Eighteenth-Century England* (Princeton: Princeton University Press, 1984): "The dimmest region of speech [in *The Bard*] is in fact the present. The poet says relatively little, and what he does say is not immediate and dramatic, like the bard's address, but narrative and descriptive" (94). And, more recently Suvir Kaul, in *Thomas Gray and Literary Authority* (Stanford: Stanford University Press, 1992), observes that when Gray's poet-figures "ventriloquize the inspired utterance of traditional personifications of poetic power," that "works actually to delimit and weaken this figure, who is represented as already considerably enervated" (74–75). In *The Bard* that "enervation" is death.

3. Almost as if conscious of what he had prophesied, Gray makes a big fuss

over Mason's questioning of the appositive "lost" and "expire." If Mason worried (actually he didn't) that "people may think Poetry in Britain was some time or other really to expire," Mason would be wrong, Gray says; "the meaning is only, that it was lost to his [the Bard's] ear from the immense distance." Besides, Gray adds, "I can not give up lost, for it begins with a L" (*CTG*, 504), surely a reflection of uncertainties about his own "warblings."

4. The information about Vida and the English translation I have taken from Lonsdale, p. 199 n.

5. David V. Erdman, ed. *The Complete Poetry and Prose of William Blake* (Berkeley: University of California Press, 1982), 702.

6. "The Contemporary Readers of Gray's *Odes*," *Modern Philology* 28 (1930–31): 61–82. See also Ketton-Cremer's *Thomas Gray*, 153–57; both of these are cited by Lonsdale as well (180). To this extent such readers may well have appreciated Kaul's argument that Gray's poems must be located "within contemporary poetic practices, and their formal and thematic elements [must be] examined as existing . . . in a (largely agonistic) counterpoint with precursory and contemporary discursive practices"—including those of Pope, *his* contemporaries, and their classical forebears. Suvir Kaul, *Thomas Gray and Literary Authority* (Stanford: Stanford University Press, 1992), 4.

7. Kaul, *Thomas Gray and Literary Authority*, 239, 244.

8. H. W. Starr and J. R. Hendrickson, eds., *The Complete Poems of Thomas Gray* (Oxford: Clarendon Press, 1966), 25. They, as well as Lonsdale later (213), indicate that though Gray copied the originals in his commonplace book, they were accompanied there by the Latin translations of Arni Magnusson in Thomas Bartholin's *Antiquitatum Danicarum De Causis Contemptae A Danis Adhuc Gentilibus Mortis* (Copenhagen, 1789), and of Thormodus Torfeaus's *Orcades Seu Rerum Orcadensium Historiae* (Copenhagen, 1697). For further proof of Gray's use of translations from the Latin versions of the originals, see Lonsdale's bibliography of discussions of the issue (213–14).

9. *A Long Story*, about which I shall say nothing, was not a favorite with Gray. It was published once in his lifetime (the 1753 edition with Bentley's designs), but not without real reluctance, for, as Gray himself wrote, it "was never meant for the publick" and he "suffer'd [it] to appear in that pompous edition because of Mr. Bentley's designs, which were not intelligible without it" (Lonsdale, 143 n). Even Mason excluded it from his 1775 edition, relegating it to the *Memoirs*.

10. *Letters from the Dead to the Living*, by Thomas Brown, Capt. Ayloff, and Henry Barker (London, 1702), 257, 13, 254–55 respectively. Lonsdale cites Brown's model, but in less specific terms (13).

11. Edward Dowden, "Milton in the Eighteenth Century (1701–1750)," *Proceedings of the British Academy* (London, 1908), 277, echoed without acknowledgment by Raymond D. Havens in his *The Influence of Milton on English Poetry* (Cambridge: Harvard University Press, 1922), 93. Edward N. Hooker, in his splendid two-volume *Critical Works of John Dennis* (Baltimore: Johns Hopkins Press, 1939), points out that among his contemporaries Dennis's admiration for Milton, and in particular for *Paradise Lost*, was "notorious" (1:511).

12. For all the private fun, or silliness, of Gray's self-fictionalizing, his later

alignment of his own friendship with Celadony/Walpole with the faithfulness of Proserpine to Pluto and Cleopatra to Mark Antony seems to pose a problem in light of my concentration in previous chapters on Gray's love "affair" with West. Jean Hagstrum, as we have seen earlier, states bluntly that Gray's letters to Walpole from their Eton days until their tour abroad are studded with verbal love-play, double entendre, and parody ("Gray's Sensibility," 16), and three years earlier Peter Watson-Smythe argued that since Gray and Walpole were "particularly devoted" to their mothers, they were both homosexuals whose greatest love was each other ("On Gray's Elegy," *The Spectator*, 31 July 1971).

Despite my admiration for Hagstrum's essay, I must respectfully disagree. Since a fully fleshed-out argument here is impossible, let me but note the tonality that bespeaks play but not love-play, silliness but not parody or double entendre, a tonality ubiquitous in Gray's letters to Walpole: (1) Gray's frequently sober closings, even to letters of foolery, gossip, chit-chat, juvenile profanity and the like: "your sincere friend & most devoted humble Servt," "Friend of yours, & just the same Servant," "your friend & Servant," or "your sincerest friend" (*CTG*, 2, 17, 18, 20); (2) aside from his addressing Walpole as Celadon and signing himself Orozmades, other silly salutations and closings include: "Honner'd Nurse," "your ever-dutifull & most obedient & most affectionate loving God-daughter," "your friend, the Defunct . . .," "To the faithful Miradolin, third Son of the Vizier-azem" (*CTG*, 27, 29, 33, 55). In fact, Gray's relationship with Walpole rarely, if ever, ventured beyond a friendliness whose circumspect contours were dictated (for Gray at least) by the radical distance between their social backgrounds and worldly status. As I argued in chapter 4 about their famous quarrel, it had nothing to do with either man's sexual inclinations or proclivities, and everything to do with what we now call their "lifestyles." As Toynbee and Whibley put it, "two men, both of difficult temper, with a diversity of tastes, who had been in each other's company for more than two years," could hardly have done other than disagree finally so sharply, seriously, and persistently that a "breaking-point" was inevitable. See their eminently sensible account in *CTG*, 1200–2.

13. In writing the final four lines of this speech by Agrippina, Gray may also have had in mind Satan's first glimpse of Paradise, "beyond expression bright" and "informed / With radiant light, as glowing iron with fire" (3.591–94).

14. It may not be too much, however, to see West in these lines of longing:

> When less averse, & yielding to Desires
> She half accepts, & half rejects my Fires:
> . . . .
> And struggles to elude my longing Eyes
> . . . .
> In brief whate'er she do, or say, or look
> 'Tis ample Matter for a Lover's Book.
>   (lines 21–28)

I follow here and in my text Toynbee and Whibley's printing (*CTG*, 197–99) rather than Lonsdale's with its minor variants and lowercased capital letters (taken from Gray's transcription in his commonplace book).

15. *The Elegies of Propertius*, ed. Walter K. Kelly (London: H. G. Bohn, 1854), 88. The translator is identified only as "Mr. Gantillon of Cambridge."

16. Lines 99–105. Propertius's original makes my point even clearer. In Kelly's edition the literal English translation of this passage is: "Whensoever, therefore, fate demands back my life, and I become a short epitaph on a slender urn, O . . . envied member of our youthful company of knights, if perchance you travel by the road near my tomb, stop your British chariot with its ornamented yoke, and with tears pay to my silent dust this tribute: An unrelenting mistress proved the death of this unfortunate" (89).

17. I give Duncan Tovey's transcription of Gray's translation taken from his commonplace book—*Gray and His Friends: Letters and Relics* (Cambridge: Cambridge University Press, 1890), 167–68.

18. *The Poems of Catullus*, trans. and ed. Charles Martin (Baltimore: Johns Hopkins University Press, 1990), xvii, xix.

19. Lonsdale, 319–20. His translation (320–21) is very close to Hendrickson's in *The Poems of Thomas Gray*, 154–56, though I do like Hendrickson's rendering of Gray's last line: "once more you were with me."

Chapter 6   The Poems (II) and the Death of West

1. Freud, of course, comes to mind here, as well as recent extensions of his *Mourning and Melancholia* by Kristeva among many others. Freud's melancholic experiences "an extraordinary fall in his self-esteem, an impoverishment of his ego on a grand scale," but at the same time the "trait of insistent talking about himself and pleasure in the consequent exposure of himself predominates." *A General Selection from the Works of Sigmund Freud*, ed. John Rickman (London: Hogarth Press, 1953), 146–47. In *Black Sun: Depression and Melancholia*, trans. Leon S. Rondiez (New York: Columbia University Press, 1989) Kristeva writes: "Riveted to the past, regressing to the paradise or inferno of an unsurpassable experience, melancholy persons manifest a strange memory: everything has gone by, they seem to say, but I am faithful to those bygone days, I am nailed down to them, no revolution is possible, there is no future . . . [*sic*]. An overinflated, hyperbolic past fills all the dimensions of psychic continuity" (60). Such analyses apply not only to Gray on the brink of learning about West's death but, in many ways, to the rest of his life's and career's herculean efforts to capitalize on "loss, bereavement, and absence" as a "trigger [to] the work of the imagination" rather than as a threat to it (Kristeva, 9).

2. J. R. Hendrickson's translation in *The Complete Poems of Thomas Gray*, ed. H. W. Starr and Hendrickson (Oxford: Clarendon Press, 1966), 119. Lonsdale translates "ingloria moles" as "ignoble hulk," but Hendrickson's "inglorious" shrewdly anticipates the *Elegy*'s "mute inglorious Milton," that poet manqué who only crept, as distinct from the one who did rise to the stars and beyond, and with whom Gray at least for a time dared to rise and soar.

3. On this point we should note that, in Gray's commonplace book transcription of West's "Ode" to May, the original end of the first stanza, which places that poem squarely in the season's and month's poetic/mythological tradition, was:

"The Winter yet is scarcely gone / And Summer comes but slowly on." Duncan Tovey, *Gray and His Friends* (Cambridge: Cambridge University Press, 1890), 165. Gray revised the lines to: "O join with mine thy tuneful lay, / and invocate the tardy May" (ibid.). That change seems to suggest that at the time of his writing his own Spring Ode Gray indeed intended it as a response to West's invitation to join with him in tuneful lay—though it may also be, of course, Gray's private recording of the powerful personal intersection he intended the two odes to enact. On the Fall at Noon see Albert R. Cirillo's fine "Noon-Midnight and the Temporal Structure of *Paradise Lost*," in *Milton's Epic Poetry*, ed. C. A. Patrides (Baltimore: Penguin, 1967).

4. William Fitzgerald, *The Pindaric Mode in Pindar, Horace, Hölderlin, and the English Ode* (Berkeley: University of California Press, 1987), 83. Much of Fitzgerald's entire discussion, particularly his analysis of Horace's "anxiety" about Pindar's prior achievement, is relevant to my view of Gray's relationship to Milton.

5. Fredric V. Bogel, *Literature and Insubstantiality in Late-Eighteenth-Century England* (Princeton: Princeton University Press, 1984), 23, 217, 211. The relevant passages from Freud may be found in vol. 14 of *The Standard Edition of the Complete Psychological Works of Sigmund Freud*, trans. James Strachey et al. (London: Hogarth Press, 1957), 244–49.

6. "How soon hath Time, the subtle thief of youth," lines 3–8. Milton, we recall (as Gray may have), after achieving some fame at Cambridge had become "for six months . . . an obscure student under his father's roof" while "his contemporaries [were] forging ahead." Douglas Bush, *The Complete Poetical Works of John Milton* (Boston: Houghton Mifflin, 1965), 104–5.

7. The translations are Douglas Bush's in *The Complete Works*, pp. 100–101.

8. Bush notes this fact in connection with Milton's first "elegy" to Diodati (15 n).

9. Walter MacKellar, *The Latin Poems of John Milton*, Cornell Studies in English 15 (New Haven: Yale University Press, 1930), 62.

10. It is perhaps not entirely coincidental that Milton delayed a year and some months after Diodati's death before writing the *Epitaphium*, which (though privately printed in 1640 or so) was not published until 1645.

11. Douglas Bush, *Variorum Commentary on the Poems of John Milton: The Latin and Greek Poems* (London: Routledge & Kegan Paul, 1970), 284. On this point see also Donald C. Dorian, *The English Diodatis* (New Brunswick: Rutgers University Press, 1950), esp. 178, as well as the extraordinary, if overwrought, "Milton and Diodati: An Essay in Psychodynamic Meaning" by John T. Shawcross in *Milton Studies* 7, ed. A. C. Labriola and M. Lief (Pittsburgh: University of Pittsburgh Press, 1975), 127–63. Pertinent here as well is Louis Crompton's interesting speculation that Byron, in the "Tirzah poems" on the death of his young male lover Edleston, may have "felt that death enhanced pathos, and weakened the taboo that set limits on protestations of devotion between males." *Byron and Greek Love: Homophobia in Nineteenth-Century England* (Berkeley: University of California Press, 1985), 71.

12. Margaret M. Smith, *Index to English Manuscripts* (London: Mansell, 1989),

vol. 3, pt. 2, p. 75. The manuscript's whereabouts is unknown, Smith's information having been derived from a Parke-Bernet sale catalog, 6 April 1982, lot 53.

13. Bush, *Complete Poetical Works of John Milton*, 164.

14. Here, and in what follows, I have opted for Lonsdale's translation (332) though Hendrickson's more elegant translation in *The Complete Poems of Thomas Gray*, 169–70, also should be consulted.

15. Bush, *Complete Poetical Works of John Milton*, 163–64 seriatim.

16. Charles E. Passage's translation in *The Complete Works of Horace* (New York: Frederick Ungar, 1983), 188. Cf. Milton's assuring Diodati that the shepherds "shall rejoice to sing your praises . . . if it means anything to have been true to ancient faith and piety, to know the arts of Pallas, and to have had a poet for your friend" (Bush, 163).

17. E.g., Geoffrey Tillotson in *Augustan Studies* (London: Athlone Press, 1961), 87–88.

18. Julia Kristeva, *Black Sun: Depression and Melancholia*, 43–44, 54–55. Needless to say, her point does not inform the common argument over the alleged overformality and stiltedness of Gray's octave, what Duncan Tovey long ago called a "music now a little trite to us" (*Gray and His Friends*, 27).

19. Kristeva, *Black Sun*, 99.

20. Suvir Kaul, *Thomas Gray and Literary Authority: A Study of Ideology and Poetics* (Stanford: Stanford University Press, 1992), 87. Kaul is, of course, merely the most recent critic to take this position.

21. *Comus*, 234–35. Citing Joseph Summers' *The Muse's Method: An Introduction to "Paradise Lost"* (Cambridge: Harvard University Press, 1962) in order to establish that "the nightingale . . . is always . . . the singer of fulfilled love" in *Paradise Lost* (98), Donald Mell reaches the odd conclusion that Gray's sorrow is less for a dead lover than for the "loss of a pastoral world" and of the joyful fulfillment of [his and West's] mutual literary interests." *The Poetics of Augustan Elegy* (Amsterdam: Rodopi N.V., 1974), 68, 73. This conclusion seems to be derived from Joseph Foladare's disappointing study of the Milton allusions in the sonnet, "Gray's 'Frail Memorial' to West," *PMLA* 75 (1960): 61–65, where what Gray laments is said to be the "joyous activities of mind and heart" that he and West engaged in together (63).

22. Peter J. Manning, "Wordsworth and Gray's Sonnet on the Death of West," in his *Reading Romantics* (New York: Oxford University Press, 1990), 56. The essay originally appeared in *Studies in English Literature* 22 (1982): 505–18. Griffin's suggestion is in "Gray's Audiences," *Essays in Criticism* 28 (1978): 209, his source being Richard Quaintance's "French Sources of the Restoration 'Imperfect Enjoyment,' " *Philological Quarterly* 42 (1963): 190–99; and Weinbrot's claim is in his "Northrop Frye and the Literature of Process Reconsidered," *Eighteenth-Century Studies* 24 (1990–91): 194.

23. On the degenderizing, even deeroticizing, of desire, especially homoerotic desire, see Michael Moon's recent study of Whitman, *Disseminating Whitman: Revision and Corporeality in "Leaves of Grass"* (Cambridge: Harvard University Press, 1991). The passage quoted is on page 118. See also Annabel Patterson's splendid

notion of "the social uses of indeterminacy," which allows writers to exploit the ungroundable quality of language in order to treat proscribed subjects with relative impunity. *Censorship and Interpretation* (Madison: University of Wisconsin Press, 1984), esp. 243. See also Linda Zionkowski's discussion of the eroticism of the sonnet on West, which she regards as revealing "Gray's nostalgia for a model of authorship that depends upon and solidifies affectional, sometimes erotic ties"—i.e., the sonnet form. "Gray, the Marketplace, and the Masculine Poet," *Criticism* 35 (1993): 599.

24. Lonsdale, 103–10; but see also *CTG*, 1214–16 (Appendix 1 on "The Composition of the *Elegy*"), and F. G. Stokes's introduction to his edition of the *Elegy* (Oxford: Oxford University Press, 1929).

25. Henry Weinfield, *The Poet without a Name: Gray's "Elegy" and the Problem of History* (Carbondale: Southern Illinois University Press, 1991).

26. Odell Shepard, " 'A Youth to Fortune and to Fame Unknown'," *Modern Philology* 20 (1923): 347–73; H. W. Starr, " 'A Youth to Fortune and to Fame Unknown': A Re-estimation," *Journal of English and Germanic Philology* 48 (1949): 97–107; Weinfield, *Poet with a Name*, 26; he goes on to argue that "one should beware of interpreting Gray's figure wholly in autobiographical terms," but "there is clearly a self-reflexive aspect to Gray's vision that reverberates with his existential situation" (97)—a tentativeness that echoes Frank Ellis's statement in 1951 that "the reconstruction of the poet's experiences from diaries, letters, accounts of friends, and public records may illuminate his poetry." "Gray's Elegy: The Biographical Problems in Literary Criticism," *PMLA* 66 (1951): 971. I sincerely hope so.

27. Unpublished paper, 10–11. Haggerty's reading of lines 53–56 strain his basically sound case even more: they are, he says, an expression of Gray's "own sexual frustration. . . . We hardly need Freud to suggest that the 'dark unfathomed caves of ocean' suggest Gray's fear of his own sexuality" and that the "waste [of] sweetness" is the "death-like masturbatory implications of the poet's lonely stance" (11). He also concludes that the epitaph "inscrib[es] his gay identity in stone" (18).

28. Kaul, *Thomas Gray and Literary Authority*, 94, 132. Kaul is clearly drawing on de Man's influential *Blindness and Insight*, 2nd rev. ed. (Minneapolis: University of Minnesota Press, 1983), 208; and though he does not cite it (as he does de Man), he may have remembered C. N. Manlove's comment, in *Literature and Reality, 1600–1800* (London: Macmillan, 1978), that the rustics of the *Elegy* "are a type of [Gray's] dead friend West, while the great are analogues of Walpole, and . . . Gray is choosing between the kind of emotionally involved relationship he had with the former and the more urbane companionship of the latter" (151). Kaul, however, regards this "choice" as the "cultural" loss inherent in the death of West (132).

29. Kaul, *Thomas Gray and Literary Authority*, 4.

30. William Empson, *Some Versions of Pastoral* (New York: New Dimensions, 1974), 5. Others, of course, have made a similar point both before and after Empson.

31. *The Divine Comedy of Dante Alighieri*, trans. Allen Mandelbaum (Berkeley: University of California Press, 1980), 47–48. The other sources, echoes, analogs

that Lonsdale cites (117–18 n) seem to me possible but less insistent. Weinfield's analysis is on pp. 46–48 of *The Poet without a Name*.

32. I see little point in identifying the "kindred spirit" as a "resurrected" West as Peter Sacks does in *The English Elegy: Studies in the Genre from Spenser to Keats* (Baltimore: Johns Hopkins University Press, 1985), 133.

33. Cf. Joshua Scodel's reference to an epitaph by Phillip Doddridge entitled "On a Young Man who died for Love; after the Manner of GRAY" as symptomatic of the fact that "some of Gray's contemporaneous readers considered the poet of the *Elegy* a traditional unhappy lover." *The English Poetic Epitaph: Commemoration and Conflict from Jonson to Wordsworth* (Ithaca: Cornell University Press, 1991), 320 n. Lines 107–8 indeed seem hardly readable any other way: "Now drooping woeful wan, like one forlorn, / Or crazed with care, or crossed in hopeless love." Gray *and* West both, perhaps?

34. Pat Rogers, *The Augustan Vision* (London: Weidenfeld & Nicholson, 1974), 138; Stephen Bygrave, "Gray's 'Elegy': Inscribing the Twilight," in his *Post-Structuralist Readings of English Poetry* (Cambridge: Cambridge University Press, 1987), 164. A slightly different version of the disappearing Gray may be found in Margaret A. Doody, *The Darling Muse: Augustan Poetry Reconsidered* (Cambridge: Cambridge University Press, 1985), 192–96.

35. Bygrave, *Post-Structuralist Readings*, 164 (which also includes the Johnson quotation).

36. Anne Williams, *Prophetic Strain: The Greater Lyric in the Eighteenth Century* (Chicago: University of Chicago Press, 1984), 104–8. The Miltonic quotation from *Il Penseroso* that she employs is absolutely on the money.

37. Richard Feingold, *Moralized Song: The Character of Augustan Lyricism* (New Brunswick: Rutgers University Press, 1989), 10–11.

Chapter 7   The Poems (III)

1. Geoffrey Hartman, "Romantic Poetry and the Genius Loci," in *Beyond Formalism* (New Haven: Yale University Press, 1970), 321, 316, 315 respectively.

2. Virtually all critics note this evocation of an Eden of one sort or another, some noting as well its Miltonic origins. One of the most thoroughgoing accounts is Dustin Griffin's in his *Regaining Paradise: Milton and the Eighteenth Century* (Cambridge: Cambridge University Press, 1988), though I have difficulty in acceding to his argument, specifically contra Harold Bloom, that there is "little compelling evidence . . . to show that Milton inhibited the poets of the eighteenth century" (46). While it is demonstrably true that Milton often empowered rather than inhibited the writing of Miltonic "imitations" in the century, those imitations, as I have argued in chapter 2, were habitually in the *L'Allegro* or *Il Penseroso* mode, a settling for middle flight rather than attempts to sublimely soar in the forbiddingly inhibitive realms of *Paradise Lost, Paradise Regained, Samson Agonistes*—and even of such shorter poems as the Nativity Ode and *At a Solemn Music*. For Griffin, Gray's thefts from Milton, as well as those by other mid-eighteenth-century English poets, merely imply "that the poet is aware of his Miltonic source, but that he conceals

it from his readers, and seeks to prevent Milton from entering the reader's mind" (4).

3. Marshall Brown, *Preromanticism* (Stanford: Stanford University Press, 1991), 25.

4. S. H. Clark, " 'Pendet Homo Incertus': Gray's Response to Locke," *Eighteenth-Century Studies* 24 (1991): 287, 291.

5. I opt for Walter Skeat's translation (which captures the implicit sense of Milton's line rather than Bush's "Farewell! remember me as you rise to the stars"). Skeat's translation is in *Milton's Lament for Damon, and His Other Latin Poems* (London: Oxford University Press, 1935), 98, Bush's in *The Complete Poetical Works of John Milton* (Boston: Houghton Mifflin, 1965), 164. With respect to Skeat's language, see Milton's earlier lines in the *Epitaphium* spoken by the nymphs to Thyrsis/Milton: "It is not for youth to have a clouded brow, grim eyes, and gloomy face. Youth rightly seeks dances and merry games and always love; twice wretched is he who loves too late" (Bush, 164)—lines with an obvious bearing on the opening scenes of *Eton College*.

6. In West's Magdalene Ode his fourth stanza concluded with the "joy" and "bliss" he misses at Oxford. The word *bliss* occurs no less than fifty-two times in Milton's English poetry, *joy* eighty-seven times, though only twice are they juxtaposed—once in Christ's colloquy with his Father ("All my redeemed may dwell in joy and bliss"—*PL* 11.43), once in the sonnet on the death of Mrs. Catharine Thomason ("joy and bliss for ever" is her final destiny).

7. As I have argued earlier, Gray was but a good friend to Walpole and vice versa. That the quarrel was not, as George Rousseau has claimed, a result of "Gray's overly aggressive professions of love" and Walpole's being able "no longer [to] tolerate Gray's sexual advances" ("Gray's Elegy Reconsidered," *Spectator* 227 [2 October 1971]: 490) clearly did not lessen Gray's (and Walpole's) regret over its occurrence. The point is that the Quadruple Alliance, itself a kind of figuration of Eton, was defunct in 1742, and was never to be revived.

8. Dustin Griffin also notes Gray's aligning of his "narrator" with Satan's "prospect" and his reaction to it, in *Regaining Paradise*, 103, but he undermines the significance of the point by his "reading" of eighteenth-century poetry as suggesting "that Satan was after all not very interesting to the eighteenth century, except as a polemical image in political satire" (x). He does not mention the *Paradise Regained* passage.

9. Needless to say, Satan's distant prospect of *his* past is of a position of power and glory, that state so "glorious" above even the sphere of the sun that he shone "In that bright eminence" but "one step" from envisioning himself as "highest" (*PL* 4.38–51).

10. *PL* 4.153–58. Griffin cites this passage as well (103), nicely characterizing Satan, *and* Gray, as approaching the "garden of innocence as one barred from it."

11. Other echoes of *Ad Amicos* include prominently West's "sunshine of my days" (Gray's "sunshine of the breast"), "Health turns from me her rosy face away" (Gray's "buxom health of rosy hue"), and "A victim yet unworthy of [death's] dart" (Gray's "The little victims play" "regardless of their doom").

12. Richard Feingold, *Moralized Song: The Character of Augustan Lyricism* (New

Brunswick: Rutgers University Press, 1989), 196. Feingold's statement of his overall thesis is pertinent here as well. What he calls the representations of "inwardness" in eighteenth-century poetry are the modes of "submerging the experience of inwardness, [of] representing that experience impersonally, or distantly, or reticently, as if to do so were to rescue it from insignificance" (viii). On the other hand, his conclusion with respect to the Eton College Ode—it registers "not so much ... what the poet felt and thought from his distant prospect ... [but] his concern for his authority to speak about the experience" (20)—seems to me to fall prey to Gray's strategic surfaces in the poem.

13. Lonsdale properly points out that Gray's catalog, as well as similar ones by other poets, derives from the *Aeneid* 6.273–81, though he may also have remembered Spenser's *Faerie Queene* 2.7.22 and/or Thomson's *Spring*, lines 278–308. The total context of the Eton College Ode, however, points primarily (not merely additionally) to Milton's postlapsarian mental and emotional "vultures"—as, not entirely coincidentally, does Thomson's Milton-derived post-Golden-Age vision. It is also worth noting that Adam warns Eve of the possible ambush: "somewhere nigh at hand" some "malicious foe, / ... seeks to work us woe and shame / By sly assault" (9.256, 253–55). In line 1079 Adam calls "shame, the last of evils."

14. Cf. Gabriel's terse summation, "Satan fell, whom folly overthrew" (4.905), and Adam's distant echo, "my folly [was] to aspire" (12.560).

15. Cf. Satan's self-torturing colloquy with himself (4.57–59).

16. Lonsdale, 69. Lonsdale goes on to suggest that in a letter to John Chute of 12 October 1747 (*CTG*, 248) Gray repeats this "part of the content" of *Adversity*. Walpole and Gray met Chute during their tour, and Chute became quite intimate with Walpole back in England while remaining, like Walpole, a confirmed bachelor. Gray's friendship with him, on the occasion of this letter (Chute's not contacting him upon his arrival in England), seems at least faintly reminiscent of his relationship with West and his guilt over West's death: e.g., he writes of those "in the World, that would have been very glad to be sorry for People they liked, when under any Pain, and could not; merely for Want of knowing rightly, what it was, themselves." Gray clearly knew no real pain till West died.

17. Stephen Cornford, ed., *Edward Young: "Night Thoughts"* (Cambridge: Cambridge University Press, 1989), p. 19. All my quotations from Young are from this edition.

Chapter 8   The Poems (IV): From *Cat* to *Progress*

1. Lord David Cecil, "The Poetry of Thomas Gray," *Proceedings of the British Academy* 31 (1945), 50; Paul Sherwin, *Precious Bane: Collins and the Miltonic Legacy* (Austin: University of Texas Press, 1977), 6; Paul Fry, *The Poet's Calling in the English Ode* (New Haven: Yale University Press, 1980), 93.

2. Wallace Jackson, "Thomas Gray and the Dedicatory Muse," *ELH* 54 (1987): 288.

3. Peter M. Sacks, *The English Elegy: Studies in the Genre from Spenser to Yeats* (Baltimore: Johns Hopkins University Press, 1985); R. W. Ketton-Cremer, *Thomas Gray: A Biography* (Cambridge: Cambridge University Press, 1955), 79; Lord David

Cecil, "The Poetry of Thomas Gray," in *Eighteenth Century English Literature*, ed. James L. Clifford (New York: Oxford University Press, 1959), 249.

4. The subtitle of Kaul's book is *A Study in Ideology and Poetics* (Stanford: Stanford University Press, 1992); the passages I've quoted are on 168–69, 172.

5. Jackson, "Dedicatory Muse," 287, 285.

6. All of these are discussed intelligently by Lonsdale (79–80). Tillotson's essay, "Gray's 'Ode on the Death of a Favourite Cat, Drowned in a Tub of Gold Fishes,' " in *Augustan Studies* (London: Athlone Press, 1961), does contain a convincing comparison between Gray's opening lines and Pope's description of Helen as the "brightest of the Female kind, / The matchless *Helen* [who] o'er the Walls reclin'd" (220), a perception that echoes J. C. Maxwell's note in *Notes & Queries* 196 (1951): 498.

7. Morris Golden, *Thomas Gray* (New York: Twayne, 1964), 64; Kaul, *Thomas Gray and Literary Authority*, summarizing the views he attacks; Ketton-Cremer, 79; *Lives of the Poets*, ed. G. B. Hill (Oxford, 1905), 3:434. Johnson went on to say, "if what glistered had been 'gold,' the cat would not have gone into the water; and if she had, would not less have been drowned."

8. *Virgil's Aeneis* 11.756, 768, 963. I quote from James Kinsley's edition of *The Poems of John Dryden* (Oxford: Clarendon Press, 1958), vol. 3. Actually Gray's allusions to Chloreus (cited by Lonsdale, 82–83 n) are more compelling by far: it is she whom Camilla, "Fond and Ambitious of so Rich a Prize," with Selima-like "ardent eyes" ogles on the battlefield (lines 1135 ff, 1144–45). Addison's splendid analysis of Virgil's Camilla (*Spectator* 15) heedlessly pursuing "glittering trifles" because of "women's weak minds and low education" is more to the point for those readers who are seduced by Gray's moralizing parable. And Gray's Agrippina, we should recall, characterizes herself as one who would "mount undaunted" to seize "the radiant prize" displayed by "bright ambition from her craggy seat."

9. Gleckner, *Blake's Prelude* and *Blake and Spenser* (Baltimore: Johns Hopkins University Press, 1982 and 1985), the latter especially in its opening pages; John Hollander, *The Figure of Echo: A Mode of Allusion in Milton and After* (Berkeley: University of California Press, 1981), 88–89. Another excellent study of this vexed issue is David Bromwich's chapter entitled "The Politics of Allusion" in *Hazlitt: The Mind of a Critic* (New York: Oxford University Press, 1983), esp. 275–85.

10. The lone exception to this "rule," as I read the many usages, is "The stars with deep amaze / Stand fixed in steadfast gaze" in *On the Morning of Christ's Nativity*, lines 69–70.

11. Blake's uncommonly shrewd "reading" of this scene in his illustrations to Gray's poems even more graphically diabolizes the fish by equipping them with Satanic batlike wings and armorlike scaled bodies (Design 1); and in Design 3, although he depicts Selima gazing at her watery image as Eve does, Blake gives that image a hair-do completely different from Selima's and no catlike features, so that the total effect is of Selima's perception of herself *as* Satan. For fuller discussion of Blake's interpretation see Irene Tayler's definitive *Blake's Illustrations to the Poems of Gray* (Princeton: Princeton University Press, 1971), 55 ff.

12. Tayler argues that Blake's Design 3, which pictures a disembodied tabby tail waving upward from the text-box centering the plate, suggests Selima's

plunge as already having taken place since three-fourths of the text-box is "under water."

13. *PL* 4.458–60, 462. See also postlapsarian Adam's glances "Of amorous intent" at Eve (9.1034–35).

14. In line with my earlier claim that the mode of Gray's "Lines Spoken by the Ghost of John Dennis" lies prominently behind that of the Cat Ode, it is noteworthy that Selima's actual "fall" in the fifth stanza is a "tumble," possibly recalling the "tumble" of Gray's "little, naked, melancholy thing / [His soul]" in the Dennis poem.

15. Unique in that history is Robert Pattison's "Gray's 'Ode on the Death of a Favourite Cat': A Rationalist's Aesthetic," *University of Toronto Quarterly* 49 (1979–80): 156–65, which reads Gray's "deflection" as exemplifying Locke's rationalistic ideas about the "behaviour of the mind understanding itself." Gray, he says, "had developed rationalism to a static dead end beyond which action seemed possible only according to a set of tested conventions so ingrained as to be commonplace" (159, 163). No comment. But see also the intelligent, brief recent analysis of the Ode's mode by Felicity Rosslyn, "Good Humour and the Agelasts: Horace, Pope and Gray," in *Horace Made New*, ed. Charles Martindale and David Hopkins (Cambridge: Cambridge University Press, 1993), 195–98.

16. Gay's jar and its shattering may account for Gray's odd opening locution: "Selima reclined" "on a lofty vases *side*" (my italics), gravitationally impossible unless Selima is part of the vase's "gayest art," which is on *its* side.

17. Rodney Edgecombe, "A Reading of Gray's 'Ode on the Death of a Favourite Cat, Drowned in a Tub of Gold Fishes,'" *English Studies in Africa* 26 (1983): 99, later included in his *Wonted Fires: A Reading of Thomas Gray* (Salzburg, 1992). Once again Tillotson, whom Edgecombe echoes, is a major "offender" in this regard (cf. note 6 above). On the other hand, as I have suggested, mock-heroic in one sense takes a back seat to the "joke" inherent in allusion's being etymologically derived from *alludere*. In her otherwise uncompelling essay "On Alluding" in *Poetics* 7 (1978): 289–307, Carmela Perri, leaning heavily on Freud's *Jokes and Their Relation to the Unconscious*, argues that jokes "economize for us by . . . lifting preexisting repressions, thereby relieving our pre-existing psychic expenditure (i.e., the psychic energy needed to repress desires)" (301). Just so. Also to the point is Felicity Rosslyn's (see note 15 above) contention that Gray may well have profited not merely from Gay but from other Scriblerians' exploitation of mock forms, in which "comedy gives a necessary home to ambivalence and contradiction," a "Serious trifling" (195, 196). I cannot agree, though, with her conclusion that the Cat Ode, "for all its real charm,. . . remains a trifle," an engagement with moralism rather than morality (197).

18. William Fitzgerald, *The Pindaric Mode in Pindar, Horace, Hölderlin, and the English Ode* (Berkeley: University of California Press, 1987), 73.

19. Elsewhere Fitzgerald points out that the *Progress* not only fails "to integrate image and narrative" (as both Pindar and Horace had done) but virtually buries its "narrative aspect . . . under the weight of the images that are the most striking parts" of the poem (*The Pindaric Mode*, 87). This argument I regard as more to the point on Gray and history than Henry Weinfield's *The Poet without a Name: Gray's*

"Elegy" and the Problem of History (Carbondale: Southern Illinois University Press, 1991). Kaul's argument in capsulated form may be found on pp. 4–6, 66, 87, 132 of *Thomas Gray and Literary Authority*.

20. *Davideis* 3.785, cited without line number by Lonsdale (161 n); Gray ignores it in his 1768 notes, citing instead (in Greek) Pindar and Psalm 57:9. Although hardly a unique usage, Gray may also have recalled the opening of Cowley's second stanza: "Hark, how the strings awake" and "A kind of num'erous Trembling make" (3.792, 795); and, given his Bard's demise (and Gray's own figurative "demise" in *The Progress*), the conclusion of Cowley's lyric interlude seems also to the point:

> Sleep, sleep again, my Lyre;
> For thou can'st never tell my humble tale,
> In sounds that will prevail,
> Nor gentle thoughts in her inspire
> . . . .
> Sleep, sleep again, my Lyre, and let thy Master dy.
> (3.806–9, 812)

Gray's reprise of his first stanza's invocative language, then, may be seen as a plea that even fails to produce "gentle thoughts," much less an achievement by a "daring spirit" who wakes the "lyre divine."

21. Charles E. Passage's translation in *The Complete Works of Horace* (New York: Frederick Unger, 1983), 310–11. Lonsdale's translation is similar (162 n), Fitzgerald's slightly different, the latter reflecting, he says, "the danger of trying to rival the inspired and lawless Pindar" and "Horace's reluctance to become the encomiast of the Augustan age" (80).

22. Fitzgerald, *The Pindaric Mode*, 34. Pat Rogers' rare dissent from the almost universal acclamation accorded *The Progress* is both interesting and provocative: except for the section on Hellenic poetry, he sees the entire poem as having "a whipped-up, galvanic quality, like the eroticizing fantasies of a man of low sexual vitality." And as for the "exclamations and apostrophes" in connection with Shakespeare and Milton, they are "absurd," language as gesture becoming language as "ham[ming] in a sort of verbal histrionics." *The Augustan Vision* (London: Weidenfield & Nicolson, 1974), 140. Cf. Fitzgerald's different, yet oddly commensurate, interpretation of the Milton apostrophe as "violently sexual," culminating "in a post-coital fall" (*The Pindaric Mode*, 92).

23. Lest my phrasing be interpreted as Gray's diminishment of Shakespeare's achievement, it is well to note Fitzgerald's fine aperçu: "Nature's self-revelation to Shakespeare occurs in a secret place hidden from Gray's view; it is an event that is impressive because it is exclusive" (*The Pindaric Mode*, 91). Nevertheless, in his early 1750s poem (just prior to *The Progress*), *Stanzas to Mr. Bentley*, Gray links Shakespeare firmly to Milton: "But not to one in this benighted age / Is that diviner inspiration given, / That burns in Shakespeare's or in Milton's page" (Lonsdale, 154–55). Even here, though, Shakespeare is the consummate artist of the pencil, and Milton does not soar. As in *The Progress*, Gray in the Bentley poem's

final lines, appears to settle for less than both, even though the last three endings
have been torn away from the sole manuscript:

> Enough for me, if to some feeling breast
> My lines a secret sympathy
> And as their pleasing influence
> A sigh of reflection

Note the extraordinary theft by Gray of his own first phrase here in the Bard's
final lines (*Bard*, 139), and my analysis of that passage in chapter 5.

24. Fry, *The Poet's Calling in the English Ode*, 86. Although it appears to be as
much an evasion as his alleged comment about always reading Spenser before he
wrote, Gray is reported to have told James Beattie that "if there was in his num-
bers any thing that deserved approbation, he had learned it all from Dryden"
(Lonsdale, 174 n).

25. Fitzgerald, *The Pindaric Mode*, 94. He goes on to argue cogently that, in his
disruption of the progress by searching for sublime images, "Gray is clearly ad-
dressing himself to Milton's *Nativity Ode*," in which "the extraordinary beauty of
the natural images is directly connected with the historical drama of the moment"
(90–91). While I don't quite see that "address" myself, Milton's success in "forging
the continuity Gray seems to reject" (91) by separating narrative and image cer-
tainly stood starkly as yet another achievement Gray may have aspired to—how-
ever much in vain.

26. Cf. also Horace's "animus infans" in his *Ode* 3.4, line 20, and Milton's
"dreaded Infant's hand" in his *On the Morning of Christ's Nativity*, line 222, both of
which Gray knew about and certainly did not ignore.

27. *Ode* 3.2 is about army service, dying for one's country, and thus about "true
manhood," while *Ode* 4.9, which does deal with poetic immortality, is more vigor-
ously positive than Gray's lines: for Horace his own words will be as imperishable
as Homer's and Pindar's—though Simonides of Ceos, Alcaeus of Lesbos, Stesi-
chorus, Anacreon, and Sappho are also included in this company. Like *Ode* 3 this
one too ends with praise for "manly worth" and those "Who for the sake of cher-
ished friends or / Fatherland [feel] unafraid of dying." The translations are by
Charles Passage, *The Complete Works of Horace*, 221, 325–26.

28. Fitzgerald, *The Pindaric Mode*, 86, 93–94.

29. *Ibid.*, 94.

30. Gray's note in the 1768 *Poems* quotes Ezekiel 1:20, 26, 28. It is also signifi-
cant that Gray's emphasis on Milton's *seeing* the throne deliberately ignores his
hearing (in *At a Solemn Music*) the "undisturbed song of pure concent, / Aye sung
before" that throne—another of Gray's efforts, then, to deflect our perception of
his self-identification with Milton's transgression.

31. Sherwin, *Precious Bane*, 68, 29.

32. Fry, *The Poet's Calling*, 84; Sherwin, *Precious Bane*, 42.

Chapter 9   Finishing

1. *CTG*, 512 n. No translation of the Greek was given in either of the two edi-
tions of the Pindaric odes, but Gray later sent one in a letter to his Pembroke

friend, James Brown (*CTG*, 797). The parenthetical quotation is from Ketton-Cremer, *Thomas Gray: A Biography*, 152.

2. Both these reports are given by Gray in a 7 October 1757 letter to Thomas Wharton (*CTG*, 532). Garrick's complimentary verses were published anonymously in the *London Chronicle* of 1 October 1757, the full text of which is in *CTG*, 535–36. For other positive responses see W. Powell Jones, "The Contemporary Readers of Gray's *Odes*," *Modern Philology* 28 (1930–31): 61–82. Gray was pleased especially with the praise accorded the odes by William Warburton, Oliver Goldsmith, and Francesco Algarotti, the last of whom wrote directly to Gray in April 1763.

3. Ketton-Cremer, *Thomas Gray: A Biography*, 157.

4. Ketton-Cremer also is uncharacteristically firm on this matter: "There can be little doubt, from the wording of the second entry [in the Cambridge register; see *CTG*, 1208] and from the embarrassment and dismay shown by [Tuthill's] friends, that he had been accused of some homosexual offense" (147). While the reputation of the college may indeed have been of concern to Gray, even more serious to him would have been the potential harm to his own.

5. The quotations here are from Leonard Whibley's account of the entire affair, in which "intimate" friend is as close as he gets to Ketton-Cremer's and my conclusion (*CTG*, 1209).

6. Cf. Stephen Cox's apposite observation that what he calls Gray's "gothic poems" are "galleries of the ideal states in which Gray imagined that the self could attain its greatest significance. But the idealization is so complete, the selves represented so autonomous, so isolated from any but a purely fabulous environment, that the characters largely lack interest as personalities; they become merely heroic gesture." *"The Stranger within Thee": Concepts of the Self in Late-Eighteenth-Century Literature* (Pittsburgh: University of Pittsburgh Press, 1980), 97. More recently, as I noted in my earlier treatment of *The Bard* and its followers, Suvir Kaul makes essentially the same point in his *Thomas Gray and Literary Authority: A Study in Ideology and Poetics* (Stanford: Stanford University Press, 1992), 74–75. In this regard Oliver Goldsmith's review of *The Progress* and *The Bard* in the *Monthly Review* of September 1757 is especially interesting since it chastises Gray (gently to be sure) for "endeavouring to force the exotics of another climate," for "being an imitator" rather than "ventur[ing] to be more an original" (*CTG*, 533 n).

7. For the particulars of Miss Speed's relationship with Gray see *CTG*, 331–33 n. The quotation is from one John Penn, *An Historical and Descriptive Account of Stoke Park* (London, 1813), noted by Lonsdale, 240 n. For an interesting analysis of the Henrietta-Lady Cobham-Lady Schaub coterie, focused on as an aristocratic audience for Gray's *A Long Story*, see Linda Zionkowski, "Gray, the Marketplace, and the Masculine Poet," *Criticism* 35 (1993): 599–602.

8. The translation is H. Rushton Fairclough's in his *Virgil*, rev. ed., 2 vols. (1916; Cambridge: Harvard University Press, 149). Virgil's passage concludes, "But if the chill blood about my heart bar me from" such love, "let my delight be the country, and the running streams amid the dells—may I love the waters and the woods, though fame be lost" (149–50).

9. For the details of the political background and Lord Hollard's role in it see Lonsdale, 243–47 and 259–61; Ketton-Cremer, 200–3 and 227–29.

10. In a letter to Mason in December 1773, *The Correspondence of Horace Walpole,* ed. Wilmarth S. Lewis et al. (New Haven: Yale University Press, 1937—), 28:118.

11. Ketton-Cremer, *Thomas Gray,* 229.

12. Ibid, 231; but see Gray's proposals for his duties in *CTG,* 1256–57, where his reward for his scholarly achievements is interpreted as the privilege of teaching what he had learned in his research. In fact, of course, he taught nothing.

13. The particular occasion for mentioning his mother's death is the serious illness of Wharton's mother, which prompts Gray to write that he "had discover'd a thing very little known, which is, that in one's whole life one never can have anymore than a single Mother"—a phrasing all the more affecting for its deliberate truism. "You may think this is obvious," he goes on, "and (what you call) a trite observation . . . [but] I was at the same age (very near) as wise as you, and yet I never discover'd this . . . till it was too late. It is 13 years ago, and seems but yesterday, and every year I live it sinks deeper into my heart" (*CTG,* 926). See also footnote 3 on the same page for Mason's account of just how deeply into his heart his mother's death sank.

14. If my suggestion of Gray's "borrowing" the sense of Milton's preludic lines seems absurd, Gray himself suggested as much in a letter of April 1769 to his lifelong friend and admirer from Eton days, James Brown: "Here a son is born unto us, and he must die a heathen without your assistance" (Brown had been ordained in 1735). The most extravagant praise of the *Ode for Music* came from Beattie, who singled out this Milton imitation as "delightful. The poetry is exquisite, and [Beattie revealing his solid Augustan principles] the imitation exact . . . I have always thought the hymn on the nativity, notwithstanding its faults, to be one of the finest poems in the world" (*CTG,* 1083).

15. *Ode for Music,* 15–22. Milton, of course, was an undergraduate at Christ's College, Cambridge.

16. Those horrors, however, are hailed by Satan in his "Farewell [to] happy fields, / Where joy for ever dwells." His fiat is to "make a heav'n of hell, a hell of heav'n" (*PL* 1.249–55).

17. Letter to Nicholls, 24 June 1769 (*CTG,* 1065). Gray applied the word earlier to *The Bard* (*CTG,* 523 n). Byron called his *Prophecy of Dante* his "Danticles."

18. Cf. *On the Morning of Christ's Nativity,* 147–48: "And heav'n as at some festival / Will open wide the gates of her high palace hall"; and *Lycidas,* 174–76, where Lycidas is "mounted high / . . . In the blest kingdoms meek of joy and love" where "entertain [him] all the saints above, / In solemn troops and sweet societies."

19. Mason, *The Poems of Mr. Gray* . . . (York, 1775), 98; Beattie, letter to Gray, circa November 1769 (*CTG,* 1083).

20. Lonsdale (272 n) properly cites as possible sources for these lines *Twelfth Night* 1.1.4: "The strain again! It had a dying fall"—the direct antecedent of Pope's "And melt away / In a dying, dying Fall" (*Ode for Music on St. Cecelia's Day,* 20–21). He also notes the biblical "still small voice" (I Kings 19:12) and Dryden's redaction of that in *Oedipus:* "now in still small tone / Your dying accents fell." All seems to me fully appropriate to Milton's "dying" here in Gray's ode to a less than solemn music.

21. *PL* 8.500–5. The ultimate absurdity of the allusion here lies in the fact that these lines preface Adam's leading Eve with "obsequious majesty" (having "approved / [his] pleaded reason") "To the nuptial bow'r / . . . blushing like the morn" (509–11).

22. Ketton-Cremer, 238. Junius caught the absurdity of it all in his letter of 8 July 1769 by predicting that Cambridge's "learned seminary," once "recovered from the delerium of an installation" will become again "what in truth it ought to be, once more a peaceful scene of slumber and thoughtless meditation.. . . The learned dullness of declamation will be silent; and even the venal muse, though happiest in fiction, will forget your [Grafton's] virtues" (quoted in Ketton-Cremer, 240).

23. *PL* 9.643, 737–38. Cf. the Lady's retort to Comus's "Obtruding false rules pranked in reason's garb": "I hate when vice can bolt her arguments, / And virtue has no tongue to check her pride" (*Comus*, 759–61).

24. Jean Hagstrum, "Gray's Sensibility," in *Fearful Joy*, ed. James Downey and Ben Jones (Montreal: McGill/Queen's University Press, 1974), 8.

25. Letter to John Hamilton Reynolds, 3 May 1818. Keats's context here is an apt one for my point about Gray: the Mansion of Many Apartments trope in which the "Chamber of Maiden Thought becomes gradually darken'd and at the same time on all sides of it many doors are set open—but all dark—all leading to dark passages."

26. The full French text of his letter to his mother about life at Cambridge is given in *CTG*, 1265–69, and the passage I've quoted from the *Souvenirs* is given (in the original French) in *CTG*, 1110–11 n. *Souvenirs de Ch. Victor de Bonstetten e'crites en 1831* was published in Paris in 1831, the passage quoted being on p. 116. I am grateful to my colleague Clyde de L. Ryals for the English translation.

27. H. Rushton Faircloth's translation in his *Virgil*, 2 vols. (Cambridge: Harvard University Press, 1947), 67–68. The shepherds' calling Lycidas "a bard" had to be a particularly wrenching recall of Gray's own bardic moment.

28. These three letters were first printed in Friedrich Matthisson's *Auserlesene Gedichte, herausgegeben von J. H. Füssili* (Zurich: 1791), 96–8, and reprinted in English translation by Anne Plumptre in *Letters written from various parts of the Continent, between the years 1785 and 1794* (London, 1799), 533–35 (*CTG*, 1117 n).

29. Marshall Brown, *Preromanticism* (Stanford: Stanford University Press, 1991), 26. On the other hand, what Brown says of the end of the *Elegy* seems to approach what I have been arguing: "Gray clear-sightedly concedes the omnipresence of bodily impulses, yet his message [in the *Elegy* at least] is that the only fruition and repose are of the mind" (47).

30. Ibid, 28.

31. Wordsworth, *The Prelude*, 5.605. It is useful here to remind ourselves that Wordsworth was a great admirer of Gray's poetry, to which he alludes more than we yet know. "Special decorum" I have taken from Bertrand H. Bronson's "On a Special Decorum in Gray's Elegy," in *From Sensibility to Romanticism: Essays Presented to Frederick A. Pottle*, eds. F. W. Hilles and H. Bloom (Oxford: Oxford University Press, 1965).

32. Brown, *Preromanticism*, 372.

33. David Simpson, *Wordsworth's Historical Imagination* (New York: Methuen, 1987), 5.

34. Geoffrey Hartman, "Romantic Poetry and the Genius Loci," in *Beyond Formalism* (New Haven: Yale University Press, 1970), 313. Moreover, as I tried to demonstrate in my analysis of the *The Bard*, it "is one long and ferocious speaking out" as Hartman says it is, but what is spoken out, as I see it, is not what Hartman implies.

35. Abrams, "Structure and Style in the Greater Romantic Lyric," in *From Sensibility to Romanticism*, ed. Hilles and Bloom, 539. Abram's conclusion is that the Eton College Ode and, by implication, the rest of Gray's poetry prior to *The Bard* and the Welsh-Norse fragments remain "distinctly . . . mid-century period piece[s]," poems of sensibility.

36. Frank Brady, introductory note to Gray's poems in his and Martin Price's anthology, *English Prose and Poetry 1660–1800: A Selection* (New York: Holt, Rinehart & Winston, 1961), p. 218.

37. Abrams, "Structure and Style in the Greater Romantic Lyric," 553.

38. Bertrand Bronson, *Facets of the Enlightenment: Studies in English Literature and Its Contexts* (Los Angeles: University of California Press, 1968), 171.

Index

LIBRARY OF CONGRESS CATALOGING-IN-PUBLICATION DATA

Gleckner, Robert F.
   Gray agonistes : Thomas Gray and masculine friendship/Robert F.
Gleckner.
   p.   cm.
   Includes bibliographical references and index.
   ISBN 0-8018-5433-4 (acid-free paper)
   1. Gray, Thomas, 1716–1771—Friends and associates.   2. Gray,
Thomas, 1716–1771—Criticism and interpretation.   3. Latin poetry—
Translations into English—History and criticism.   4. Homosexuality
and literature—England—History—18th century.   5. Love poetry,
English—Men authors—History and criticism.   6. West, Richard,
1716–1742—Friends and associates.   7. Friendship—England—
History—18th century.   8. Poets, English—18th century—Biography.
9. Masculinity (Psychology) in literature.   10. Milton, John,
1608–1674—Influence.   11. Male friendship in literature.   12. Men
in literature.   I. Title.
PR3503.G48 1997
821'.6—dc20   96-17083